MOTHER TONGUE THEOLOGIES

Mother Tongue Theologies

Poets, Novelists, Non-Western Christianity

Edited by Darren J. N. Middleton

☙PICKWICK *Publications* • Eugene, Oregon

MOTHER TONGUE THEOLOGIES
Poets, Novelists, Non-Western Christianity

Copyright © 2009 Wipf and Stock Publishers. All rights reserved. Except for brief quotations in critical publications or reviews, no part of this book may be reproduced in any manner without prior written permission from the publisher. Write: Permissions, Wipf and Stock Publishers, 199 W. 8th Ave., Suite 3, Eugene, OR 97401.

Pickwick Publications
An imprint of Wipf and Stock Publishers
199 W. 8th Ave., Suite 3
Eugene, OR 97401

www.wipfandstock.com

ISBN 13: 978-1-55635-965-1

Cataloguing-in-Publication data:

Mother tongue theologies : poets, novelists, non-Western Christianity / edited by Darren J. N. Middleton

xvi + 236 p. ; 23 cm. Includes bibliographical references.

ISBN 13: 978-1-55635-965-1

1. Globalization—Religious aspects—Christianity. 2. Christianity and literature. 3. Theology in literature. I. Title.

PN49 .M75 2009

Manufactured in the U.S.A.

In memory of
Rev. Henry Dearman Martin (1923–2009)
and in honor of
Margaret Anne McMullen Martin,
Baptist missionaries to Nigeria,
where they served twenty-six years,
and cherished friends.

Contents

Introduction / ix

PART ONE: Eastern Christianity

ONE The Ambiguity of Suffering: Dostoevsky and the Russian Orthodox Tradition / 3
Evgenia V. Cherkasova

TWO The Unorthodox Greek Orthodoxy of Constantine Cavafy / 16
John Estes

THREE In Lieu of Logos: Creation and Redemption in the Poetry of Scott Cairns / 32
J. A. Jackson

PART TWO: Christianity in Africa and the Caribbean

FOUR The Collision of Two Cultures: Chinua Achebe's *Things Fall Apart* and Christianity's Coming to Nigeria / 47
Catherine Winn Merritt and Eric J. Sterling

FIVE Jesus of Nazareth in Ghana's Deep Forest: The Africanization of Christianity in Madam Afua Kuma's Poetry / 61
Darren J. N. Middleton

SIX Essential Being: Reflections of Christianity and Human Survival in Caribbean Literature / 77
Mozella G. Mitchell

PART THREE: Christianity in Central and South America

SEVEN "They Come Smiling Out of the Morgue": Historical Resurrections in Ernesto Cardenal's Nicaragua (1934–70) / 95
Ellin Sterne Jimmerson

EIGHT   The Syncretism of Candomblé and Feminism in
Helena Parente Cunha's *Woman between Mirrors* / 110
Isabel Asensio-Sierra

PART FOUR: Christianity in Asia and the Pacific Islands

NINE   The Pilgrims's Progress: Ayemenem House and
the Syrian Christian Church in Kerala, India / 127
Mini Chandran

TEN   Converting the Idolatrous Heathens: British
Missionaries in the South Sea Islands and India in
Children's Fiction / 140
Ymitri Mathison

ELEVEN   Conflicts between Christianity and Korean
Shamanism in Nora Okja Keller's *Comfort Woman* / 157
J. Stephen Pearson

TWELVE   Christianity's Cross-cultural (Mis)Translation in
Amy Tan's Fiction / 172
Di Gan Blackburn

THIRTEEN   Images of Religion in South Pacific Fiction:
An Interpretation of Albert Wendt's *Pouliuli* / 189
Jack A. Hill

PART FIVE: Christianity in Native America

FOURTEEN   Native-Christian Syncretism in Two Louise Erdrich
Novels / 211
Sinéad Moynihan

Contributors / 225
For Further Reading / 229

Introduction

WE LIVE IN AN exceptional religious climate. Today, most Christians practice their faith outside Europe and North America, and recent books chart as well as explain the growth of such "Global South" or "Non-Western" Christianity in sociological, anthropological, and historical terms.[1] Some scholars, like Todd M. Johnson and Kenneth R. Ross, note that the dramatic and lively transition away from Global North Christianity has been happening since the "Edinburgh 1910" World Missionary conference.[2] Other commentators, such as Philip Jenkins, Lamin Sanneh, and Andrew F. Walls also recognize this ecumenical gathering's importance yet accentuate the important issues emerging from Christianity's recent locational shift.[3] Such issues include—but are not restricted to—Christianity's inherent vernacularizing tendencies and its translatability; the dynamics of trans-cultural interactions within religiously plural settings; the multifaceted, frequently messy contextualization process; the initiatives of indigenous persons as well as groups; and, the momentous manner in which grassroots or mother tongue theologies are shaping, even revitalizing, twenty-first century Christianity.

Utilizing these and other non-fictional works, the fourteen essayists in *Mother Tongue Theologies* explore how fiction also depicts Christianity's dramatic movement South and East of Jerusalem as well as North

---

1. The idea for assembling and editing a collection of essays devoted to non-Western Christianity and literature came to me whilst attending Andrew F. Walls's Calvin College Summer seminar in Christian scholarship, "From Tertullian to Tutu: Africa's Place in Two Millennia of Christian History," June 17–July 5, 2002. I thank Calvin College and Texas Christian University for making it possible for me to attend.

2. Todd M. Johnson and Kenneth R. Ross, editors, *The Atlas of Global Christianity* (Edinburgh: Edinburgh University Press, 2009). See also Brian Stanley, *The World Missionary Conference, Edinburgh 1910* (Grand Rapids: Eerdmans, 2009). The 1910 conference is widely recognized as initiating the contemporary ecumenical and world missionary movement(s).

3. For details, see Philip Jenkins, *The Next Christendom: The Coming of Global Christianity*, rev. and expanded ed. (New York: Oxford University Press, 2007); Lamin Sanneh, *Whose Religion Is Christianity?: The Gospel beyond the West* (Grand Rapids: Eerdmans, 2003); and Andrew F. Walls, *The Cross-Cultural Process in Christian History: Studies in the Transmission and Appropriation of Faith* (Maryknoll: Orbis, 2002).

and West. Our collection thus joins a small but growing list of edited texts tackling Christianity's global story through literary art.[4] Structured by geographical region, it captures the numerous and dissimilar ways in which people around the globe receive Christianity. It also celebrates postcolonial literature's diversity. And it highlights non-Western authors' biblical allusions, paying attention to how and why locally rooted Christians invoke scripture in their pursuit of personal as well as social transformation. Individual authors rightly come to different conclusions about Christianity's global character. Some connect missionary work with colonialism as well as cultural imperialism, for example, and yet others accentuate how indigenous cultures amalgamate with Christianity's foreignness to produce mesmerizing, multiple identities. Differences exist, then, but our volume centers around honoring the many moral and theological issues that arise out of the cut and thrust of native responses to Western Christian presence and pressure. Ultimately, we believe the reward of listening for as well as to such responses, particularly in story, will be a wider as well as deeper discernment of the merits *and* demerits of post-Western Christianity, especially for Christians living their faith in the so-called post-Christian West.

With approximately three hundred million members globally, the Eastern Orthodox Church is the world's second largest single Christian communion. Our anthology's first three chapters treat this tradition and, in the first essay, Evgenia V. Cherkasova uncovers the Russian Orthodox roots in Fyodor Dostoevsky's novels. She shows how a complex rhetoric of suffering descends from the work of the Fathers in the Christian East, was embraced by eighteenth-century Russian thinkers, and, to some extent, continues to influence national identity. For Dostoevsky, as well as for the religious tradition he belongs to, suffering's psychological, ethical, and spiritual significance appears ambiguous—while purification through suffering is praised, for example, suffering of the innocents is vehemently opposed. "Ultimately, Dostoevsky's novels demonstrate that by suffering with others we do not increase the ills of the world but partake in a genuinely humane communion, sustained by love and mutual responsibility," Cherkasova says.

4. See John C. Hawley, editor, *Christian Encounters with the Other* (New York: New York University Press, 1998); Seodial Frank H. Deena and Karoline Szatek, editors, *From Around the Globe: Secular Authors and Biblical Perspectives* (Lanham, MD: University Press of America, 2007); and Susan VanZanten Gallagher, editor, *Postcolonial Literature and the Biblical Call for Justice* (Jackson: University of Mississippi Press, 2007).

While John Estes concedes that Constantine Cavafy's poems are, at least on the surface, unsympathetic to Christianity, even openly hostile, his luminous verse may profitably be seen to incarnate the religious and cultural spirit of Eastern Christian civilization. "To make this reading possible requires an assertion that the core of Orthodoxy is not a set of theological statements," Estes declares, "but a stillness that looks upon humanity and the world with love." He then notes some compelling points of consanguinity between Cavafy and two gifted personalities associated wth Orthodox mystical spirituality, Maximus the Confessor and Gregory Palamas. By examining Cavafy's poignant vision through the perspective of an Eastern spirit he in part inherited and in part resisted, Estes hopes that the Greek poet's words can be models and guides for individual readers toward a more conscious love for the universe.

Like the fourth and fifth century Desert Fathers, who often elucidate scripture by telling stories (a sort of Christian *Midrash*), Scott Cairns's verse also defies classification. According to J. A. Jackson, it is both literature and exegesis, or, better still, an icon that points not to the poetry itself, nor to the biblical or liturgical text, but to that which all of these texts—indeed, all of the material world—is never not pointing: "the necessity of a synergistic divine-human relationship, a theanthropic existence." In Jackson's reading, Cairns challenges Western Christian soteriology—with its robust belief in sacrificial atonement, justification, and then sanctification—by upholding *theosis*, the Christian East's creation-redemption model of salvation as deification, explicit in 2 Pet 1:4 and frequently associated with Athanasius and Ephrem the Syrian. In Cairns as well as the Eastern tradition *theosis* is ecclesial, not simply personal, and comes to us as sheer Gift, the absolute generosity of God.

The volume's second part transports us to Africa and the Caribbean where, since the last century, Christianity has been expanding rapidly. In chapter 4, Catherine Winn Merritt and Eric J. Sterling examine Christianity's evolution in Chinua Achebe's *Things Fall Apart* and in modern Nigeria. During most of Achebe's novel, the complex and contentious interplay between the Igbo villagers and the Anglican missionaries creates a cultural disturbance; the once homogeneous society becomes bifurcated. Clergy seem to consort with government officials and soldiers, furthermore, and colonialism's confusion of gospel values and European cultural values creates serious problems, not the least of which is the belief among the villagers that the church plans to use

Christianity to coax the Nigerians into accepting colonialism. In some cases, though, missionary Christianity appears to help many Igbo, especially the osu—the undesirables with little or no social standing—to secure confidence, feel dignity, and to practice the power of self-determination. By the novel's end, then, the plot has moved from "the monologue level, with both cultures effectively talking to themselves, into the more complex—and ultimately more important—dialogue," Merritt and Sterling aver, and this scenario anticipates much of what we now see in post-missionary Nigeria.

Darren J. N. Middleton notes that in the twentieth century's second half, as more African countries gained independence, Christianity in Africa began to change. Several African churches abandoned beliefs and behaviors that they had acquired from Western missionaries. They retained their religious commitment, but began Africanizing their Christianity. Such churches are now called African Independent Churches (AIC) and their convictions as well as customs differ enormously throughout the continent. One AIC, West Africa's Church of Pentecost, which is located in Ghana's Eastern Region, embodies the process of Christianity's Africanization by way of the transcribed prayers and praises of Madam Afua Kuma. Familiar biblical themes and allusions are present in her work, *Jesus of the Deep Forest*, so scripture, which was taught to her in her native language, shapes her understanding. Yet she adapts some of the more recognizable biblical characters and teachings to her Ghanaian setting. She reconfigures them in a way that reflects and affirms her culture. Middleton claims that while contextualization is an inescapable characteristic of religious communities, the oral nature of Afua Kuma's Christianity, indeed rooted in the oral nature of African storytelling and sacred mythologies, enables a fluidity of boundaries that aids the process of contextualization.

Since the Caribbean constitutes an important aspect of the African diaspora, chapter 6 probes and evaluates Caribbean Christianity in two modern novels, Earl Lovelace's *The Wine of Astonishment* and V. S. Reid's *New Day*. In her reading of both, Mozella G. Mitchell shows how various and different characters employ scripture to challenge colonialism and emancipate the disvalued black self. Lovelace depicts how Trinidadian Spiritual Baptists work to decolonize the faith by valorizing the way God moves among them, by dignifying ancestral modalities, and by refusing to mimic European or North American church authorities. A vivid account of Jamaica's 1865 Morant Bay Rebellion, Reid's story examines how one fictional family constructs as well as models their religious and cultural identity under colonialism's oppressive spectre, gives agency to their version of Caribbean humanness, and, ultimately, quests for a community that enlivens as well as empowers all.

The third part of *Mother Tongue Theologies* examines Christianity in Central and South America. In chapter 7, Ellin Sterne Jimmerson addresses one of the most widely-read poets in the Spanish language, Ernesto Cardenal—Roman Catholic priest, liberation theologian, and onetime Minister of Culture in Sandinista Nicaragua. She shows how he uses the documentarist style he calls *exteriorismo* to stress the historical and theological ramifications of U. S. political, cultural, and economic dominance of Central America. In Nicaragua a man of God cannot avoid political struggle, Cardenal proclaims, and thus, as Jimmerson makes clear, his work consistently grapples with such issues as the theological legitimacy of violence in the Nicaraguan context, such themes as the resurrection (the resurrection of Jesus argues for the resurrection of the Nicaraguan people), and such personalities as U.S. backed Nicaraguan dictator Anastasio Somoza García and his National Guard. An interdisciplinary exploration of Cardenal, Jimmerson's work offers a window onto the Christians of the 1979 revolution, inspired and supported by many clergy, like Cardenal, and suggests how liberation theology then, as now, gives ordinary people power in their communities, pride in their lives, and much else.

Isabel Asensio-Sierra highlights Brazilian folk Christianity in chapter 8. An African-derived religion, Candomblé was carried by African priests and other devotees who were brought to South America as slaves. Upon its arrival, Candomblé was banned and prosecuted by the Roman Catholic Church for many years. In addition, it has been illegalized and criminalized by some governments. Nevertheless, Candomblé constitutes an integral aspect of Brazilian popular culture and it is associated mainly with the Afro-Brazilian population. Today, it enjoys millions of adherents from several social classes and racial groups. Asensio-Sierra notes that a significant feature of Brazilian culture is that Brazilians do not see religions as exclusive; thus, many people of different faiths participate in Candomblé ceremonies. Moreover, influence has been reciprocal and for centuries Candomblé has incorporated many Christian elements. Such syncretism was in part due to religious persecution and to Candomblé's polytheistic as well as multi-ethnic nature, in contast to the centralized, monotheistic Christianity of the Old World. Candomblé appears in the work of several recent Brazilian writers. For her part, Asensio-Sierra concentrates on Helena Parente Cunha's novels, especially *Woman Between Mirrors*, which illustrates how Candomblé´s syncretism fosters the identity formation—spiritual, racial, sexual, and national—of Afro-Brazilian women. At the same time, Asensio-Sierra approaches Candomblé as a manifestation of resistance by the Afro-Brazilian woman in a largely Catholic country, which already implies the conservative role of women as opposed to the patriarchal, dominant role of men.

Part four asks us to travel in the mind's eye to Asia and the Pacific Islands. And this section's first two chapters focus on India. Mini Chandran explains how Arundhati Roy's *The God of Small Things* depicts the cultural ethos surrounding the Syrian Christians of Kerala, a faith community that is perhaps older than most other Christian denominations. The novel is set in the late 1960s and early 1970s, when communism's entrenchment, the rise of the extreme leftist faction of the Naxalites, and the caste-ridden political situation were to pose challenges both to the city and the church. In this context, the fluctuating fortunes of the inhabitants of Reverend John Ipe's Ayemenem House, especially Chacko, capture the Christian faith in its interactions with Kerala's socio-political reality. In the next chapter, Ymitri Mathison surveys children's evangelical tract fiction of the last two centuries, and she notes how various novels reflect the tensive alliance between colonialism, Christian missionaries, and the conversion of natives into Christianity. Mathison scrutinizes Mary Martha Sherwood's *Little Henry and His Bearer*, Marguerite Butler's *Tulsi, the Story of an Indian School Girl*, R. M. Ballantyne's *The Coral Island*, and Rudyard Kipling's *Kim*. While such novels assess the mission movement critically, they also invoke the strategies of various missionary agencies, especially the largest and most influential, the London Missionary Society, and their basic theme is the major British characters' angst of living and surviving in the colonies among the heathens with the natives to some extent secondary. We also learn that women missionaries were crucial to the imperial project as only they had access to the secluded female natives—a means of converting the men and thus insuring their loyalty to the empire.

J. Stephen Pearson's chapter explicates how Soon Hyo, the title character in Nora Okja Keller's novel *Comfort Woman*, captures the discord between Korean traditions and Christianity. With the help of a Christian mission in Pyongyang and her marriage to Rick, the American missionary, Soon Hyo escapes the horrors of the Japanese comfort camps and finds refuge in America, where she eventually raises a daughter. However, in spite of the help she receives from Christians, Soon Hyo never embraces Christianity herself, and it becomes a steady source of tension in her life, especially through the attitudes of her husband, who represents both the ambitions of the Western church and its limitations. Pearson tackles three areas of concern to Keller—the processes by which Korean indigenous religions intermingle with Christianity; the church's role in Korean history, especially with regards to the Japanese occupation; and, the clashes of culture that occur between the American and Korean characters regarding the human body and language.

In the volume's twelfth chapter, Di Gan Blackburn recognizes that recent Christian theologians and historians define Christianity as a cross-culturally translatable religion, by which they mean that it can and should be translated out of its Western cultural embodiment to receptor cultures. In Amy Tan's novels, however, Christianity is never translated well into the Chinese culture—the white missionaries present it as part of a Western cultural enterprise while the Chinese and Chinese American Christian characters interpret it through their deep-rooted Chinese religious mindset. In *The Joy Luck Club*, *The Kitchen God's Wife*, and *The Bonesetter's Daughter*, Christianity becomes so syncretistic and pragmatic that it bears a stronger resemblance to folk Chinese religions than to what is initially presented by Western missionaries. In addition, a substantial portion of *The Hundred Secret Senses* can be read as a satire of Christian mission. Always lacking a proper translation, the Christian message presented by Western missionaries appears absurd and comical to its Chinese receptors. Judged by post-colonial literary theories, Tan's Chinese and Chinese American characters are "de-colonizing" warriors who "subvert" and "ironize" Western Christianity. In the light of Christian literary theories advocated by scholars such as Robert Detweiler and David L. Jeffrey, however, none of Tan's characters is a qualified translator who understands basic Christian doctrine. In Blackburn's view, then, Christianity fails its cross-cultural translation in Tan's novels because the Word is never made flesh to her characters.

Proceeding out from a broad phenomenological perspective, Jack A. Hill concludes our collection's fourth part by showing how the fiction of Albert Wendt, one of the South Pacific Islands most prolific writers, helps us comprehend the many as well as various intricacies in the region's religious experience. In particular, Hill reads Wendt's *Pouliuli* as a postcolonial novel, ground-breaking literary art that not only questions invasive Christian missionary forms and values, it also evokes powerful contemporary images of transformation that are fully continuous with traditional cultural forms. Wendt is not a conventional or orthodox religious voice, as Hill admits, but "his critical approach to Christian motifs presupposes a complex moral and spiritual sensibility that is rarely articulated in the region today."

In the volume's fifth and final part, which examines Christianity in Native America, Sinéad Moynihan probes Native-Christian (specifically, Roman Catholic) syncretism in two novels by Louise Erdrich, who claims German American and Ojibway ancestry. Moynihan holds that Erdrich's *Tracks* and *The Last Report on the Miracles at Little Horse* together pose the question of whether Catholicism's colonialist function necessarily distances it irreconcilably from Native beliefs, or if the two might, in some contexts, actually prove compatible. Erdrich's account of the promise and/or shortfall of Native-Christian relations are mapped upon the bodies of two women who "pass" in order to take up their Catholic vocations. By offering us two alternative—one "positive," one "negative"—incarnations of Native-Christian alliances, Erdrich's evaluation of religious syncretism emerges as ultimately ambivalent, Moynihan deduces.

The essayists in *Mother Tongue Theologies* think that with globalization's advent, Western literacy in non-Western Christianity is intellectually obligatory if we are to comprehend the wider world and the many forms the Christian religion takes within it.[5] Our contributors also recognize that most of us simply do not have the means to travel to places far from Europe and North America, to learn from Global South Christian communities directly. On such grounds, we regard literary art that showcases several embodiments of a newly emerging World Christianity as potentially intriguing alternatives. Poems and novels can never replace the real thing, to be sure, but if we delve into the story and mentally migrate, learning to travel to dissimilar territories of belief and behavior, the chance to view life differently heightens and the choices in how to think about matters of the spirit multiply.

---

5. In this respect we share the observations made by Susan VanZanten Gallagher in her splendid essay, "Reading and Faith in a Global Community," *Christianity and Literature* 54.3 (Spring 2005) 323–40.

PART ONE

Eastern Christianity

ONE

The Ambiguity of Suffering

Dostoevsky and the Russian Orthodox Tradition

Evgenia V. Cherkasova

Introduction

A DISTINCTIVE FEATURE OF Russian Orthodox spirituality is its emphasis on the immanence of suffering in moral and religious consciousness. In its many manifestations—in Russian kenoticism, ascetic monasticism, the canonization of passion bearers, and the adoration of the holy fools—the Orthodox tradition accentuates suffering's spiritual value. The tradition of sanctifiying suffering descends from the earliest hagiographic accounts of the first Russian saint-martyrs in the eleventh century and continues across the years in a variety of religious teachings, practices, and in social life in general. In the nineteenth century, Russian philosophers and writers frequently evoked the theme of suffering. Paradoxically, even during the aggressively anti-religious Soviet era the archetypal rhetoric of suffering, allegedly so dear to the "Russian soul," was routinely employed, albeit to some dubious ends.[1]

---

1. In a penetrating study of the post-revolutionary narratives of the working-class Russian writers, Mark Steinberg writes: "The image of the proletarian as 'crucified martyr' was pervasive after the October Revolution, though now the 'road to Golgotha' was also seen as passing not only through the factories but also through the bloody fields of revolutionary struggle" ("Workers on the Cross: Religious Imagination in the Writings of Russian Workers, 1910-1924," *Russian Review* 53.2 [1994] 222). Many Soviet ideologues, notably Lenin's minister of education, Lunacharski, consciously used the power of the deeply rooted religious symbolism in their ideological projects.

In this chapter I trace this influential theme in Russian culture, identify its religious and social roots, and analyze some of its expressions in Russian literature. Due to the magnitude of the proposed study I have to limit myself to just a few most characteristic examples. In this context, one thinker, Fyodor Dostoevsky, stands out in particular. The novelist's vivid and quite radical artistic depiction of the problem of suffering both reflects and challenges the Orthodox tradition he belongs to. It is widely acknowledged that the rich and engaging philosophical content of Dostoevsky's work helped shape the thinking of future generations of philosophers, writers, psychologists, and political theorists. Specifically, his treatment of the problem of suffering is often considered emblematic of the uniquely "Russian" way of approaching the subject. My work will therefore address the following interrelated themes: the significance of suffering in Russian Orthodox culture, and Dostoevsky's perspective on suffering and the contradictions it introduces.

Suffering as a Prominent Theme in Russian Orthodox Spirituality

Cultural historians and theologians observe a tendency in the Russian spiritual tradition to ascribe profound significance to the experience of suffering—notably, the voluntary acceptance of suffering is often praised unconditionally, irrespective of its causes and consequences. This peculiar attitude toward suffering is sometimes superficially extended to the so-called Russian national character in general; ostensibly, Russians are gloomy creatures who tend to glorify their misery and derive pleasure from it. The famous "psychologism" of Russian literature, much admired by numerous commentators, is sometimes attributed to the "typically Russian" sado-masochist leanings. Thus, Dostoevsky's novels, which I discuss shortly, have been routinely subjected to such criticism.[2] However, as is always the case with sweeping generalizations, the whole picture is more subtle and complex.

---

2. Classic examples of such criticism include: N. K. Mikhailovsky, *Dostoevsky: A Cruel Talent* (New York: Ardis, 1978); and two essays by Maxim Gorky, "On Karamazovism" and "Once Again About Karamazovism," in N. P. Zhdanovskii and A. I. Ovcharenko, editors, *Gorky, O Literature. Literaturno-criticheskie Stat'i*, [*Gorky, About Literature. Literary-critical Essays*] (Moscow: Sovetski Pisatel, 1953).

The Orthodox ethics and rhetoric of suffering do indeed oppose the modern ideals of hedonism, utilitarianism, and rationality. Russian kenotic tradition, for instance, not only acknowledges suffering as an important spiritual experience; it urges believers to embrace suffering as a genuinely Christian way of life. Kenoticism in the context of Russian Orthodoxy refers to a religious tenet based on the mystical identification with Christ. The term derives from the Greek word *kenein*, which literally means "empty" and evokes Christ's "emptying himself, taking the form of a servant, being born in the likeness of men" (Phil 2:6–7). Kenoticism is therefore metaphorically linked to nonresistance and the humble acceptance of suffering. For Russian Orthodox Christianity, *kenosis* signifies the supreme expression of religious devotion and represents a path that intimately links the sufferer to the image of Christ.

Since Orthodox kenotic tradition venerates suffering irrespective of what is accomplished by it, it stands in sharp contrast to both the ancient Hellenistic cultures and to Russia's own pagan past. First, it emphasizes that God can and did suffer. Second, human suffering does not need justification as some kind of cathartic experience for the purposes of spiritual purification, attainment of a higher wisdom, or moral receptivity. Finally, in contrast to the ethics of the warrior cultures, the moral emphasis is shifted from heroism, practical intelligence, and strength to the virtues of humility and nonresistance. Consequently, one of the central features of Russian spirituality has always been the "evaluation of suffering as a superior moral good, as almost an end in itself."[3]

From the earliest days of Christianity in Russia, the kenotic ideal is most poignantly expressed in the acts of supreme humility in suffering and its ultimate form—nonresistance to violent death. The first saints canonized by the Russian Orthodox Church were two young princes, Boris and Gleb. They were mercilessly killed by their older brother Sviatopolk in an attempt to usurp power after the death of their father, prince Vladimir. It was Vladimir who brought Christianity to pagan Russia in the eleventh century and his children thus belonged to the first generation of Christians. Boris, despite being a successful warrior, freely succumbed to his tragic fate without any attempt to flee or fight back. His younger brother Gleb met the murderers sent by Sviatopolk with the same humility. According to their hagiographer Nestor, both brothers were fully informed about the

---

3. George P. Fedotov, *The Russian Religious Mind: Kievan Christianity, the 10th to the 13th Centuries* (Belmont, MA: Nordland, 1975) 341.

plot. In their last hours they prayed and reflected on the old days when an honorable end meant death in a battle; they decided, however, to be true to their father who underwent a remarkable transformation from a ruthless conqueror to a conscientious Christian ruler. Thus they both intentionally chose to fall victims to their brother's sinister plan, rather than repudiate the newly established Christian order.

Historian George Fedotov stresses an interesting detail in the canonization of the "sufferers" Boris and Gleb: neither of the brothers was, strictly speaking, a martyr for faith. They died in a political power struggle—yet their names have always been among the most cherished in the tradition. From Boris and Gleb there begins a long line of saints—"sufferers," or passion bearers (*strastoterptsy*)—revered with love and awe by the Orthodox believers. Fedotov writes:

> Saints Boris and Gleb created in Russia a particular, though liturgically not well defined, order of "sufferers," the most paradoxical order of the Russian saints. In it are included some victims of political crimes among the princes or simply victims of a violent death. Among them one finds many infants . . . in whom the idea of innocent death is blended with the idea of purity.[4]

Kenotic tradition also finds various expressions in ascetic monasticism in the Middle Ages. Thus, Saint Theodosius, the founder of monasticism in Russia, was a proponent of the kenotic Christ in his earthly incarnation as a poor, suffering human being. Drawing on the evangelical image of the humiliated Christ, Theodosius developed a teaching and monastic practice that emphasized, above all, the self-offering of the believer and readiness to undergo severe hardships as a way of life in Christ. Beginning with Theodosius, the ideals of simplicity and humble service to all people, strong rejection of social hierarchy, and independence from the worldly power became the hallmarks of Russian kenoticism. Further developments of this tradition, not surprisingly, occur for the most part outside of the official religious institutions.

The ultimate outsiders were, of course, the holy fools (*yurodivy*), or, as they were sometimes called, "fools for Christ's sake." A culture of holy foolishness, a peculiar blend of insanity and saintliness, abject poverty and charisma, flourished in Russia up to the beginning of the last century, even though the Orthodox Church stopped the official canonization of holy fools in the eighteenth century. With no roof over their heads,

4. Ibid., 104–5.

hardly any clothes to cover their bodies, and no possessions whatsoever, *yurodivy* nonetheless commanded wide as well as significant respect. They often performed absurd, offensive public acts and they spoke openly to anyone, be it a beggar or a monarch. Thus, the legendary Saint Basil the Blessed would fearlessly reproach Ivan the Terrible for his merciless executions and conquests. Stunningly, the Tsar, who would not think twice before subjecting an opponent to torture or sentencing him to death, was not only moved by Basil's harsh words but also feared his condemnation. The people's love for and veneration of Basil is reflected in the fact that he was buried in a beautiful Cathedral on the Red Square, which has become known as Saint Basil's Cathedral. Basil the Blessed was canonized by the Russian Orthodox Church in 1588 and to this date remains one of the great icons of Orthodox spirituality; his final resting place represents an architectural symbol of Russia itself.

As a social and moral phenomenon, holy foolishness survived even the Bolshevik Revolution. It can be said to represent the extreme form of kenoticism—standing as it does for radical asceticism, rejection of earthly possessions and ambitions, chastity and purity of intention (represented by insanity), and the tireless challenging of the moral and social *status quo*. Russian literature in the eighteenth and nineteenth centuries responded to this phenomenon with a pleiad of memorable characters, the most famous of whom is perhaps Prince Myshkin, the protagonist in Dostoevsky's *The Idiot*.[5] Interestingly, in this particular character the novelist decides to combine traditional features of a martyr-prince and a holy fool in order to create an image of a "perfectly good human being." Such artistic choice only seems natural in the context of a culture where moral perfection is strongly associated with the image of the humiliated, suffering Christ.

Finally, closely linked to kenoticism is the Orthodox eremitic tradition of *pustynniks* (literally, "desert dwellers"). Note the etymological connection between *pustynya*—"empty, deserted place"—and the spiritual practices of *pustynniks*: in solitude and prayer one reaches the "desert of one's heart" and, through emptying oneself, seeks communion with God. Christian eremitism, which originated in the practices of early desert fathers such as Paul of Thebes and Antony of Egypt (Antony the Great) and was advanced by the Byzantine theologians, was introduced

---

5. Among the writers who depicted the holy fools were Alexander Pushkin, Leo Tolstoy, Nikolai Leskov, and many others.

in Russia by St. Nilus of Sora in the fifteenth century. St. Nilus's own hermitic life, his teachings, and ardent service in establishing semi-hermit communities of believers in Russia became the foundation of the ascetic culture of *pustynnichestvo* and the interrelated, rich tradition of religious elders (*startsy*).

Both traditions suffered greatly during the "governmental secularization" of the Russian Orthodox Church under Peter the Great, but were resurrected in the eighteenth century by St. Paisy Velichkovsky, a devoted theologian whose asceticism and unprecedented commitment to the restoration of the Eastern Patristic tradition in Russia bore remarkable fruit. In the eighteenth and nineteenth centuries the influence of revered elders reached far beyond the walls of their monasteries or deserted dwellings. People from all walks of life—men and women of all ages, peasants, intellectuals, aristocrats—sought the elders' advice, guidance, or consolation for their woes. The practices of kenotic contemplation of Christ's suffering and remembrance of his voluntary self-abasement constituted an integral part of the elders' message and consequently shaped the spiritual culture of the time. *Startsy's* writings and personal examples influenced many contemporary thinkers and writers. Thus, the teachings of two remarkable elders, St. Tikhon of Zadonsk and Amvrosy of Optino, provided Dostoevsky with inspiration and models for central characters in his novels, most notably for the *starets* Zosima in *The Brothers Karamazov*.[6] Specifically, St. Tikhon's commitment to humility and meekness (not so easily achieved, given the elder's naturally explosive temperament), and his preaching of universal forgiveness and acceptance of suffering as humble recognition of guilt and responsibility, featured prominently in Dostoevsky's literary art. I now turn to the novelist's treatment of suffering and its sources.

Dostoevsky on Suffering

"Suffering is necessary for the deep consciousness and heart," ponders the main character in *Crime and Punishment*, Rodion Raskolnikov. The protagonist in an earlier novel, *Notes from the Underground*, makes an even stronger claim that suffering is the sole source of all consciousness.

---

6. Sven Linnér, *Starets Zosima in the Brothers Karamazov: A Study in the Mimesis of Virtue* (Stockholm: Almqvist & Wiksell, 1975). See also John B. Dunlop, *Staretz Amvrosy, Model for Dostoevsky's Staretz Zossima* (Belmont, MA: Nordland, 1972).

Ippolit, a terminally ill youth in *The Idiot*, speaks of himself as "unworthy" of his own affliction, while Ivan Karamazov bases his rebellion against God's world on the irreconcilable suffering of innocent children. Ivan's literary creation, the infamous Grand Inquisitor, claims to have taken suffering upon himself for humanity's sins so that his subjects could enjoy carefree, childlike existence under his paternalistic tutelage. Throughout Dostoevsky's voluminous work—from the earliest novellas of the pre-Siberian period to his crowning novel, *The Brothers Karamazov*; from socio-political commentaries in the *Diary of a Writer* to personal correspondence—the novelist investigates the meaning and significance of affliction and spiritual anguish.

While Dostoevsky the artist paints an arresting picture of human suffering and explores a broad spectrum of responses to it, ranging from the openly sadistic to the genuinely compassionate, Dostoevsky the thinker also offers his readers insightful, albeit controversial, reflections on the cognitive, ethical, and spiritual significance of suffering. One aspect of the novelist's view may appear particularly troubling: at times he seems to prescribe suffering not only as a means for spiritual transformation, but as an end in itself. This stance seems all the more radical in light of Dostoevsky's well-deserved reputation as an advocate of the "insulted and injured." Indeed, the novelist was one of the first intellectuals in Russia to draw the public's attention to outrageous cases of domestic violence and crimes against children. He tirelessly commented on contemporary court cases and even took active part in some of them, meeting personally with abusers and their victims. Further, Dostoevsky's powerful words about the "unavenged tears of a little child" in *The Brothers Karamazov* are still considered by many the last word on the subject in world literature. In our century, as in Dostoevsky's time, the question remains: who would dare, in a world torn by wars, crime, cruelty, and violence, to speak of the positive value of suffering or, what is worse, glorify painful experiences and promote self-inflicted torment?

In his book *Dostoevsky the Thinker*, James Scanlan attempts to dispel the apparent ambiguity of the writer's views on suffering by claiming that "far from accepting all suffering as good, Dostoevsky excluded whole classes of it from the moral sphere, including some of the suffering most common in human life."[7] In support of this view, Scanlan

---

7. James Scanlan, *Dostoevsky the Thinker* (Cornell: Cornell University Press, 2002) 110.

distinguishes between different types of suffering depicted in Dostoevsky's work. The first category includes masochistic suffering (allegedly inherent in the Russian national character) and the anguish associated with the possession of free will, neither of which, in Scanlan's view, had positive moral value for Dostoevsky. A different type of suffering, one which may promote higher understanding and moral awareness, corresponds to a familiar conception, invoking "little more than a commonsense approval of negative experiences as having spiritual benefits."[8] The remaining two categories are related: one includes the "notion of suffering as an instrumental value of great moral significance," linked to redemption and regeneration of personality; the last category encompasses voluntary self-sacrifice, accepting suffering as an end in itself. Summarizing, Scanlan writes:

> Suffering serves to counter egoism, humbling the individual and enlivening conscience, and in that respect it is instrumentally valuable as promoting observance of the moral law. But suffering has a more intimate connection with the law when, in Christlike fashion, it is freely accepted for the good of others. Then it is itself a manifestation of the law; it is not an aid to altruism but an active instance of it in its most sublime form, the paradigm of which is Christ's suffering for the good of all.[9]

Scanlan's study offers a helpful conceptual framework for understanding Dostoevsky's complex views on suffering. Although Scanlan makes no reference to the connection between choosing suffering as a terminal good and kenoticism, his analysis clearly implies this link.[10] For Dostoevsky, Christ always remains the ultimate spiritual example of selfless sacrifice as well as compassion, and Christ's suffering is love's supreme expression.

Compassion in particular plays a crucial role in Dostoevsky's artistic world. The Russian word *sostradanie* literally translates as "co-suffering" or "suffering with." The positive value of suffering could make sense only in the context of one's voluntary acceptance of it, never as projected on

---

8. Ibid., 113.

9. Ibid., 117.

10. For a detailed study of this connection see Margaret Ziolkowski, "Dostoevsky and the Kenotic Tradition," in *Dostoevsky and the Christian Tradition*, edtied by George Pattison and Diane Oenning Thompson (Cambridge: Cambridge University Press, 2001) 31–40.

the suffering of the other. Accepting suffering has nothing to do with remaining indifferent to human affliction, not to mention affirming it on the grounds that such experience is beneficial to the sufferer. In accepting one's own suffering a person (however modestly) likens himself to Christ; in prescribing suffering to others he likens himself to Christ's tormentors. Dostoevsky's *Notes from the Underground* contains an intricate depiction of this dynamic in the novel's climactic scene, which focuses on the underground man's last interaction with the prostitute Liza. When Liza responds to the underground man's abuse with love and understanding; when she shows penetrating insight into his unhappy, bitter, excruciatingly self-conscious personality; when, despite all the pain he causes her, she tries to console him, his heart "turns over" and he bursts into tears. But just a few moments later he is once again overcome by hatred and jealousy of this meek, helpless woman who turns out to be the "heroine."

The underground man, for whom all human relationships are power struggles, chooses to see Liza's compassionate gesture as a strategic move in a game. In a desperate attempt to take revenge, he presses a five-ruble bill in Liza's hand thinking that by insulting her he would finally prevail. But his illusion quickly evaporates for he finds the money on the table after Liza's departure. He is "crushed" and races after her in order to "to weep in repentance, to kiss her feet, to beg forgiveness . . ."[11] Needless to say, all these prospects turn out to be no more than an echo of the artificial, "bookish" romanticism on which he was raised. Upon returning to his room, the underground man occupies himself by constructing theoretical justifications for his monstrosities. In order to stifle "the living pain in his heart," he quickly develops a theory of the purifying power of insult, which is supposed to elevate Liza, "however vile the dirt that awaits her." "Such were my reveries," he reports,

> as I sat at home that evening, barely alive from the pain in my soul. Never before had I endured so much suffering and repentance; . . . Never have I met Liza again, or heard anything about her. I will also add that for a long time I remained pleased with the *phrase* about the usefulness of insult and hatred, even though I myself almost became sick then from anguish.[12]

---

11. Fyodor Dostoevsky, *Notes from the Underground*, translated by Richard Pevear and Larissa Volokhonsky (New York: Vintage Classics, 1993) 128.

12. Ibid., 128–29.

The underground man did suffer, but he used all his power to deaden it with mockery, doubt, sarcasm, and rationalizing. For Dostoevsky, the moral deficiency of his anti-hero consists in his active resistance to the call of his aching heart, sincere sympathy, and co-suffering. In his refusal to open himself to a loving relationship with another human being the underground man condemns himself to hellish existence, which elder Zosima in *The Brothers Karamazov* aptly defines as the "suffering of being no longer able to love." The anti-hero reasoned that suffering is the root of all consciousness but the moral potential of his own torment is effectively overturned by hatred and pride. His sinister justification of Liza's suffering, which he himself caused, points unambiguously to his moral deficiency, which springs from a grievous inability to love and co-suffer.

Writing *Crime and Punishment*, Dostoevsky devotes much care to developing this theme in its many variations. The two main characters, the ambitious murderer Raskolnikov, and his unlikely companion, the prostitute Sonia, whose character combines features of a sinner and a holy fool, are both sufferers. However, while Sonia's pain originates in love and compassion for her family and results in self-sacrifice, Raskolnikov's torment initially comes from his wounded pride; indeed, he fails to prove that he could place himself above the law. Dostoevsky's subtle depiction of Raskolnikov's struggle with the consequences of the crime is designed to prove that, despite his hero's conscious pursuit of spiritual superiority, the murder he commits causes tremendous moral torment in him, the torment that can only be addressed by an admission of guilt and the free acceptance of punishment. Raskolnikov is portrayed as a person capable of deep feeling, and it is this moral sensibility that eventually leads him from the "murk of separation" to the confession of his crime and sincere repentance. Sonia's example, her refusal to judge Raskolnikov, and her infinite patience and kindness play a crucial role in Raskolnikov's moral resurrection. Vyacheslav Ivanov's penetrating analysis of the sinner's suffering in *Crime and Punishment* sums up Dostoevsky's general view:

> She who brings salvation to the murderer, the teacher of repentance, the meek-hearted Sonia, who becomes a prostitute in order to save her parents, brothers and sisters from starvation, is also a victim for the sins of others . . . Sonia is at the same time herself a great sinner; for, albeit to save others, she deliberately and overweeningly takes upon herself not only suffering, but also

the curse of another's deed, by making it her own. In the sinner who expiates his sin by suffering, there is an antinomy of curse and salvation—unless it happens that love has not been extinguished within him; unless, like Svidrigailov [the novel's ultimate villain] he has not become incapable of loving. For inability to love is Hell itself, as Zosima teaches; and he who is incapable of loving breaks away entirely from the partnership of all men in both sin and salvation.

The act of suffering finds a recognition appropriate to its dignity in Raskolnikov's prostration of himself before Sonia, and in the obeisance made by Father Zosima before Dmitry [in *The Brothers Karamazov*].[13]

"We are both cursed, so let us go together," says Raskolnikov to Sonia. And while he is still unsure at that point where exactly they should go, his choice of Sonia as a confidant and companion indicates his desperate need to expiate his horrible deed. Raskolnikov's gradual realization of guilt is accompanied by grandiose spiritual and physical torment. Throughout his ordeal he simultaneously resists the pain and is drawn to its redeeming power. Step by step, diffidently, he is lead through the murk of his cultivated separation to the very end where he suddenly finds himself at Sonia's feet, his heart overflowing with love. While some readers question the credibility of Raskolnikov's moral resurrection in the novel's epilogue, Dostoevsky's moral message is transparent: truth and justice claim their rights, so that the criminal himself accepts suffering in order to atone for his deed.[14]

It is clear that Dostoevsky's "ethics of suffering" is at the same time the ethics of love and compassion. Suffering's regenerating power comes not only from repentance but from recognition of one's belonging to a community. Where a person forcefully cuts himself off from others, where love is no longer possible, suffering is unredeemable. In *The Brothers Karamazov* we find the fullest development and culmination of this idea. It would require a book-length study to cover all the aspects of Dostoevsky's doctrine of suffering in his last, most elaborate novel. Here I limit my comments to a brief account of elder Zosima's teaching, which effectively unifies the ethics of suffering with the ethics of humility and love.

---

13. Vyacheslav Ivanov, *Freedom and the Tragic Life* (New York: Straus and Giroux, 1968) 81–82.

14. K. Mochulsky, *Dostoevsky: His Life and Work*, translated by M. Minihan (Princeton: Princeton University Press, 1971) 272.

In elder Zosima Dostoevsky aspired to portray "a majestic, positive, holy figure" whose closest prototype was St. Tikhon of Zadonsk. While depicting Zosima's path Dostoevsky calls upon the hagiographic tradition of recounting a life (*zhitie*). Both literally and allegorically, Zosima's teaching bears witness to his life and the lives of those who played major roles in his spiritual journey from a proud army officer to the revered religious elder. The reader receives the message from Alyosha, Zosima's "dear, quiet boy," who does not merely record the teaching of the *starets*, but bears witness to his love. In one of his letters, Dostoevsky predicts that some people would shout at Zosima's words and call them "absurd, since too elated." But, he continues, "they are of course absurd in the everyday sense, but in another inner sense, they seem justified."[15] In a "homily" recorded by Alyosha, the elder addresses the theme of sin and the legitimacy of indignation:

> If the wickedness of people arouses indignation and insurmountable grief in you, to the point that you desire to revenge yourself upon the wicked, fear that feeling most of all; go at once and seek torments for yourself, as if you yourself were guilty of their wickedness. Take these torments upon yourself and suffer them, and your heart will be eased, and you will understand that you, too, are guilty, for you might have shone to the wicked, even like the only sinless One, but you did not. If you had shone, your light would have lighted the way for others...[16]

Zosima's response to Ivan Karamazov's terrifying question about the unavenged tears of a little child is indirect. Ivan famously argued that God's world is intolerable so long as the innocent children suffer in it. Even if all torment is destined to disappear in some very distant future, the pain, tears, and humiliation of children who suffer today and suffered in the past can never be justified by any future harmony. Dostoevsky himself considered the question of his hero unanswerable, but through Zosima and Alyosha he offers an alternative to Ivan's indignation. This alternative involves one's conscious, tireless fighting of the world's injustices by means of active, humble love. As Robert Belknap

---

15. Letter from Fyodor Dostoevsky to Konstantin Pobedonostsev, August 24, 1879, in F. M. Dostoevsky, *Complete Collection of Writings in Thirty Volumes* (in Russian), edited by G. M. Fridlender, vol. 30, bk. 1: *Letters* (Leningrad: Nauka, 1988) 122; translation mine.

16. Fyodor Dostoevsky, *The Brothers Karamazov*, translated by Richard Pevear and Larissa Volokhonsky (New York: Farrar, Straus and Giroux, 1990) 321.

points out, instead of "answering" Ivan's question, the elder redirects it to the questioner; instead of asking why God allows suffering, Zosima urges you to ask yourself why you allow it.[17] According to Dostoevsky's design, the intellectual Ivan falls short of the task of nurturing in himself a heedful, active love. Unlike Alyosha, who devotes himself to his family and becomes a spiritual guide to a group of young boys at the end of the novel, Ivan holds on to his drawing room discussions of divine injustice and resists the role of his brother's keeper.

The theme of universal responsibility unfolds on various levels in the novel: the oldest brother Dmitry, inspired by the mystical vision of the "suffering babe," accepts punishment for the crime he did not commit; Alyosha befriends a group of school boys who initially gang up on one of their classmates but who, with Alyosha's guidance, begin to learn the values of mutual love and compassion; and, lastly, the seductress Grushenka overcomes her pride as well as self-centeredness and resolves to share Dmitry's ordeal. These characters, themselves abandoned children in the past, transform their own torment into healing relations to others. Ivan's suffering, on the other hand, leads him to delirium for he continues to treasure his acute sense of injustice at the expense of real, heart-felt connections to people around him. His passionate search for the answer to the paradox of senseless suffering leads him into a deadlock; it becomes a self-fulfilling prophecy, confirming the sheer destructiveness of undeserved pain. In Ivan's world, then, suffering is purposeless and will always remain so.

While continuing the Orthodox tradition of venerating suffering, Dostoevsky puts it in a concrete social-ethical context and presents co-suffering as a powerful antidote to grave social injustices. Dostoevsky's heroes suffer with and for others, seek suffering for its own sake, suffer to expiate their guilt, prostrate themselves before a sinner who represents the suffering humanity, and even offer false confession in pursuit of the purifying power of hardship. Ultimately, Dostoevsky's novels demonstrate that by suffering with others we do not increase the ills of the world but partake in a genuinely humane communion, sustained by love and mutual responsibility.

---

17. Robert Belknap "The Rhetoric of an Ideological Novel," in *Literature and Society in Imperial Russia, 1800–1914*, edited by William Mills Todd III and Robert L. Belknap (Stanford: Stanford University Press, 1978) 186.

The Unorthodox Greek Orthodoxy of Constantine Cavafy

John Estes

Introduction: The Poetics of Humility

CONSTANTINE CAVAFY IS KNOWN, by those who know him, as many things: a Greek poet, an erotic poet, a gay poet, a historical poet. Those who knew him in life, where he lived in Alexandria, knew him as a singular character with a distinctive voice and a gift for friendship; in E. M. Forster's famous description of him he was a "gentleman in a straw hat, standing . . . at a slight angle to the universe."[1] One adjective by which neither he nor his work has been known, however, is religious. While many of his historical poems set in Alexandrian and Hellenistic antiquity cannot but engage the Orthodox Church, they are, at least on the surface, unsympathetic to the faith or are plainly antagonistic, even if satirically so. In Robert Liddell's biography, between Cavafy's first-chapter baptism and his deathbed reception of the sacraments from the patriarch in the book's penultimate paragraph, the few mentions of Orthodoxy emphasize his personal indifference to it. Though he would position himself outside the cathedral each Good Friday to watch the "beautiful and touching" funeral procession, Liddell cannot conclude, from any evidence, "if this was only a love of Greek forms, or if he had any religious conviction."[2] Cavafy's mature style—distant, ironic, unfigured—welcomes this restrained interpretation, and it would be impossible to argue some hidden allegiance to his cultural faith. That

---

1. E. M. Forster, "The Poetry of C. P. Cavafy," in *The Mind and Art of C. P. Cavafy: Essays on His Life and Work* (Athens: Denise Harvey, 1983) 13.
2. Robert Liddell, *Cavafy: A Critical Biography* (London: Duckworth, 1974) 250.

is not my program. While Cavafy's poetry is hardly orthodox in the literal sense of expressing "right beliefs," his poems embody a spirit that is continuous with the historical, and even literary, heart of the Orthodox tradition. To make this reading possible requires an assertion that the core of Orthodoxy is not a set of theological statements but a stillness that looks upon humanity and the world with love.

Cavafy's poems construct what Edmund Keeley calls a "universal perspective" that, defined by a stylistic modesty and detached stance, may seem to a reader singularly unpoetic: a flow of facts and gestures with the barest sinew of obvious feeling, emanating from a place beyond (or prior to) judgment and ideology.[3] They are a kind of close reading—idylls as much as poems, "little pictures"—of moments in time; the utter simplicity of the vision proffers a world where, paradoxically, ecstasies are among our most permanent possessions. By suppressing his own personality behind the flat statements and the masks of characters, Cavafy achieves an ascetical feat, despite his poems amounting to a passionate defense of the sensual life. When he reveals himself his bias is for the human *qua* human; even his satires and critiques use humor in a way that evoke compassion for fools. In representing everyone as equally frail and fumbling in their attempts to live, without prejudice for religious, political, or economic station, Cavafy's voice—as mysterious as it is unmistakable, as unique as it is catholic—embodies an erotic humility.

This conflation of desire and meekness is what becomes most suggestively Orthodox in Cavafy's accomplishment, which is perhaps less scandalous when eros is understood in its broader sense, including but not eclipsed by the sexual. Stanley Rosen defines eros as "a striving for wholeness or perfection, a combination of poverty and contrivance, of need mitigated by a presentiment of completeness."[4] Similarly, Christos Yannaras defines it as "the dynamic movement of loving self-offering," as the essential energy of the cosmos binding all things together.[5] What activates this energy is a realization of one's impoverishment, and an openness to what may come, what Olivier Clement defines simply as

---

3. Edmund Keeley, *Cavafy's Alexandria: Study of a Myth in Progress* (Cambridge: Harvard University Press, 1976) 147.

4. Stanley Rosen, *The Quarrel Between Philosophy and Poetry: Studies in Ancient Thought* (New York: Routledge, 1988) 103.

5. Christos Yannaras, *Person and Eros*, translated by Norman Russell (Brookline, MA: Holy Cross Orthodox Press, 2007) 118.

humility, "the acceptance of self in openness to the Other."[6] Cavafy's relationship to the world is compassionate, egalitarian insofar as he recognizes this need in everyone. After Isaac of Ninevah, he "considers all human beings good, and no created thing appears impure or defiled to him."[7] Not that he does not have favorites: those committed to love for its own sake come out better than those who seek it for ego aggrandizement. But in his understated approach, free of absolutes, Cavafy grants the subjects of his attention an autonomy that amounts, in most cases, to a benefit of doubt. His hesitancy to judge adds to the sense that the poems are moments of possibility realized, but also possibility reborn; his histories often ache with the charismatic quality that hope remains for everyone. By observing human behavior from a position of pre-valuation, he can report with authority the follies in which all theological, moral, and political self-righteousness eventuates, and why he cherishes above all erotic desire, which is as natural to the soul as being itself, and thus worthy of trust.

The poem "Growing Strong" makes explicit tenets that remain implicit in other poems, an antinomianism that favors the immediately knowable because inhabitable: sensuality, primal energies, unconditioned being:

> He who wishes to strengthen his spirit,
> must abandon reverence and submission.
> He will honor some laws,
> but mostly he will break both law and custom,
> and he will stray from the accepted, inadequate straight path.[8]

These values have a literary history that Robert Bly describes as "a vigorous awareness of what language is like when it reaches outward to plants and metals, as well as inward to night-intelligence and sleep."[9] Cavafy extends integrity into the smallest quarters, and in its relation to the lyric speaker, this poetic amounts to what Bly later calls a "struggle against narcissism," exemplified by a "serene and transparent style," which cor-

---

6. Olivier Clément, *The Roots of Christian Mysticism: Text and Commentary* (London: New City, 1993) 149.

7. Ibid., 283.

8. Constantine Cavafy, *The Collected Poems of C. P. Cavafy: A New Translation*, translated by Aliki Barnstone (New York: Norton, 2006) 20.

9. Robert Bly, *News of the Universe: Poems of Twofold Consciousness* (San Francisco: Sierra Club Books, 1980) 80.

responds to Cavafy's typical self-effacement.[10] This humility, it should be stressed, is not a moral program but a kind of proto-morality. The same movement inward, throwing off scales of thou-shalts along the way, may lead one to a Nietzschean will to power, but under a different calculus may also lead one toward Christian piety. Cavafy continues:

> He will be taught much by sensual pleasures.
> He will not fear the destructive act;
> half the house must be torn down.
> This way he will grow virtuously toward knowledge.[11]

The return to self—the fearless reckoning with one's natural person as given—is the central action of the Orthodox contemplative tradition, and for the monk and layperson alike, stripping away the layers of accumulated, received belief is necessary to reach the illumined interior.

The Alexandrian Tradition

There are traditions of Alexandrian thinking that both clarify this sensibility and throw light on Cavafy's artistic strategies. What most defined the Alexandrian school's contribution to Orthodox theology, represented by the famed and misunderstood heretic Origen, is an emphasis on the unified nature of Christ as man and God. Concomitant to that is the defense of the individuals' unique soul which, by the process of deification, is brought to a similar condition, a dual human and divine nature. Deification, or *theosis*, is most succinctly defined in Athanasius's formula: God became man so that man may become God.[12] According to Edward Moore, what was lost over time in the church's thinking about this process was Origen's emphasis on the persistent individuality of the soul, which remains fully idiosyncratic even under transformation. He credits Maximus the Confessor for most persuasively "describ[ing] salvation as the replacement of personal ego with the divine presence."[13] Most important to Moore is the dynamic process (and responsibility) this entails, committing to history a cooperative activity between God

---

10. Ibid., 127.
11. Cavafy, *Collected Poems*, 20.
12. St. Athanasius *On the Incarnation* 54.3.
13. Edward Moore, "Origen of Alexandria and St. Maximus the Confessor," PhD diss. (St. Elias School of Orthodox Theology, 2004) 104. Available for download online at http://dissertation.com/book.php?method=ISBN&book=1581122616.

and individuals. As he quotes Nicolas Berdyaev: "The creative act of man is needed for the coming of the kingdom . . . God is in need of and awaits it."[14]

The belief that God deals with persons as individuals immersed in a specific relational context is best exemplified by the tradition of *oikonomia*, where a priest, in his role as caretaker of souls, exercises "pastoral flexibility according to the particular situation of each person."[15] Cavafy's poetry can be read as demonstrating—unlike historians such as Herodotus, Plutarch, and Augustine in whose lineage he viewed himself—that history does not unfold according to an inherent order called Nature, or Fortune, or Justice. Rather it keeps pace with, and shifts in accord with, human choices that are inherently imperfect. Peter Bien compares Cavafy to the ancient Alexandrians who were defined by their territorial marginality and the confluence of Christianity and paganism that existed in their city. "What was natural to him, and therefore interested him poetically, was compromise, dilemma, indecision, bewilderment: the true, weak, and 'human' reactions of the average man caught between antagonistic loyalties."[16] Cavafy's poems follow the drama of desire as shaped in history, and argue that, through small yet decisive acts, eros makes destiny.

Another Alexandrian literary tradition that informs his work is that of Theocritus's bucolic idylls. Cavafy does not, on the surface, appear to fit in what we commonly consider (after Virgil) the pastoral genre; his poems do not allegorize, do not idealize rustic landscapes, or contrast country virtue with urban venality. There are no shepherds, no sheep or cows, and no one plays a pipe. But William Empson's designation of the pastoral as "putting the complex into the simple" has helped define the pastoral as a mode marked by internal structure rather than generic conventions, and suggests a schema, as well as a context, for reading Cavafy's typical strategy of narrative and tonal reduction. As Empson says, "The simple man becomes a clumsy fool who yet has better 'sense' than his betters and can say things more fundamentally true; he is in contact

---

14. Nikolai Berdyaev, *The Beginning and the End*, translated by R. M. French (New York: Harper, 1952) 152.

15. Kallistos Ware, *The Inner Kingdom* (Crestwood, NY: St. Vladimir's Seminary Press, 2000) 52.

16. Peter Bien, *Constantine Cavafy* (New York: Columbia University Press, 1964) 27.

with nature ... speak[s] the truth because he has nothing to lose."[17] By adopting an anti-heroic stance, Cavafy opens a literary space that projects a poetic ethos. Kathryn Gutzwiller has shown how the Theocritean cowherd is equated, by analogy, to the poet: sensual, playful, marginal, skilled at song. The keeper of livestock is uniquely qualified to order and guard divine thought.[18] The bucolics were a "creative response to the epic tradition," according to David Halperin; insofar as Homer depicted war and political struggle with domestic and erotic life as a distant foil—the life Achilles chose against—Theocritus inverts the equation.[19] Similarly, Cavafy mutes epic concerns and foregrounds private agonies; he locates in history moments other chroniclers would deem insignificant. And like Theocritus, Cavafy refused "to accept the roles of teacher, prophet or sage"; rather than seeking public acclaim he distributed his poems among friends, written "to gratify himself and others."[20]

The Iconic Imagination

The crux of Cavafian perception turns on an insight that humans are social and relational beings prior to their individuality. Our personhood is conditioned by our bodies, our dependence upon others, our environments, and the cultural beliefs we inherit. Cavafy's moral scheme privileges relationship over isolated subjectivity, feeling over principle; to use Edmund Husserl's phrase, experience is intersubjective, and not surprisingly the pre-eminent emotion Cavafy explores is empathy, or the lack of it. In his lifeworld, people are divided, quite unequally, between those who act from their hearts and those who live by their heads, by calculation and conformity in service of self-advancement. The Orthodox tradition claims as its central ecclesial analogy a hospital—therapy and healing—as opposed to a court of justice. In the East imagination precedes reason, experience trumps explanation, worship produces theology. Kallistos Ware phrased it in terms of an attitude toward God:

17. William Empson, *Some Versions of Pastoral: A Study of Pastoral Form in Literature* (Harmondsworth: Penguin, 1966) 14.

18. Kathryn J. Gutzwiller, *Theocritus' Pastoral Analogies: The Formation of a Genre* (Madison: University of Wisconsin Press, 1991) 30.

19. David M. Halperin, *Before Pastoral, Theocritus and the Ancient Tradition of Bucolic Poetry* (New Haven: Yale University Press, 1983) 238.

20. Ibid., 243.

"[The] joy and beauty of the Kingdom cannot be properly expounded in abstract arguments . . . it has to be experienced, not discussed."[21] Imagining emerges in Cavafy's poems as the supreme force of life, an energy capable of shaping a workable relation between one's body and everything outside of it, and through memory the realm of spiritual succor. As Denis Donoghue explains, "Imagination is the power by which that which is considered natural, conventional, or axiomatic is transfigured to become truly known, possessed in the form of knowledge and action." [22] It is the soul itself.

These factors can be seen at work in the poem "Before Time Changed Them—," which tells of two lovers who were forced to part, as "circumstance . . . drove one of them / far away to New York or Canada." Although their "attraction cooled," and they continued to acknowledge that they would not have chosen to part, Cavafy offers a solace:

> Or perhaps Chance
> turned out to be an artist, parting them now
> before their feelings were snuffed out, before Time changed them.
> For each the other will always stay
> the twenty-four-year-old beautiful boy.[23]

A cynical reading is that the memories of people are valued over the people themselves; memories, selective as they are, can be made perfect. But that distinction does not exist in Cavafy's poems; contents of the mind and contents of the physical world are fused. An image, even a mental image, is formed in the body and remains part of the body, and one like this, made by the impression of love, especially carries with it salutary effects. In another poem he calls these images "the joy and perfume of my life . . . the memory of the hours / when I found and held sensual pleasure as I wanted it."[24] History, chance, accident: these are but interpretive constructs manufactured after the fact, but to follow the lead of eros is to produce memories beyond the need for interpretation, true images in the mind that contain real presence. In Cavafy's poems memories and dreams are as visceral as physical or historical evidence.

---

21. Ware, *Inner Kingdom*, 65.

22. Denis Donoghue, *The Sovereign Ghost: Studies in Imagination* (Berkeley: University of California Press, 1976) 28–29.

23. Cavafy, *Collected Poems*, 152.

24. Ibid., 93.

The image as a consolation for the absent beloved is a frequent trope in Cavafy's poems, and bears a similarity to the Orthodox theology of the icon. It is worth noting that iconography is not a mere cultural attribute of the Eastern liturgy but identified with the essence of the faith; the triumph over the iconoclasts in 787 was called the Triumph of Orthodoxy. The central dispute was over how the practice of the mind's interaction with images worked in service to the religious imagination and in turn aided the deification of the soul. The iconoclasts focused strictly upon what Milton Anastos calls "the ethical theory of the image," that knowledge of the image's subject is efficacious but degraded by the image itself. Their arguments at the council of Nicea (754) presaged Protestant iconoclasm of the seventeenth century and what remains a common religious belief: that "it is shameful to put trust in colors and not in the heart, for that [faith] which is in colors is easily washed away, while that which is in the depth of the mind is dear."[25] A central analogy upon which the controversy turned was the status of the written text. The iconoclasts approved of the study of words while denouncing the veneration of images, but as Daniel Sahas points out, "the word for 'scripture' in Greek (*graphe*) means both 'writing' and 'painting'; in the Greek Orthodox mind there is no separation, no division, between these two forms of communication, let alone abrogation of [one by the other]."[26] Artistic representations and the "ethical image" were coherently linked, in keeping with the incarnational theology that bound heaven and earth in Christ's body. As it was decreed, "The more often [images of Christ, the Theotokos and the saints] are seen in figural representation, the more readily men are lifted up to remember their prototypes and long for them."[27]

Verbal and imagistic indeterminacy mark Cavafy's anti-dualism, and evinces his interest in representing minute complexities of feeling, particularly the epistemological ambiguities where desire and belief intersect. "In Church" begins, "I love the church—with its sacred banners, / the silver of its vessels, its candelabra, / the lights, its icons, its

25. Milton Anastos, "The Ethical Theory of Images Formulated By the Iconoclasts in 754 and 815," *Dumbarton Oaks Papers* 8 (1954) 154.

26. Daniel J. Sahas, *Icon and Logos: Sources in Eighth-Century Iconoclasm: An Annotated Translation of the Sixth Session of the Seventh Ecumenical Council* (Toronto: University of Toronto Press, 1986) 14.

27. J. M. Hussey, *The Orthodox Church in the Byzantine Empire* (Oxford: Clarendon, 1986) 48–49.

pulpit," and continues to list other sensuous and beautiful events encountered in "the church of the Greeks." Reflexive dualism instructs us to view this emphasis on outward appearance with suspicion. Perhaps the tone is ironic, and the fact that this experience sends his mind "to the great honor of our people, / to our glorious Byzantium" should be read as an indictment of the Church as merely a pageant, a historical relic, outwardly beautiful but spiritually bankrupt.[28] But read under the assumption that an erotic response to beauty is spiritually authentic, the physical beauty marks the presence of inward beauty, and our desire for identification with or possession of the beautiful is a moral act. Aliki Barnstone says about this poem that Greeks love the Church "not for theology, but for identity and ecstasy . . . the past erotically merges with the present, and becomes myth."[29] Cavafy credibly preserves both readings, leaving us suspended in the irresolvable question of why we are drawn to what draws us.

Poetry and Hesychasm

One way to understand Cavafy's detachment, both as a principle and a narrative strategy, is by analogy to the hesychastic formulations about the nature of the world and human knowledge that emerged in the fourteenth century. *Hesychia*, literally "stillness," is a form of contemplative prayer practiced by monks in solitude and silence, often called "prayer of the heart." It became a definitive part of Orthodox spirituality through a dispute between Barlaam, a philosopher who sought to bring Western humanism to Byzantine theology, and Gregory Palamas, who, in his defense of Eastern prayer and the tenets that sponsor it, articulated the relation between God and creation that instituted hesychasm into Church dogma. Motivated by the good intention of bridging East and West and a sincere advocacy for apophatic mysticism, Barlaam nonetheless represented a trend toward philosophic nominalism long ascendant, arguing that since God is ultimately unknowable human reason alone is the province, and arbiter, of theological understanding. At stake, as John Meyendorff explains, was the East's integral approach to philosophy-as-theology. Had Barlaam succeeded in separating theology from its prophetic roots, as had happened in the Christian West, "a whole whirlwind

---

28. Cavafy, *Collected Poems*, 57.
29. "C. P. Cavafy: Eros and History as Prophesy," in ibid., xxxv.

of the new ideas of modern times would have broken down the framework of medieval society" and led to its own version of renaissance and reformation "in the spirit of the new nominalist philosophy."[30]

Palamas's refutation of Barlaam was that while it may be true that God's essence is inaccessible to human perception—sensual or otherwise—God's energies were not; that although God, the uncreated, is entirely distinct from creation, lines of interior communication remain. The central dispute, introduced by Greek philosophy and as actively disputed today, revolved around the dualism between knowledge and sense experience, or just how fundamentally divided the knowing self is from material reality. "Barlaam's criticism of hesychastic prayer is in reality based on a spiritualistic presupposition . . . that identifies the supernatural with the immaterial. Even to think of the human body as a possible receptacle of grace seemed an intolerable outrage."[31] Palamas successfully defended the sanctity of matter on incarnational grounds, and preserved the possibility of prophetic encounter between the divine energies and the soul. Simply put, the doctrine that Palamas established and which, like icons in the eighth century, became equated with Orthodoxy itself, is that God is met in the body.

That perception is confined to the body—that we are our bodies—is an insight as contrary to the dominant strains of Western tradition as it is central to Orthodoxy. Our comprehension of the world is inextricable from the historical, material, social, and political. No sharp divide between spirit and matter exists, and what happens to one happens through the other. As Palamas writes, "When spiritual joy comes to the body from the mind, it suffers no diminution by this communion with the body, but rather transfigures the body, spiritualizing it."[32] However distinct the creation may be from God, so long as the cosmos is divided into God and not-God just one more dualism has been instituted. What spares the Church fathers from this dead-end dialectic is a Trinitarian logic that posits a constant motion—*perichoresis*—between the three persons. The being that defines God is not a static being but the dynamic activity of constant relation, ever in the process of creation; "being is not a genus whereunder God as 'a being' might be subsumed, but is the act

---

30. John Meyendorff, *St. Gregory Palamas and Orthodox Spirituality* (Crestwood, NY: St. Vladimir's Seminary Press, 1998) 99.

31. Ibid., 111.

32. Ibid., 113.

through which beings are given form by the God who is never without form and beauty."[33]

Cavafy's poems dramatically evoke this existential, if not natural, condition. While his interest is not in paths of salvation—at least not as traditionally conceived—nearly all his poems find their tension in the dramatic possibility of transformation. He recognizes that our primal instinct is to identify and join ourselves in communion, but that how we do this and with whom can enlarge as well as diminish us. The people in his poems are either at the cusp of choosing for or against these creative energies, or else confronting the consequences of their choices. All Cavafian characters suffer, but what distinguishes the barren suffering of those who look outward for help that never quite arrives and the fruitful anguish of others is the presence of eros, an animating desire, a spiritual and physical craving for transfiguration.

The contrary examples are perhaps most telling. In "Ioannis Kantakouzinos Triumphs," the central figure is a nobleman experiencing fear of retribution for having sided with Anna—the widow of the Emperor Andronikos III—in the civil war (1341–47) against Kantakouzinos who, now victorious, has become Emperor (the former Grand Domestic for Andronikos, Kantakouzinos had presided over the council of 1341 condemning Barlaam and officially adopting the hesychast theology of Palamas). One cannot help but pity the fellow, a useful idiot by all accounts:

> He looks at the fields he still owns—
> the wheat, the animals, the fruit-laden trees;
> and farther away, his ancestral home,
> full of clothing, precious furniture, and silver vessels.
>
> They'll take it all away—Jesus Christ!—now they'll
> take it all away.[34]

A Cavafian type, this man's suffering is rooted in misguided calculation, his faith misplaced as he traded genuine feeling for presumed safety and security. He reveals no aesthetic allegiance, no devotion to one side or another, but merely sought to be on the right side of political power. He is no different than the citizenry in Cavafy's most famous poem, "Waiting

---

33. David Bentley Hart, *The Beauty of the Infinite: The Aesthetics of Christian Truth* (Grand Rapids: Eerdmans, 2004) 235.

34. Cavafy, *Collected Poems*, 155.

for the Barbarians." Commerce, government, and daily life have ceased while everyone awaits the arrival of an invading horde. It is revealed at the end, as news from the border arrives in the city, that the barbarians no longer exist. "Now what will become of us without barbarians? / Those people were some kind of solution."[35] One cannot avoid politics, but to strategize one's loyalty, as opposed to being lead by one's heart, is to be met with frustration, impotence, or failure.

Conclusion: Poetry as Theology

An old patristic adage is that "The theologian is one who knows how to pray," and Paul Evdokimov claims it expresses the central tenet of Orthodoxy, which begins with worship and only later "translates into theological terms the experience of God."[36] The *Philokalia*, that central text of Orthodox prayer and spirituality, defines theology as an "active and conscious participation in or perception of the realities of the divine world," which "presupposes the attainment of the state of stillness and dispassion."[37] The attitude presupposed is *nepsis*, or watchfulness—alertness, vigilance, attention. As I have said, it is neither accurate nor helpful to ascribe to Cavafy an Orthodox agenda, or a concern for particularly Christian virtues. When Yannaros describes the Church fathers' opinion that "for us to encounter the world's true beauty—'not the imaginary beauty of the flesh'—we must draw back from the physical demand for beauty," we sense a brand of asceticism in conflict with the Cavafian ethos.

But if prayer is seen as a form of attention, and we follow Paul Celan in defining attention as the "natural prayer of the soul," then the notion that Cavafy's poems are a kind of proto-theology is not only defensible but circumscribes a view of his overall achievement. Simone Weil defines attention as "directed desire," and sees it as a prerequisite to prayer: both require one be situated in ambiguity, between a now and a not yet, and require attunement to the finite particular. "Attention consists in suspending our thought, leaving it detached, empty, and ready to be penetrated by the object; it means holding our minds, within reach of

---

35. Ibid., 28.

36. Paul Evdokimov, *In the World, of the Church: A Paul Evdokimov Reader* (Crestwood, NY: St. Vladimir's Seminary Press, 2001) 139.

37. Nicodemus et al., *The Philokalia: The Complete Text* (London: Faber, 1983) 367.

this thought, but on a lower level and not in contact with it."³⁸ Cavafy aims toward intimate contact with his subjects, and through subtle attention reveals how they traverse pain, uncertainty, failure or loss.

"In the Bars" is spoken by of one of his saddest youths: "I wallow in the bars and brothels / of Beirut," he begins, heart broken because Tamidis left him for the Prefect's son, who can also provide him with a villa on the Nile. But despite living a "low life" in "cheap debauchery," he clings to the purity of his memory—it saves him "like lasting beauty, like lingering perfume" on his flesh—of Tamidis, who was his for two years "and not for a house or a villa on the Nile."³⁹ One cannot help but conclude that despite his admittedly wretched life, the nakedness of his spiritual condition is praiseworthy, and his memory of Tamidis true iconic solace. Compare to "A Byzantine Nobleman in Exile Composing Verses": equally cast out of the life he most desired, this man who insists "no one knows the Church Fathers / or the Scriptures or the rules of the Synods better than I do" finds it "not inappropriate that I would amuse myself / writing sextets and octets" versified in "strict iambs."⁴⁰ As opposed to the libertine above, this fatuous man fails, despite his lack of dissembling, to see himself as anything more than his accomplishments and the regard powerful people once had for him. He lacks any imaginative or erotic space to find solace, much less healing. The difference between self-pathos and self-pity is the difference between making what good one can of life and a living hell.

In suspending us directly within the lives of characters as different as these two, Cavafy achieves a depth of attention, the perspective that Keeley calls "universal," and which renders him less a poetic speaker than a *conscience* "that sees any individual success and any specific historical movement subject to reversal by the gods and that shows wisdom and courage residing in the recognition of human limits."⁴¹ When he denies the world of his poems the consolations of cosmic time, and specifically a transcendent God who redeems and restores all things, the tragic horizon of death gives no one a way out. Without an eternal backstop, one's character is all there is; one either knows oneself, or not. The bracketing off of that comfort—even if one believes in it—for the

---

38. Simone Weil, *Waiting on God* (London: Routledge & Kegan Paul, 1979) 111.
39. Cavafy, *Collected Poems*, 165.
40. Ibid., 133.
41. Keeley, *Cavafy's Alexandria*, 148.

sake of confronting one's nature is a central method of Eastern spirituality, from the zen koan that instructs one to kill the Buddha if one meets him on the road, to the message of Christ who, when asked in a vision by the Athonite monk Silouan, "What must I do that my soul will grow humble?" answered, "Keep thy mind in hell and despair not."[42] By framing every choice as tragic within the horizon of death, Cavafy demonstrates a response to life that recommends an "honest and honorable stance" that attends to and celebrates "the passions [life] held, even as one sees the death it bears."[43]

Keeley cites "The God Abandons Antony" as a touchstone for how this plays out in Cavafy's mythos. As recounted in Plutarch, Antony, the night before he leaves Alexandria for the last time—the scene of his affair with Cleopatra and his defeat at the hands of Octavius—sees a group of musicians pass beneath his windows and enter the enemy's camp, which he interprets as his protective god, Dionysius, departing from him. The poet counsels him:

> When suddenly at the midnight hour
> you hear the invisible troupe passing by . . .
> don't futilely mourn your luck giving out, your work
> collapsing, the designs of your life
> that have all proved illusions.
>
> Above all don't fool yourself . . .

This is not a call to stoicism, but rather to "go stand by the window / and listen with feeling . . . / and hear the voices—your last pleasure—"[44]: to embrace the life granted him (which he will soon end atop his own sword). It may strike one as an odd, if not a perverse, eroticism to hand oneself over to fate in such a way, even to death. Is such love possible? Perhaps it is precisely the fleeting nature of physical beauty and sensual pleasure—its natural alignment with death in our imaginations—that makes it an effective trope. To die, according to Yannaras, is the transformation of the personal into the transpersonal, "*absence* as existential affirmation of the person."[45] Eros, the drive to meet and overcome the

---

42. Archimandrite Sophrony, *Saint Silouan, the Athonite* (Crestwood, NY: St. Vladimir's Seminary Press, 1999) 430.
43. Keeley, *Cavafy's Alexandria*, 149.
44. Cavafy, *Collected Poems*, 45.
45. Yannaras, *Person and Eros*, 125.

egoistic self, is both vehicle and tenor: the mode of our relation as well as the direction of its perfecting, however imperfect.

Poetry, in the widest sense, is the art of making something out of what would otherwise pass into non-existence. Triumphant moments offer little information but, as W. H. Auden famously said to Stephen Spender, "Art is born of humiliation."[46] One of Cavafy's most moving poems, "Come, O King of the Lacedaimonians," surrounds the parting of King Kleomenis and his mother, Kratisiklia, who, along with Kleomenis's children, must go to King Ptolemy as a hostage in exchange for wartime aid. She has tried to compose herself, but at the last minute goes to the temple of Poseidon with her son where "she embraced him / and kissed him, 'in great pain,' said / Plutarch, 'and deeply afflicted.'" Then, "the marvelous woman" turned with her son to exit the temple, toward the waiting ships, she took hold of herself and said:

> Come, O King
> of the Lacedaimonians, so when we go out
> no one will see us in tears
> nor doing anything unworthy of Sparta.
> For this is between us alone;
> on the other hand, fate will be as God gives it.

And she boarded the ship headed toward "the given."[47]

This is somewhere beyond an Emersonian triumph of principles, beyond a mere conformity to codes of honor for the sake of appearance, although those pressures are operative. Kratisiklia's decision to hand herself over for the sake of Sparta, and the manner in which she goes, is the consummation of her desire (and habit) to be immersed in energies that both compose her sense of self and exceed it. These energies are as real as they are imagined. Analogous to the poet's longing for beauty, and the monk's for holiness, these endeavors lead us toward humiliation, or humbling, in the etymological sense of being brought to the ground, literally *humus*, the earth. This erotic quest for contact with something beyond the conventions of polite society and beneath, or more accurately within, the physicality of the known world, unite these three figures. To quote Auden again, "The primary function of poetry, as of all the arts,

---

46. James Fenton, *The Strength of Poetry* (New York: Farrar, Straus and Giroux, 2001) 209.

47. Cavafy, *Collected Poems*, 193.

is to make us more aware of ourselves and the world around us . . . and I am quite certain it makes us more difficult to deceive."[48] There can be neither pleasure nor hope nor salvation of any kind for the self-deluded. And if there is an Orthodox theology to be drawn or made from Cavafy's poems, it is contained in that hope for clear sight, the capacity to abide, so understood, in prayer.

48. Ibid., 246.

THREE

In Lieu of Logos

Creation and Redemption in the Poetry of Scott Cairns

J. A. Jackson

> Blessed is he
> for whom Paradise yearns.
> Yes, Paradise yearns for the man whose goodness
> makes him beautiful.
>
> St. Ephrem the Syrian, *The Hymns on Paradise*.[1]

WHEN ASKED IN A 2004 interview to define his notion of "sacramental poetics," Scott Cairns responded: "Like the holy mysteries, then, poems—if they are truly poems—have agency, bear energy, are concerned more with making something with and of the observer than they are with referring her to a past event, or to a proposition, or to any previously discovered, temporally circumscribed, static matter."[2] One discovers in much of Scott Cairns's poetry a transformational, incarnational, even sacramental, theology of Eastern Orthodox Christianity. Cairns's poetry always points to something else, not in an allegorical or metaphorical way, but in a traditional typological sense—a historical, diachronic, participatory way. While typological exegesis of the

---

1. St. Ephrem the Syrian, *Hymns on Pardise*, translated by Sebastian Brock (Crestwood, NY: St. Vladimir's Seminary Press, 1990) 84.

2. Scott Cairns, "A Conversation with Scott Cairns," *Image: Art, Faith, Mystery* 44 (Winter 2004) 56. I urge the interested reader to read this interview, in which Cairns articulates his own theory of writing; and I think it is a treat to see a poet discuss the integrated life of prayer and poetry.

Old Testament looks for Christ in various passages, images, even words themselves, Cairns's poetry takes for granted that God has become man, that the world has already been transformed, that Paradise stands not in a spiritual nether region, nor solely as a promised beatified future, but that Paradise is here, now—and is to be experienced here, now—a rupturing of the finite world, an eschatological "already but not yet."[3] What stands at the crux of Cairns's poetry, and what I hope to demonstrate, is Eastern Orthodoxy's reliance upon a creation-redemption model of salvation as *theosis* (deification) versus a modern over-emphasis of salvation in terms of juridical sacrificial atonement, justification, and then sanctification.

Cur Deus Homo: An Eastern Approach

Though I have not the space to flesh out fully the stark and subtle differences between Orthodox soteriology and much of the soteriology found in Western Christian models, I shall sketch out some of the more obvious distinctions and the ones most pertinent to my discussion of Cairns's poetry. This discussion is not meant to act as an introduction to Orthodox theology, and I fully admit that many of the differences outlined below may not be as great as my brief sketch will indicate; yet, at the same time, some of the differences mentioned here between Eastern and Western soteriology could be even greater.[4] Since all of this theological discussion is pointing towards poetry (and vice versa), perhaps the most appropriate way to underscore some of the differences between Eastern and Western models of salvation is to quote one of the most prolific hymnographers in the East, Saint Ephrem the Syrian: "The Most

---

3. I'm borrowing this phrase from John D. Zizioulas, *Being as Communion: Studies in Personhood and the Church* (Crestwood, NY: St. Vladimir's Seminary Press, 1985) 62.

4. For two classic introductions to Orthodox Christianity, see Metropolitan Kalistos Ware, *The Orthodox Church*, new ed. (New York: Penguin, 1997), esp. 195–328; and idem., *The Orthodox Way*, rev. ed. (Crestwood, NY: St. Vladimir's Seminary Press, 1995). For a more detailed and comprehensive introduction to Orthodox Christianity, see John McGuckin, *The Orthodox Church: An Introduction to the History, Doctrine, and Spiritual Culture* (Malden, MA: Wiley-Blackwell, 2008), esp. 120–379. See also Dumitru Staniloae, *The Experience of God: Orthodox Dogmatic Theology*, 2 vols., translated and edited by Ioan Ionita and Robert Barringer (Brookline, MA: Holy Cross Orthodox Press, 2000). For a focused study on the mystical foundations of Eastern Orthodoxy, see Vladimir Lossky, *The Mystical Theology of the Eastern Church* (Crestwood, NY: St. Vladimir's Seminary Press, 1976).

High knew that Adam wanted to become a God, / so He sent His Son who put him on in order to grant him his desire."[5] If we were to pause at the first line of this hymn—"The Most High knew that Adam wanted to become a God"—and ask Christians to predict what was to follow, one can imagine a Miltonesque response: God would have to come and punish Adam for his hubristic overreaching, for his Luciferian desire to be like God. Then an articulation of the classic juridical understanding of salvation would follow: because God has been "dishonored" by Adam's sin, and infinitely so because God's honor is infinite, this honor must in some way be restored; that is to say, the relationship between God and man must be restored (especially since Adam has been justly punished by being separated from God). Christ the God-man (*theanthropos*) acts as the perfect sacrifice to restore God's honor; as the New Adam, he stands sacrificially in place of the old Adam to appease/restore the honor of God; or, to be more bold, Christ comes to appease the wrath of God that was and should have continually been justly visited upon man.[6]

Yet the very opposite of this sort of juridical reading is found in Ephrem's second line: "so He sent His Son who put him on in order to grant him his desire." One can see immediately that Ephrem's notion of the incarnation, his answer to *cur deus homo* (why the *theanthropos*) is relatively simple: to restore to man his original desire, the *telos* of his being created—to be sons of God, or, to use Saint Peter's language, to "become partakers of the divine nature," to participate synergistically with the Divine, and so to become divine. Ephrem sees nothing wrong with Adam's desire to be divine; in fact, this is why man is created. For Ephrem, and for much of the East, the problem lies in the fact that he reached for those heights too soon. He was not prepared for the knowledge borne of the tree, but perhaps someday he would have been. In fact, rather than seeing the expulsion from the garden solely as a punishment (or even worse, and bordering on the blasphemous, as seeing death introduced into the world as a punishment from God), many

---

5. Quoted in Sebastian Brock, "Introduction," in *Hymns on Paradise*, by St. Ephrem the Syrian, translated by Sebastian Brock (Crestwood, NY: St. Vladimir's Seminary Press, 1990) 73.

6. This is what I believe to be at the heart of the substitutionary model of atonement. There are obviously various versions within this model—from the *felix culpa*, to Anselm's *Cur Deus Homo*, to Calvinism's penal substitution. For a brilliant and sympathetic Orthodox reading of Anselm's *Cur Deus Homo*, see David Bentley Hart, *Beauty of the Infinite* (Grand Rapids: Eerdmans, 2003) 360–72.

commentators in the East see the expulsion as an act of divine mercy.[7] Ephrem understands Adam and Eve's disposition towards God as one of suffering and near despair, for their eyes have been opened both to their own shame and to the Divine Glory. But with this exposure to the Divine Glory, their shame becomes even more heightened. Herein lies the paradox: the more one experiences the Glory of God (the Uncreated Energies of God), the more of one's unworthiness one experiences. Such is the magnified case of Adam and Eve. In Hymn II.7, Ephrem describes Paradise as torment for Adam and Eve because of their exposure to the Divine Glory:

> But when Adam boldly ran
>   And ate of this fruit
> this double knowledge
>   straightway flew toward him,
> tore away and removed
>   both veils from his eye:
> he beheld the Glory of the Holy of Holies
>   and trembled;
> he beheld, too, his own shame and blushed,
>   groaning and lamenting
> because the twofold knowledge he had gained
>   had proved for him a torment.[8]

And so, out of mercy, God cuts them off from the Tree of Life, lest they suffer eternally, experiencing and thus transforming Paradise into Hell.

The incarnation, then, is a response to the fruit of that original transgression: death. Man is created with both body and soul, and this is his natural condition. Death is an unnatural and, it turns out, historically temporary condition, for when God became man, was crucified, and was resurrected, he healed that ontological rift. In becoming man, God healed man; or, in the Church's Paschal language: "Christ is risen from the dead, trampling down death by death, and upon those in the tombs

---

7. St. Basil writes: "To the extent that man stood apart from life, in like amount he also drew closer to death. For life is God, and the deprivation of life is death. Thus Adam prepared death for himself through his withdrawal from God, as it is written, 'Those who separate themselves from you are lost.' Therefore, God did not create death, but we brought it upon ourselves by our wicked purpose. Neither did he prevent the dissolution, for the reasons already stated: so that illness would not be preserved immortal in us" (quoted in John Romanides, *The Ancestral Sin*, translated by George S. Gabriel [Ridgewood, NJ: Zephyr, 2002], 31).

8. St. Ephrem the Syrian, *Hymns on Paradise*, 93.

bestowing life." We see Saint Athanasius make this point repeatedly in his *On the Incarnation*: "The supreme object of His coming was to bring about the resurrection of the body. This was to be the monument of his victory over death, the assurance to all that he had Himself conquered corruption and that their own bodies would eventually be incorrupt."[9] Or one can find its succinct formulation in Athanasius's most famous proclamation: "He, indeed, assumed humanity that we might become God."[10] We see then in Orthodoxy a sense of atonement that very much takes literally the notion of at-one-ment: the human and divine relationship is one of participation, a synergistic relationship where the human and divine meet.[11] One could go so far as to say that man was created for atonement; indeed, to be fully human is to participate with the Uncreated Divine Energies—to be made one with God. As Ephrem will point out, God became man to grant us our desire (which also turns out to be God's original desire), to make it possible for us to become divine, to bridge the chasm that death (caused by Satan and Adam and Eve) wrought—the separation of man from God. Repentance, prayer, fasting, the participation in the sacraments of the Church—these are the offerings the faithful sacrificially give back to God, an asymmetrical reciprocal gesture on the part of the faithful returning that which has been offered to us in the incarnation, crucifixion, and resurrection. For salvation finds itself in the reciprocal gesture of this dual offering: our insufficient gesture to God in response to his infinitely excessive gesture of self-emptying love.

"At the glib horizon's edge": A Sacramental Poetics

In composing his "sacramental" poetry, Cairns utilizes many inter-related spiritual traditions within Eastern Orthodoxy. Apophaticism saturates his poetry, and one can see in his poetry an attempt to achieve a certain

---

9. St. Athanasius, *On the Incarnation*, translated by a religious of C.S.M.V (Crestwood, NY: St. Vladimir's Seminary Press, 1993) 52 (¶ 22).

10. Ibid., 93 (¶ 54).

11. "Atonement" is first used theologically in the English language by William Tindale in 1526 in his translation of 2 Cor 5:18. See "atonement" in the *Oxford English Dictionary*. In the fourteenth century, mystics such as the author of the *Cloud of Unknowing* and Julian of Norwich would use the verb "onyd" or "oned" to mean "united," though they no doubt had the sense that it would mean "at-one-ment."

apatheia in its relation to the world and even to the reader.¹² Like the desert fathers (or like Ephrem above) who often comment on Scripture by telling stories (a sort of Christian *Midrash*), Cairns's poetry also defies classification: it is both literature and exegesis.¹³ Cairns's poetry stands as a mediator, an icon, that points not to the poetry itself, nor purely to a concrete linguistic referent, nor to a biblical or liturgical text, but points to that which all of these texts—indeed, all of the material world—is never not pointing: the necessity of a synergistic divine-human relationship, a theanthropic existence. The richness of Cairns's poetry is the near effortlessness—his own developed poetic *apatheia*—with which he both depicts and encounters the divinized life in his poetry.¹⁴ He can articulate with awe the simplicity of creation, with both remorse and joy the blissful sadness inherent in *metanoia* (repentance), and with a fullness that is excessive and overflowing yet also tinged with a spirit of self-emptying, always longing for more of a redemption found already within creation when lived within the fullness of a life of repentance.

In his poem "Adventures in New Testament Greek: *Metanoia*," Cairns attempts to sketch out the difference between a mundane understanding of repentance—"of thought revisited," "compunction with a pledge / of recurrent screw-up"—and *metanoia*.¹⁵ While he sees in *metanoia* a sense of compunction, a sense of guilt for a wrong done, and perhaps in this a pledge to sin no more, the significance of *metanoia* for Cairns is not so much about the past, "of thought revisited," about the turning away from one's sins, but of a turning "*toward*" something else: toward one's true pilgrim self, toward the "man alive" (to use Saint Irenaeus's term), toward the Glory of God. In an elegant twist, he concludes his poem with a succinct thesis on the nature of sin, tapping into, I believe, the true spirit of the Greek *hamartia* ("missing the mark"). Cairns observes that the problem with sin is not that it is "bad," which it

---

12. Cairns notes the importance of the apophatic theologians—St. Dionysus the Areopagite, St. Gregory of Nyssa, St. Maximos the Confessor, St.Isaac the Syrian, and St. Gregory Palamas—to his poetry (Cairns, "Conversation," 59).

13. In my own conversation with Cairns, he expressed how deeply interested he is in rabbinic literature and its approach to, its constant wrestling with, Scripture. Indeed, Cairns's poem "In Lieu of Logos" is a meditation on his own relationship with this body of literature.

14. Having heard Cairns read his own poetry, I can attest to the apathetic intonation (and I mean this in the fullest, most positive sense) with which he reads his poetry.

15. Scott Cairns, *Philokalia* (Lincoln, NE: Zoo Press, 2002), 15, lines 7; 11–12.

surely is, but that it is "a waste of time" (l.20). Cairns envisions life—and a life lived in sin—not in a juridical mode, where transgressions are tallied up, forgiven, and then simply committed again—a repetitious cycle in which, perhaps, one finds no sense of time at all but an existence eked out between acts of sin. This, of course, is no life at all. Rather, sin is an affront to time, a waste of time, precisely because it hinders one from participating in the divine life, a divine life ushered into this world at the incarnation, the new creation, where all was assumed and therefore healed, all was recapitulated and united unto Christ, and this would include time itself. A sinful life lived repetitiously refuses to partake in the divine life and therefore lives outside of true time, i.e., outside of divinized time. The time of sin that Cairns rejects is time which is predicated upon only the past and the future, a time frame in which one can only dwell on one's sins and hope to be forgiven for a future time.

The playfulness of Cairns's assertion that sin is a waste of time means that he has imagined that time has also been assumed and healed at creation. Since the aim of *theosis* is a participation in the life in of the Divine Energies, and since God has assumed and therefore redefined time, indeed healed time itself, then a participation in sin is a waste, a throwing away of time fully recapitulated. *Theosis*, then, can be understood as standing at the crux of both created time (*chronos*) and Uncreated Time (*kairos*), the synergistic participation of the immanent and the transcendent, the human and the Divine. For Cairns, this mystical union is none other than salvation itself—an event not of the future (unless we envision the future, the *eschaton*, as potentially always already present), not of an undoing of the past, but of an experience of the present, a rupturing of finite time by the Infinite.[16]

In envisioning the world and all of its components as having been assumed and therefore healed by God, Cairns participates in a long Orthodox tradition of imagining the world as always already a paradise waiting to be discovered, to be enjoyed, to assume as one's own. In his famous death-bed speech/conversion, the *starets* Zosima's elder brother Markel both sings the praises of creation and yet laments the present condition: "'Mother, don't cry, life is paradise, and we're all in paradise,

---

16. See Zizioulas, *Being as Communion*, 61. He finds an expression of the fullness of the eschatological in the Eucharist: "The eucharist is not only an assembly in one place, that is, a historical realization and manifestation of the eschatological existence of man; it is at the same time also *movement*, a progress towards this realization."

though we don't want to acknowledge it; but if we only acknowledged it, there'd be paradise on earth tomorrow."[17] The paradisiacal existence named here by Fyodor Dostoevsky Cairns envisions as sacramental time, that is, the fullness of time, the fullness of a divinized existence itself. Like other writers in the East (Russian, Greek, Syriac), Cairns will continue to flesh out, to push to the limits of, the ever-presence of redemption, of Paradise itself.

In his "Adventure in New Testament Greek: *Apocatastasis*," Cairns alludes to a Syriac belief that "everyone will be redeemed—or, more nearly, / *have been* redeemed, always, have only to notice."[18] In this poem, one finds Cairns's strongest sense of redemption through recapitulation—or an incarnational model of atonement. A sense of doubleness saturates the language employed in this poem, a doubleness that articulates an ever-present deification always already begun—a proclamation that when the Word became flesh everything was immediately transformed, redeemed, healed, and redefined according to their unique "inner essences"—including even the notion of the Greek Logos.[19] Creation is not subverted but healed, redefined, re-experienced; or, better yet, one is finally able to experience the fullness of creation.

In this poem, Cairns sees in the incarnation itself as "Divine Excess," a pouring forth of God's being-into-the-world so that "all creation came to be," but with such a self-emptying excess, such a Divine gesture of *kenoitic* excess, that in this excessive self-emptying "He will mend the ancient wound completely, for all."[20] The wound referred to here, of course, is the original transgression in the Garden, an act that separated the human body from the soul, and consequently the human from the Divine. So, by a self-emptying gesture, by taking his place on the life-giving cross, Christ as *theanthropos* heals the original wound of separation with the "mending" wound of the cross. God becoming man "mends" our whole nature (body and soul) with the Divine. Or, to use

17. Fyodor Dostoevsky, *The Karamazov Brothers*, translated by Ignat Avsey (Oxford: Oxford University Press, 1994) 360.

18. Cairns, *Philokalia*, 39, lines 7–8.

19. I refer here to Maximos Confessor's notion of inner essences (*logoi*) which are contained within the *Logos* and which always seek to participate fully within Him. See in the introduction in *On the Cosmic Mystery of Christ*, translated by Paul M. Blowers and Robert Louis Wilken (Crestwood, NY: St. Vladimir's Seminary Press, 2003). See also Joseph P. Farrell, *Free Choice in Maximus the Confessor* (South Canaan, PA: Saint Tikhon's Press, 1989).

20. Cairns, *Philokalia*, 39, line 17.

the language employed in Hebrews, "Since therefore the children share in the flesh and blood, he himself likewise partook of the same nature, that through death he might destroy him who has the power of death, that is, the devil, and deliver all those who through fear of death were subject to lifelong bondage" (2:14–15).

Cairns goes to such subtle lengths to communicate the excessiveness of Divine (re-) creation that his poem appropriates the very excessiveness of which he speaks:

> So it's not a far stretch from *that* Divine Excess
> to advocate the sacred possibility
> that in some final, graceful *metania* He
> will mend that ancient wound completely, and for all.[21]

His final line—"[He] will mend that ancient wound completely, and for all"—refers explicitly to a mending borne of a "graceful *metania*" (as if God bows before creation, his own icon, before his own priests), yet this single last line stands on its own, separated from the four-line stanzas that precede it.[22] The poem performs for the reader the very excessiveness, the very possibility, the very hope the poem sees in the incarnation itself. The line ruptures the crafted symmetry of the rest of the poem, the apparent ordering of strict stanzaic moderation. Cairns's last line of his poem appropriates and then acts out "the gross immoderation" (of a heresy borne of an excessive belief of the excessiveness of love witnessed in the incarnation) named in the second line of the poem. In this excessive, immoderate last line, this attempt to subvert a clear sense of balance, of justice, Cairns quite literally hollows out a place for hope, for prayer.[23]

---

21. Ibid., lines 14–17.

22. In Orthodoxy a *metania* is a deep bow performed first by the believer crossing himself, then bending deeply at the waist, and touching the ground with the right hand. One often performs a *metania* before an icon or before one receives a blessing from a priest or a bishop.

23. One is reminded here of St. Basil's Third Kneeling Prayer, prayed at Pentecost Vespers, in which one offers prayers on behalf of those who suffer torment in Hades; or of the prayer of Isaac the Syrian: "And what is a merciful heart? It is the heart burning for the sake of all creation, for men, for birds, for animals, for demons, and for every created thing. . . . For this reason he offers up tearful prayer continually even for irrational beasts, for the enemies of truth, and for those who harm him, that they may be protected and receive mercy . . . because of the great compassion that burns without measure in his heart in the likeness, in imitation of God" (quoted in Hilarion Alfeyev, *The Spiritual World of Isaac the Syrian* [Kalamazoo: Cistercian, 2000], 43).

Cairns's most sustained meditation on creation comes not from a poem *about* creation or *about* various scenes in Genesis, but through his retelling of Scripture itself. Cairns taps into a tradition of Jewish biblical commentary (midrash) in his selection of poems, "The Recovered Midrashim of Rabbi Sab."[24] Though he calls the poems midrash, and they are no doubt midrash in practice, they are also unquestionably Christian midrash—and even more to the point, Orthodox Christian midrash. Like Ephrem the Syrian, Cairns takes scenes from the Bible and recasts them poetically to get at the spirit of repentance, humility, and *agape* therein. Like all midrash, Cairns's poetry says only what Scripture says, but will say it anew, shifting our perspective, will add images, details, dialogue—whatever he has at his disposal as both a poet and an exegete—to tease out the kernel of the spiritual teaching of the given scriptural passage.

In his poem on Genesis 1:26, "YHWH's Image," Cairns establishes immediately a christological foundation in his first line: "And YHWH sat in the dust, bone weary after / days of strenuous making . . ."[25] The hyper-anthropomorphization here is striking, and yet nuanced enough so that the christological point is both unmistakable and subtle. One must note how Cairns utilizes the Tetragrammaton, the name of the ineffable God. Yet the ineffable, utterly transcendent, unknowable God sits in the dust. The dust in which he sits, of course, is the dust (*adamah*) from which the human (*adam*) will be created. The connection between this God who sits in the dust and his soon-to-be creation made of this same dust is made even more evident as Cairns describes God as "bone weary." This phrase is echoic of the words uttered by Adam at Eve's creation: "bone of my bones, flesh of my flesh" (2:23). Cairns gives to God the same physical trait that Adam refers to at the creation of Eve. Whereas the ancient exegetes focus on the way in which man is made in the image and likeness of God spiritually, Cairns begins his investigation of the Divine-human relationship by hyper-literalizing this connection, by making "the image and likeness" already incarnate. He reverses the traditional spiritual connection between the image and likeness of the

---

24. For Cairns's "Midrashim," see *Recovered Body* (Wichita, KS: Eighth Day, 2003) 35–55. For a thorough introduction to the world of midrash, see Jacob Neusner, *Invitation to Midrash* (San Francisco: Harper, 1989). For an overview of rabbinic literature, see Neusner, *Introduction to Rabbinic Literature* (New York: Doubleday, 1994).

25. Cairns, *Recovered Body*, 39, lines 1–2.

divine and human, as it were, by making the physicality of YHWH come to the fore, so as to announce that this original physical "image and likeness," this original pre-creation at-one-ment, will be healed at the incarnation—that all will be recapitulated at the incarnation.

We then see Cairns move to the spiritual image and likeness in the third stanza as he imagines the breath of God (*ruah*) of Genesis, traditionally understood by early exegetes as the Holy Spirit: "As He exhaled, a sigh and sweet mist spread / out from him, settling over the earth."[26] He then describes for us "the trembling clay" in front of YHWH's lips, lips which then part "to avail another breath."[27] There is obviously already something "living" about the clay even before YHWH breathes his life into it the clay this moment, perhaps a life imbued by the first breath, "sigh and sweet mist." The "trembling" clay, I imagine, has little to do with God breathing on it, since its trembling precedes God's second breath. Rather, one ought to see here the Pauline image of a "fear and trembling" before God (Phil 2:12), a trembling borne out of an awe before the Creator, a trembling borne out of awe prior to any transgression of Law. Indeed, we must imagine in this "trembling" before the Creator something quite intimate, anticipatory, a first response from the to-be-beloved to the overwhelming love of the Creator.

Cairns then pushes to the extreme this notion of being made in "the image and likeness" of God by having YHWH take the clay into which he has just breathed life (the Holy Spirit), clay which was just trembling in his hands, and start coating his "shins," "thighs," and "chest."[28] Cairns describes the process as a "layering," until "He had been wholly interred." And then Cairns finishes the poem with dizzying christological connections: "He parted the clay at His side, and / retreated from it, leaving the image of Himself / to wander in what remained of that early / morning mist."[29] We witness here a slow, careful process by which YHWH has made himself man in the Garden. YHWH leaves, of course, but he also leaves something behind, something of himself, a remnant of the Divine, excessive, yet, nevertheless, wholly Divine. Like the image of YHWH's being "bone weary" prefiguring Eve's being made from Adam's bone, here too we see the same connection: God slips out from the side of the

---

26. Ibid., lines 13–14.
27. Ibid., lines 21–22.
28. Ibid., lines 23–24.
29. Ibid., lines 25–29.

human here as the woman (*ishah*) will be taken from the man (*ish*), the intimacy between the Divine and the human palpable—the very image of marriage itself.

Perhaps most striking in these final lines is the christological connection here in the Garden of Paradise to the Garden of Gethsemane: the image of the crucifixion here is unmistakable, the wound from the spear Longinus already prefigured in the part from which God leaves the human. The exegetical precision here really is remarkable: just as Christ is the Logos incarnate and in becoming so assumed and healed humankind, so too God has thus begun the project already here in Cairns's Garden. It seems Cairns depicts in a very poetically literal, fleshly fashion the typological prefiguration of what is to be restored at the incarnation; just as at the crucifixion, when Christ dies and is then resurrected on the third day, taking with him and restoring his human body and soul, and thus "leaves behind" humanity to rejoin the Father, so too does YHWH depart from his clay "icon," leaving his creation to "wander in what remained of that early morning mist." Yet in both scenes—Cairns's creation scene and the biblical crucifixion—something of the Divine is left behind as well and offered to and assumed by the human (through YHWH's slathering clay all over his body; through God becoming man at the incarnation), and something of the human is brought back with the Divine (Christ's resurrected body and soul). So even before the creation of the first man—or perhaps more accurately, *at this very moment*—Cairns has already traced Christianity's soteriological narrative.

While his "In YHWH's Image" prefigures the incarnation, the crucifixion, and the resurrection (all three of which take for granted the original transgression in the Garden), Cairns's second midrash, "The Entrance of Sin," takes up that moment of the original transgression and maps out for the reader the ongoing ancestral curse of humankind. Yet for Cairns the moment of that original transgression is not the taking of the fruit, nor is it the sting of pride in Adam's desire to ascend to the heights of divinity. Rather, in Cairns's recasting, we observe something far simpler, sneakier perhaps than a snake armed with beautiful fruit, a sin revisited every day, perhaps, unfortunately at almost every moment. Cairns describes the invisible entrance of sin, during a walk in the garden, "when the woman had reached to take the man's hand and he with- / held it."[30] The neglect of the other human, the turning away

---

30. Ibid., 40, lines 13–14.

from another, a sense and enjoyment of isolation, "developing a habit of resistance"—in Cairns's retelling this is the original transgression, the first act that will make possible the eating of the prohibited fruit. This same spirit of "irresistible," enjoyable isolation marks also the ancestral curse of humanity—the way in which we turn to ourselves, into ourselves, and become entirely isolated. Cairns names explicitly this sin as a "turning away," and I imagine he has in mind an inverted sense of *metanoia*, of a turning back to God. True *metanoia*, a true turning back to God, then, involves a breaking free from solipsistic isolation. But how is this sin to be undone? True *metanoia* involves a self-emptying, humility, a participation in the divine *kenosis*; to truly turn back to our fellow man, we must follow the model of Cairns's hyperbolic, self-emptying God in "Adventure in New Testament Greek: *Apoctastasis*": we must extend to the neighbor before us what God extended to humankind—a "graceful *metania*." Liturgically, one is reminded of the beginning of Lent at Forgiveness Vespers where every member of the parish does a full prostration before every other member and asks for forgiveness. In this way, we extend and participate in the Divine project, existing not in isolation but in community, made in the image and likeness of a Trinitarian God. Here when our isolation and our turning away from others, from God, gives way to *metanoia*, our own turning back, we meet in the face of our neighbor the face of God. And for a brief moment we stop wasting time.

PART TWO

Christianity in Africa and the Caribbean

FOUR

The Collision of Two Cultures

Chinua Achebe's *Things Fall Apart* and Christianity's Coming to Nigeria

Catherine Winn Merritt and *Eric J. Sterling*

Introduction: Achebe's Purpose in Writing

IN *THINGS FALL APART* (1958), Chinua Achebe describes life in Nigeria before the Colonial Period and the effects of the arrival of the British missionaries, offering a new perspective on two colliding cultures while providing insight into the immediate and long-term consequences of the missionary process in Nigeria. Rather than judging these two distinct forces and the religious beliefs to which they adhere, Achebe draws parallels between the two societies and allows some of the native characters to waver between their deep-rooted beliefs and the emergent appeal of Christianity. The missionaries sent by British churches are also granted a certain amount of humanity that they have been denied in recent literature. They are not purely destructive forces, bent on destroying any trace of native religious traditions. Because Achebe portrays the harmony that existed before the missionaries arrived and offers new ways of interpreting pre-colonial Africa, this novel occupies a significant place in the postcolonial literary movement and continues to influence the popular perceptions of both traditional African culture and the destructive effects of Christian imperialism.

With the previous standard for literary depictions of Africa in mind, postcolonial authors such as Achebe began embarking upon a different journey into the heart of Africa. In some ways, Achebe penned *Things Fall Apart* as a response to the unsympathetic and dehumanizing portrayals of Africans by writers such as Joseph Conrad. By writing the novel in an accessible and engaging manner, Achebe attempts to rectify the perceived shortcomings and inadequacies of the preceding colonial literature in regard to the portrayal of native Africans and their religious faith. He presents a picture of Africa that defines Nigeria independently of Western values, without demolishing the humanistic message inherent in the Christian movement. Instead of building his story around the Western presence and the political aspects of colonialism, Achebe begins his novel with the conflicts of everyday life in the village of Umuofia. Okonkwo's story does not begin with the arrival of the white missionaries from the West, much as African history does not begin with the Colonial Period. Achebe carefully highlights the rich and deep-rooted inheritance of cultural tradition among the Igbo people that existed before foreign influences, a concept which was not widely held or frequently taught during this time.

Life before the Missionaries

Early in his novel, Achebe establishes a clear correlation between spiritual faith and everyday society in the Igbo tribes. Okonkwo becomes angered during the Week of Peace when one of his three wives, Ojiugo, neglects to make his dinner and feed the children because she is plaiting her hair. Incensed by Ojiugo's maternal neglect, Okonkwo beats her, despite the fact that he knows it is the Sacred Week, when people are explicitly forbidden to hit others. The narrator reports that "Okonkwo broke the peace, and was punished, as was the custom, by Ezeani, the priest of the earth goddess. . . . His first two wives ran out in great alarm pleading with him that it was the sacred week. But Okonkwo was not the man to stop beating somebody half-way through, not even for fear of a goddess."[1] His fiery temper and his unconscious desire to demonstrate his manhood supersede his spiritual devotion to the gods. Ezeani subsequently rejects Okonkwo's offer of hospitality and atonement, a kola nut, because he is insulted by Okonkwo's misdeed—not the beating of his wife, but rather the beating of his wife during the Sacred Week, which is

---

1. Chinua Achebe, *Things Fall Apart* (New York: Knopf, 1992) 24–25.

interpreted as an affront to the gods, thus endangering the entire village. Ezeani lectures Okonkwo:

> [O]ur forefathers ordained that before we plant any crops in the earth we should observe a week in which a man does not say a harsh word to his neighbor. We live in peace with our fellows to honor our great goddess of the earth without whose blessing our crops will not grow . . . Your wife was at fault, but even if you came into your *obi* [hut] and found her lover on top of her, you would still have committed a great evil to beat her . . . The evil you have done can ruin the whole clan. The earth goddess whom you have insulted may refuse to give us her increase, and we shall all perish.[2]

Ezeani then orders Okonkwo to bring sacrifices to Ani's holy shrine to atone for his sin. The priest of Ani, the earth goddess, manifests the Igbo belief that the spiritual sins of one person can result in devastating ramifications for the rest of the village and that the adherence to spiritual laws is necessary for the benevolence of the gods, such as a god that brings a fruitful harvest. Ezeani would ordinarily condone wife-beating, but not during the Week of Peace because violence of any kind angers the gods and can lead to a poor annual crop. The narrator of *Things Fall Apart* never mentions that Umuofia suffered a poor or a good harvest that year, despite Okonkwo beating his wife during the Sacred Week, indicating that the gods actually do not exist or have no power, or (what the Africans wish to believe) that Ani has accepted Okonkwo's sacrifice at his shrine and has forgiven the hot-tempered villager.

This passage concerning the Week of Peace and Ezeani's warning instructs the readers that the Igbo possess a polytheistic spiritual belief—a belief system that is attacked later in the novel by the missionary Mr. Brown. When an old man in Mbanta asks the missionary, "'Which is this god of yours, . . . the goddess of the earth, the god of the sky, Amadiora of the thunderbolt, or what?'" Mr. Brown replies, "'All the gods you have named are not gods at all. They are gods of deceit who tell you to kill your fellows and destroy innocent children. There is only one true God and He has the earth, the sky, you and me and all of us.'"[3] Brown does not understand—partly because he never asks—that the Igbo do believe in one supreme being, the Creator, Chineke (also known

2. Ibid., 26.
3. Ibid., 126.

as Chukwu), although they also believe in other, lesser deities related to nature, such as the Sun, the Sky, Thunder, and the Earth, as well as the priests who represent them. Brown counters what he considers the Igbo polytheistic religious faith with his conviction that there is only one God, with monotheism. Brown, however, confuses the Africans in the audience, who are listening to his call for converts, when he mentions Jesu Kristi (Jesus Christ). When Okonkwo innocently asks about God's wife, Brown declares that God has a son but no wife, which Okonkwo and his fellow villagers fail to comprehend. Brown mentions the Holy Trinity, but the villagers, like the narrator struggling with his faith in John Donne's Holy Sonnet XIV ("Batter my heart, three person'd God"), cannot conceive that God can be one and simultaneously three (Father, Son, and Holy Spirit). Brown "went on to talk about the Holy Trinity. At the end of it Okonkwo was fully convinced that the man was mad. He shrugged his shoulders and went away to tap his afternoon palm-wine."[4] Achebe manifests how the missionaries fail to explain to the satisfaction of the villagers how the Holy Trinity is understood. Okonkwo and his neighbors seek rational explanations that they can verify empirically, not realizing introspectively that their own invisible gods can only be accepted through spiritual faith. Similarly, the missionaries expect that the villagers will accept Christianity and the Holy Trinity through faith yet refuse to make an effort to understand or believe in the Igbo gods. Instead, even the tolerant and understanding missionary Mr. Brown immediately dismisses the African gods: "Your gods are not alive and cannot do you any harm [if you convert to Christianity] . . . They are pieces of wood and stone."[5] Both the African villagers and the Christian missionaries from Europe decline to make a strong effort to understand the religious beliefs and customs of the other side and refuse to investigate why the other group believes so strongly in its deities.

The Conflict between Faiths

As in reality, two conflicting and unyielding forces cannot exist within the same space, and the tension cannot last. In "The Second Coming," the poem from which Achebe took his title, William Butler Yeats writes:

4. Ibid., 127.
5. Ibid., 126–27.

"Things fall apart; the centre cannot hold."[6] Once the two spiritual ideologies meet, there can be no peaceful resolution without some level of effort and understanding from either or both parties. Obviously, this is not the case in *Things Fall Apart*, so "Mere anarchy is loosed upon the world."[7] In Achebe's novel, the turning point in the prominent role that Christianity plays in the Igbo culture occurs when the natives of Mbanta, Okonkwo's home during his exile, agree to relinquish part of their land, a section of the Evil Forest, to the missionaries. Achebe borrowed the idea from a true story involving Samuel Ajayi Crowther, bishop of the Niger, who "courageously cut a road through Bonny's 'bad bush'—the same sort of haunt of wandering spirits and abominations described by Achebe as Umuofia's Evil Forest—so that boys going to school could walk to the mission."[8] The Evil Forest is where the Igbo bury those who die of leprosy and smallpox and where the charms of the medicine men are placed upon their death. The Evil Forest is considered a cursed place, only fit for the disposal of unwanted and unclean people whom the culture believes are unloved by their gods. The villagers believe that this test will destroy the will of the missionaries and show them that the Christian God is no match for the Igbo deities. The natives are surprised that the missionaries gladly accept the lot, sing praises of God, and then clear the land. The villagers of Mbanta express surprise and concoct excuses when the Christians do not die while building their church in the Evil Forest. Some natives, inspired by the Christians's survival, convert. Mbanta villagers conceded

> that their gods and ancestors were sometimes long-suffering and would deliberately allow a man to go on defying them. But even in such cases they set their limit at seven market weeks or twenty-eight days . . . And so excitement mounted in the village as the seventh week approached since the impudent missionaries built their church in the Evil Forest. The villagers were so certain about the doom that awaited these men that one or two converts thought it wise to suspend their allegiance to the new faith. At last the day came by which all the missionaries should

---

6. Ibid., ix.

7. Ibid.

8. Robert M. Wren, *Achebe's World: The Historical and Cultural Context of the Novels of Chinua Achebe* (Washington, DC: Three Continents, 1980) 95.

have died. But they were still alive . . . That week they won a handful more converts.⁹

This passage narrates a pivotal moment in the progression of Christianity in the Nigerian villages. The natives anticipate the wrath of their deities upon the Christians for defying the cultural taboos by building their church upon cursed land. Yet the Christians survive and prosper, causing the Igbo to question the power and even the existence of their own deities. The villagers obey oracles and priests because of their faith and their fear of punishment, but the ability of the Christians to defy these gods—something the natives have never dared to do—and experience no punishment allows the natives to think that they can also defy their own gods and even convert to Christianity without fearing divine retribution. The Christians, through their faith in God and their ability to survive the Evil Forest, demystify the Igbo deities, showing the people that their own gods are harmless, if they even exist. The natives begin to flock to the missionaries, partly because they believe that the Christian God and his Son have demonstrated unequivocally, through the survival of their devotees in the Evil Forest, that they are more powerful than the Igbo gods.

Once the missionaries survive the forest, their first female convert to Christianity is Nneka, who has, unfortunately, given birth to four sets of twins. In the indigenous religion, the birth of twins is considered an abomination because twins are considered to have divine powers that can hurt people. In an effort to protect the culture, twins are killed. Nneka, therefore, has lost all eight of her children to death because of the religious laws. In each pregnancy, "she had borne twins, and they had been immediately thrown away. Her husband and his family were already becoming highly critical of such a woman [for consistently giving birth to twins] and were not unduly perturbed when they found that she had fled to join the Christians. It was a good riddance."¹⁰ Devastated by what she considers the unwarranted murder of her four sets of twins and pregnant for the fifth time (and thus perhaps fearing that she will give birth to twins for the fifth time and lose her children to the forest yet again), she flees the clan for the missionaries' church after realizing that the Igbo deities have been unable to destroy the missionaries and their

9. Achebe, *Things Fall Apart*, 131.
10. Ibid., 131.

church in the Evil Forest. If the gods cannot harm the Christians or their church, she feels safe when converting to Christianity.

This scene is crucial in Achebe's novel because it manifests one of the primary reasons why the missionaries came to southeastern Nigeria to spread Christianity: the indigenous religious practice of murdering innocent twin babies. Missionaries, particularly female missionaries, were appalled by this practice and desired to stop it, which they eventually did in the 1930s. It is noteworthy that after the conversion of the Igbo and the Yoruba to Christianity and the cessation of the practice of killing twins, the incidence of births of twins has risen markedly; today the rate in this region is more than quadruple the world average. Some attribute this high incidence to the eating of yams, but another possibility is the people's conversion to the Christian faith.

Similarities and Differences between the Two Faiths

The fact that the Europeans and Africans subscribed to markedly different cultures is indisputable. Just as the missionaries were horrified by the practice of infanticide, the villagers must have been just as suspicious of the white man's lifestyle, which included technology (such as the "iron horse" [bicycle] that the first missionary arrives on) that must have seemed dangerously alien. Nevertheless, the modern reader might be surprised by the complete lack of understanding between the two cultures, especially considering that Achebe takes such care to weave recognizably Christian beliefs and symbols into the Nigerian tapestry of faith and ritual. By creating an interconnected web of ideas and religious symbols shared by both groups of people before they begin the long conflict of spiritual conversion and conquest, the author diminishes any preconceived notions a reader might have regarding spirituality in either of the cultures. In order to maintain two distinct spiritual backgrounds for the cultures, the similarities between the Christian and Nigerian religions are often subtle rather than obvious. Achebe's goal was not to create an image of Africa that disregards all similar themes between Western and Nigerian practices, but rather to paint a more holistic and integrated portrait of the pre-colonial culture of Nigeria.

Although the religious beliefs and practices within the village of Umuofia and the lands mentioned in the Old Testament feature several similarities, inhabitants of the two cultures react and interpret the similar aspects in different ways. The Nigerian village, for instance, greets the swarm of locusts with great enthusiasm and jubilation, as a rare occurrence and a divine source of sustenance. To the village of Umuofia, the cloud of locusts is a sight "full of power and beauty" and the Nigerian people know "by instinct that they were very good to eat."[11] Within the Judeo-Christian tradition, swarms of locust in the Book of Exodus are viewed as one of the ten plagues of Egypt, sent from God as punishment for the enslavement and maltreatment of the Jews (Exod 10:4–6). The fact that Achebe wrote his novel in English suggests not only something about his intended audience, but also the religious knowledge he anticipates that they carry. By integrating the locusts within a story concerning religious conflict between members of two contrasting faiths, Achebe suggests a sense of shared symbols and indicates that the people of the two distinct cultures live within the same world, wherein the same phenomena are experienced, so that the difference lies not in the experiences themselves but rather in the manner in which they are interpreted.

Consider also the similarities between the tale of Okonkwo and his son Ikemefuna, and the Old Testament story of Abraham and his son Isaac. In both cases, the son joins the patriarch in an unusual way and is soon demanded as a divine sacrifice. The similarities are further accentuated when Nwoye, Okonkwo's biological son, adopts the name Isaac upon conversion. Abraham's willingness to sacrifice his only son manifests his complete faith in God, rendering the religious sacrifice unnecessary. Abraham passes God's test not with his sacrifice of his beloved son but rather with his willingness to fulfill God's commandment unquestioningly. In Okonkwo's case, however, the oracle who speaks on behalf of the gods demands Ikemefuna's death in order to maintain peace and to allow the villagers to demonstrate their unmitigated faith. Although Ogbuefi Ezeudu warns Okonkwo against participating in his adopted son's death, declaring, "I want you to have nothing to do with it. He calls you his father," the protagonist decides, nonetheless, to accompany the men into the woods and kills his son with his matchet to prove his manhood, courage, and faith.[12] Because of Abraham's devotion to the Lord, he becomes a biblical hero. Okonkwo's sacrifice of Ikemefuna causes his life to descend into tragedy; as the title of Achebe's novel suggests, things fall apart for Okonkwo after he kills his son: he is exiled because of an

11. Ibid., 48.
12. Ibid., 49.

accident, his other son, Nwoye, deserts him, and he commits suicide. The distinction is that he carries out the sacrifice, yet Abraham does not. Other villagers, such as Ezeudu, consider him a murderer because of the killing, yet he simply fulfills the order of the oracle.

Perhaps the difference between Abraham and Okonkwo is not that one loves his son while the other murders his child, but rather that in the Bible, and not in *Things Fall Apart*, God intervenes and makes his presence known, thus releasing the father from committing the sacrifice. The deity in Achebe's novel is absent after the oracle is declared, which results in Okonkwo being forced to assume the blame for following the orders of his faith. Perhaps Achebe uses the lack of divine intervention to suggest that the Igbo gods do not exist (or do not play a major role) and that the oracle is not the word of the gods but rather the indiscriminate ideology of a cultural construct embodied by powerful people in the village who, pretending to be the oracle, speak the words of the gods.

Rhonda Cobham also notes the biblical parallel "between Okonkwo's situation and the New Testament story about God's sacrifice of his son Jesus for the greater good of all humanity (itself a version of the Abraham/Isaac motif). What is important here, however, is that Achebe has picked the form of human sacrifice most compatible with Judaeo-Christian myth as the centerpiece of his examination of human sacrifice in Igbo culture."[13] Achebe employs the arrival of the locusts and the story of the sacrifice of a beloved son in the name of the gods to foster a sense of shared cultural baggage, while allowing the differences of interpretation and reaction to distinguish the two religious faiths. If the missionaries had put forth a small amount of effort and energy in an attempt to understand the culture of the Nigerian people, they would have recognized these spiritual connections and perhaps gained a greater level of respect for the native culture. While the missionaries might have chosen to ignore certain aspects of the Nigerian heritage in order to make their own cause seem superior, Achebe's audience is expected to recognize the similarities for what they are and grant the African nations the respect they have previously been denied. The British missionaries might not have known about the oracle's cave and the burning logs that glow without flame, but Achebe describes the cave in detail and perhaps expects his readers to make the connections denied by the missionaries in their

---

13. Rhonda Cobham, "Problems of Gender and History in the Teaching of *Things Fall Apart*," in *Modern Critical Interpretations: Chinua Achebe's "Things Fall Apart*," edited by Harold Bloom (Philadelphia: Chelsea House, 2002) 25.

Western-centric quest to pacify, subjugate, and convert the inhabitants of the Nigerian villages.

Achebe perhaps illuminates his own ambivalence toward the Igbo religion and acknowledges the spiritual complexity of religious conflict by demonstrating how the Igbo faith in the gods also has merit. Okonkwo's daughter Ezinma is considered an *obanje* child: a child who dies at a very young age and is then considered to be reborn periodically in the mother's womb during the mother's next pregnancy, until the child dies again. The villagers suspect that when a mother loses several of her children, she actually has one child who dies, only to be reborn and to die again and again. Perhaps it is the culture's manner of dealing with the high child mortality rate, blaming it on malevolent spirits. The religious leaders attempt to scare the *obanje* children from reappearing by mutilating the bodies of the deceased children, yet the child will continually be born and die until its *iyi-uwa*, the *obanje* child's personal stone that connects her to the gods, wrapped in a handkerchief, is found. When Ezinma's parents, Okonkwo and Ekwefi, decide that she is an *obanje*, they find a medicine man, Okagbue, who seeks her *iyi-uwa* so that she may survive and no longer live as an *obanje* child who torments her parents. Although Western readers of Achebe's text might be skeptical of such a belief, the medicine man does in fact find Ezinma's stone, wrapped inside a handkerchief, buried deep inside the earth, so deep that she could not have buried it herself; with such a find, Achebe leads his readers to consider the possibility that the Igbo faith in this spiritual practice could be justified. If the concepts of *obanje* children and the *iyi-uwa* are Nigerian polytheistic religious myths and not based in reality, how, Achebe's readers should ponder, can one explain the existence of the stone wrapped in a handkerchief that is found at the exact spot that Ezinma pointed out to the medicine man?

Recent Studies on the Igbo

Little unbiased research is available concerning the more intricate aspects of Igbo religion, for most of the published material focuses on the political and economic aspects of Igbo life. The paucity of reliable research has been observed by many scholars, who occasionally note that the most reliable account of Nigerian culture comes in a novel rather than in a scientific essay. Elizabeth Isichei states, perhaps a little sadly, that the majority of sources that revolve around Igbo religion are literary rather than scholarly. In this statement, Isichei specifically references Achebe's novel as one of the most "illuminating."[14]

Despite the recent shortage of scholarly material, there are a few key factors that are recognizable as native Nigerian beliefs. By looking at the modern church in Nigeria, researchers can trace certain spiritual traditions and symbols to sources beyond the recognizably Christian and Islamic influences. Some aspects of modern Nigerian Christianity, such as the presence of various Earth symbols that have been adapted to symbolize different aspects of Christianity and ritualized prayers, are uniquely and inherently African in origin. Even the belief in sorcery and witchcraft has persisted in spite of severe opposition from Western churches.[15]

However, given the process of conversion and the nature of colonial expansion, the phenomenon of incorporating existing beliefs and symbols into an emergent Christianity is hardly confined to Africa. In the earliest stages of Christianity, pagan symbols were incorporated across the Roman Empire in an effort to make the foundling religion more appealing to the masses. In some ways, the spread of Christianity has followed a formulaic path, regardless of continent or people. As in Nigeria and Achebe's narrative, the first to accept the new religion have historically been the outcasts and the underprivileged, the *osu* (undesirables) in *Things Fall Apart*. With the message of brotherly acceptance, those who previously felt shunned by the existing religion flocked toward the promise of universal fraternity. However, as David Pratten has noted, some African chiefs have sacrificed their power in the process of their conversion because their faith was strong. Chief Egbo Egbo "began to take instruction and was ministered to daily. Once he had renounced the gin trade and had pensioned off eleven of his twelve wives he was baptised. His power in village politics and in the 'palaver-house' fell considerably, but Egbo Egbo became one of the first church elders appointed to oversee the expanding congregation in Ibeno."[16] As evinced by the

---

14. Elizabeth Isichei, "Ibo and Christian Beliefs: Some Aspects of a Theological Encounter," *African Affairs* 68:271 (1969) 121.

15. Toyin Falola, *Culture and Customs of Nigeria* (Westport, CT: Greenwood, 2001) 30.

16. David Pratten, "Conversion, Conquest, and the Qua Iboe Mission," in *Christianity and Social Change in Africa: Essays in Honor of J. D. Y. Peel*, edited by Toyin Falola (Durham, NC: Carolina Academic Press, 2005) 416.

crowd's reaction in Umuofia, the first to join the new religion do not, and indeed cannot, understand the more complex concepts of Christianity in such a short span of time. For instance, the immediate appeal of Christianity is felt by Nwoye as soon as the missionaries burst into song. Although the boy's village is rich with song, Nwoye hears answers to his deepest, unspoken questions in the missionaries' voices. As the narrator describes, the music is "one of those gay and rollicking tunes of evangelism which had the power of plucking at silent and dusty chords in the heart of an I[g]bo man."[17] Nwoye is not attracted to what he considers "the mad logic of the Trinity,"[18] but rather by the poetry of the Christian religion. The first generation converts cannot be expected to learn all of the intricacies of Christian theology, and although they accept the new faith, many of the old traditions linger alongside Christianity.

Jude C. Aguwa, a theological anthropologist, describes the levels of communication and give and take between the indigenous and Christian practices as a process of dialogue. In the first level, the domineering attitudes and prejudices of the missionaries force the conversation into a monologue, where the native voice is all but silenced. The next level, which begins with the first generation of converts, begins with what Aguwa calls a "rudimentary" dialogue. At this level, the converts begin blending Nigerian and Christian practices, symbols, and beliefs; the Independent Churches, those that built off of this combination, became very popular during this period.[19] The appeal of syncretism has evidently lasted to modern day Nigeria, where Independent Churches have become influential and maintained sizeable congregations. The appeal of these churches lies in their focus on Nigerian nationalism and on the preservation of their inherited culture. In *Things Fall Apart*, the plot effectively follows this pattern, moving from the monologue level, with both cultures effectively talking to themselves, into the more complex—and ultimately more important—dialogue.

---

17. Achebe, *Things Fall Apart*, 127.

18. Ibid, 128.

19. Jude C. Aguwa, "Christianity and Nigerian Indigenous Culture," in *Religion, History, and Politics in Nigeria*, edited by Chima J. Korieh and G. Ugo Nwokeji (Lanham: University Press of America, 2005) 14.

Conclusion: Repercussions in Modern Nigeria

Of course, the influence of Christian missionaries in Africa extends beyond Achebe's novel. Modern day Nigeria reflects many aspects of the missionary process, including an overwhelmingly large population of Christians and an abundance of churches. Western and eastern Nigeria are primarily Christian, yet the "Northern region, mainly Hausa, tend[s] to be aggressively Muslim."[20] As of 2000, the Nigerian Christian community was one of the largest in the world, with 50 million self-described Christians and a projected growth of 73 million by 2050. In fact, the nations of sub-Saharan Africa account for nearly half of the Christians worldwide.[21] In addition to the growing community of converts, the missionaries influenced other aspects of Nigerian history and development. The road to Nigerian independence was, at least in part, paved by the Christian missionaries and the institutions they put in place. The Western education system introduced by the missionaries trained the native men in basic literacy skills and the mechanisms they needed to play the Western system and succeed within the changing political landscape. As the educated men became more powerful and achieved influential positions, they realized that there was, in effect, a glass ceiling where Africans were concerned. Despite the natives' education and ambition, the government and high-powered institutions were run exclusively by Westerners. However, because the Nigerian men were well-trained and understood how the apparatus functioned, they were able to organize more effective independence movements, eventually liberate their country, and seize the positions they had once coveted. Although the early Christian missionaries—whether intentionally or inadvertently—changed much of the indigenous culture, the foundation laid by the foreigners ironically led to the independence and empowerment of the Nigerian people, despite decades of repression with the church's implicit approval. As Achebe indicates, the missionaries clearly spread their cultural influence on the indigenous people. Andrew F. Walls notes:

> cross-cultural diffusion has been necessary to Christianity. It has been its life's blood, and without it faith could not have survived

---

20. Steven Paas, *The Faith Moves South: A History of the Church in Africa* (Zomba [Malawi]: Kachere, 2006) 155.

21. Philip Jenkins, *The Next Christendom: The Coming of Global Christianity* (Oxford: University Press, 2002) 90.

> ... One of the few things that are predictable about third-millenium Christianity is that it will be more culturally diverse than Christianity has ever been before, and thus have more capacity for blessing, and more capacity for disaster, than any previous era. We need to reflect on the implications of Africa and Latin America and Asia becoming the home of representative Christianity, that is, mainstream, norm-setting Christianity.[22]

---

22. Andrew F. Walls, *The Cross-Cultural Process in Christian History: Studies in the Transmission and Appropriation of Faith* (Maryknoll, NY: Orbis, 2002) 67–68.

FIVE

Jesus of Nazareth in Ghana's Deep Forest

The Africanization of Christianity in Madam Afua Kuma's Poetry[1]

Darren J. N. Middleton

Introduction: Africa's Ancient and Future Faith

BOTH SCHOLARS OF RELIGION and popular journalists have spoken of the explosion of Christianity in Africa, particularly in sub-Saharan Africa where traditionalism, they claim, once ruled. Yet African Christianity is not a new-fangled occurrence. Indeed, it substantively begins in the rural areas of the Nile Valley, circa the third and fourth centuries CE, with figures such as Antony, Pachomius, and Frumentius establishing the Coptic Church and the Ethiopian Orthodox Church. The king of the Congo professed Catholic Christianity as early as the late fifteenth century. Portuguese missionaries pursued Portuguese colonizers to West Africa, followed by hundreds of mainline Protestants during the nineteenth-century mission movement, even if high death rates somewhat limited their effectiveness. Africa truly became the domain of evangelical missionaries during both 1880–1920 and the post-WWII period.[2]

---

1. Brill Academic Publishers has kindly granted permission to reprint "Jesus of Nazareth in Ghana's Deep Forest: The Africanization of Christianity in Madam Afua Kuma's Poetry," *Religion and the Arts* 9-1/2 (2005) ISSN 1079-9265, pp. 116–34.

2. Details may be found in Kwame Bediako, *Christianity in Africa: The Renewal of a Non-Western Religion* (Maryknoll, NY: Orbis, 2002); Jehu Hanciles, *Euthanasia of a*

Today, Christianity spans the southern two-thirds of the continent and Madagascar, prompting some scholars to observe that Africa has taken the place formerly occupied by Europe. This Christianity is, of course, as multi-faceted as its history. But perhaps the least examined angle is the African Independent Church movement, whose deepest roots lie in those African churches that broke from mission churches to incorporate African beliefs, practices, and stories with those received from Westerners. In this chapter, I offer a theological reading of one African Independent Christian: the Ghanaian (more specifically, Akan) woman Madam Afua Kuma (1900–87), spokesperson of her local Christian community, the fellowship of the Church of Pentecost. Using her transcribed folkloric narratives, I focus on her own images and symbols regarding the personality of Jesus Christ relative to the Ghanaian Christian condition, and I argue that her prayers and praises enable scholars and other observers to speak of the Africanization of Christianity in the same breath as the Christianization of Africa.[3]

An illiterate farmer and traditional midwife from the forested hills of Obo-Kwahu, which is situated in Ghana's Eastern Region, Madam Afua Kuma (Christiana Afua Gyan) has authored a collection of prayers and praises, *Jesus of the Deep Forest*, which exemplifies African Independent Church approaches and beliefs. Her book demonstrates an oral, everyday African narrative theology. I stress the word "oral" because Afua Kuma first spoke her prayers and praises in Twi, her mother tongue, which many Akan (Ashanti [also: Asante] and Fante) groups use as their first or second language, both for herself and her church community.[4] Peter Kwasi Ameyaw tape-recorded these spoken words, and then Vincent Adjepong and Michael Owusu Nimako wrote them down. They were

---

Mission: African Church Autonomy in a Colonial Context (Westport, CT: Heinemann, 2002); Elizabeth Isichei, *A History of Christianity in Africa: From Antiquity to the Present* (Grand Rapids: Eerdmans, 1995); Philip Jenkins, *The Next Christendom: The Coming of Global Christianity* (Oxford: Oxford University Press, 2002); Andrew F. Walls, *The Cross-Cultural Process in Christian History* (Maryknoll, NY: Orbis, 2002); and, Kenneth L. Woodward, "The Changing Face of the Church," *Newsweek*, April 16, 2001, 46–52.

3. This chapter's primary focus is the Africanization of Christianity. However, I do recognize that I argue for this process by suggesting that Afua Kuma's images and symbols for Jesus embody such a phenomenon. In my mind, then, Jesus is Africanized also.

4. Afua Kuma worshipped at the Church of Pentecost, which is located at Asempaneye (Atuobikrom), also in Ghana's Eastern Region.

translated into English in 1980 and then published (in Twi and English) in Accra, Ghana, in January 1981.⁵

An African Jesus: Four Images

Like all Christianities, African Independent Churches have grown by using local languages, customs, symbols, and rituals to articulate their own distinctive Christology. One of the quickest ways for outsiders to penetrate this Christology is to consider the names, titles, and portraits African Christians use for Jesus Christ. For some African churches he is "the light" who scatters the dark and evil powers, for others he is "the healer" and "giver of life." Most understand him as containing multiple dimensions, and picture him through countless images.⁶ In this section, I look at some of Afua Kuma's prayers and praises, isolating four of her numerous images for Jesus to show how she indigenizes the Christian gospel.

Jesus and Ghana's Eastern Region

While much of Ghana lies flat, the Eastern Region's forested hills are lushly vegetated and support many different birds and animals. Most visitors here comment on the spectacular switchbacks amidst the jungle-clad slopes, which afford some of Ghana's most scenic sights. For the locals, however, this awesome green expanse appears to stimulate mixed feelings. While many farm the forest for food, and thus rejoice over its beneficence, they also approach it with trepidation, because they believe evil spirits often creep stealthily among the forest's stultifying thickets and gangly plants. In traditional Akan wisdom, these evil spirits are known as the *sasabonsam*, the so-called forest monster, and the *mmoatia*, the diminutive, human-like forest creatures who create havoc for hunters and gatherers alike.⁷

According to Afua Kuma, Jesus relates to the forested hills of Ghana's Eastern Region in at least three separate yet interrelated ways. First, she praises Jesus for disclosing his being and presence as "the great

5. Afua Kuma, *Jesus of the Deep Forest*, translated by Fr. Jon Kirby (Accra, Ghana: Asempa, 1981).

6. For details, see Diane B. Stinson, *Jesus of Africa: Voices of Contemporary African Christology* (Maryknoll, NY: Orbis, 2004). See also Volker Küster, *The Many Faces of Jesus Christ: Intercultural Christology* (Maryknoll, NY: Orbis, 2001) 57–76.

7. For background information on religion in Ghana, see Robert B. Fisher, *West African Religious Traditions: Focus on the Akan of Ghana* (Maryknoll, NY: Orbis, 1998).

forest canopy that gives cool shade / the Big Tree which lifts its vines / to peep at the heavens, / the magnificent Tree whose dripping leaves / encourage the luxuriant growth below."[8] She celebrates him as "the deep forest which gives us tasty foods. / The forest of cane and thorns, / where wander *kente* weavers, / in search of shuttle and loom."[9] And she exults him as "the fertile forest-land / on which farmers labour, cutlasses in hand."[10] Now, many Africans—both Christian and non-Christian—associate God with natural objects and phenomena, and Afua Kuma, who believes Jesus is God-for-us, is no exception to this axiom.[11]

Second, Jesus relates to the forest because he is "the hard-working Farmer" who offers the land's first fruits to others, especially the disadvantaged.[12] In developing this farming image Afua Kuma, who often farmed the Obo Kwahu forests, reconfigures the Gospel accounts of the feeding miracles. Here are three brief examples of her imagistic indigenization:

> You [Jesus] take a single grain of corn, grind it, roast it,
> and then go and plant it and, look!
> now the grain has borne fruit, and filled two hundred bags,
> with some left over!
> Farmer,
> who generously gives to all in need;
> Farmer,
> who slays hunger,
> Only in you will we be satisfied.[13]

---

8. Kuma, *Jesus of the Deep Forest*, 5.

9. Ibid., 37. *Kente* is the intricately woven and splendidly colorful cloth associated with the Ashanti (also spelt "Asante"). One of the most storied sub-Saharan African peoples, the Ashanti's fame stems from their elaborate mythology, their influential royalty, and their single-minded resistance to late-nineteenth-century British colonialism. To this day, Ashanti royalty employ the most skilled *kente* weavers, who use the finest fabrics to create the most arresting designs. See Fisher, *West African Religious Traditions*, 51–54. In associating Jesus with *kente* weavers, Afua Kuma links Jesus to royalty. Significantly, she also says that Jesus is so generous that he gives us "*adwinasa* [the best kind of *kente* cloth] to wear in the morning" (ibid., 10).

10. Kuma, *Jesus of the Deep Forest*, 39.

11. Ibid., 38. See also Philip T. Laryea, "Mother Tongue Theology: Reflections on Images of Jesus in the Poetry of Afua Kuma," *Journal of African Christian Thought* 3:1 (2000) 50–60; and John S. Mbiti, *African Religions and Philosophy* (Portsmouth, NH: Heinemann, 1969) 51–57.

12. Kuma, *Jesus of the Deep Forest*, 10.

13. Ibid., 15.

And again:

> Jesus! you light a bush-fire to clear a farm,
> and look: the oceans are ablaze,
> while the dry grass remains untouched.
> Only one acre was burnt,
> but three days later, it takes five hundred men,
> strong and mighty, to carry the harvest back to the house.[14]

Finally:

> He [Jesus] uses a needle to dig a wild yam.
> It feeds the army of the land
> for three days,
> and still some is left over.[15]

Like any other African villager, Jesus enters the forest to farm the land and hunt for game. Whatever else he is, then, Jesus is "a Man among men," to use Afua Kuma's words.[16] Having said this, his hunting courage makes him stand apart from others. Leading the way, Jesus is the fearless Hunter, the only one brave enough to take charge and descend into the deep forest. He is "the brightest of Lanterns / who helps us hunt [for elephants] at night."[17]

According to Afua Kuma, Jesus also stalks and kills the forest's evil spirits. He is the only one able to accomplish this task, she suggests, and such singular skill illustrates his distinctiveness. Ridding the forest of these spirits, thus securing its protection, brings us to the third and final way in which Jesus relates to the forested hills of Ghana's Eastern Region. In her own words:

> He [Jesus], the sharpest of all great swords,
> has made the forest safe for the hunters.
> The *mmoatia* he has cut to pieces;
> he has caught *sasabonsam*
> and twisted off its head!
> He is the Hunter gone to the deep forest.
> *Sasabonsam*, the evil spirit,
> has troubled hunters for many years.
> They ran in fear,

14. Ibid.
15. Ibid., 15.
16. Ibid., 19.
17. Ibid., 7, 32, 33.

> leaving their guns behind.
> Jesus has found these same guns,
> and brought them to the hunters
> to go and kill the elephant.
> Truly, Jesus is a Man among men,
> the most stalwart of men!
> He stands firm as a rock.[18]

Africa pulsates with a lively sense of the spiritual world in which good and evil forces operate. Many scholars therefore think we cannot even begin to comprehend African life and literature without first recognizing how intensely Africans feel that cosmic powers, some of them evil, both regulate and constrain behavior.[19] When Afua Kuma therefore describes Jesus's victory over the *sasabonsam* and the *mmoatia*, and how his victory helps hunters overcome their forest fear, if not their fear of life, we must try to absorb the full theological force of her words and imagery. When Jesus kills both spirits, that is, he establishes his spiritual and therefore cosmic lordship. Put differently, Afua Kuma's Jesus is *Christus Victor*.[20] He annihilates the evil powers many Africans view as sociologically and ideologically destructive, and so Jesus is an African.

For the Ghanaian theologian Kwame Bediako, Afua Kuma "provides clear evidence that Christianity in Africa is a truly African experience."[21] This is because her lively sense of spiritualized nature, which signifies the *African* side of her African Christianity, informs the *Christian* side of her African Christianity, her claim that Jesus presides over spiritualized nature. Jesus is Lord because he meets African people where they need him most—namely, in life's deep forest, highest among its principalities and powers, installing hope where fear once reigned. "This is theology which comes from where faith lives and must live continually," Bediako declares, "in the conditions of life of the community of faith, the theology of the living church, reflecting faith in the living Lord as present reality in daily life."[22]

---

18. Ibid., 19.

19. Fisher, *West African Religious Traditions*, 100–102; Mbiti, *African Religions and Philosophy*, 74–89.

20. Küster, *The Many Faces of Jesus Christ*, 57–76.

21. Kwame Bediako, *Jesus in Africa: The Christian Gospel in African History and Experience* (Akropong-Akuapem, Ghana; Oxford: Editions Clé and Regnum Africa, 2000) 9.

22. Ibid.

Jesus as the Chief among Chiefs

The *Christus Victor* model that upholds our first African Jesus-image also supports our second. Expressed another way, Jesus reigns as Chief among chiefs as well as the deep forest's Lord. He is *Okokurokohene*—the powerful Chief.[23] And by using this Twi counterpart to the Greek *kyrios* (Lord), one of Jesus's numerous New Testament titles, Afua Kuma once more indigenizes the gospel.

The historian of African religions Philip T. Laryea holds that "background knowledge of the chief's status and position [in Akan society] is necessary for an understanding of how the image is used in Afua Kuma's poem."[24] He informs us, for example, that the Akan divinize their chiefs. This is because they believe *Onyame* (or more popularly, *Nyame*), that is, God, dwells within the chief's heart. Once the people therefore install a chief, he represents *Onyame* to them. And he has *Onyame*'s authorization to rule. Laryea further explains that so-called chief executioners frequently compose *apae*, which is akin to court verse, in praise of the chief. These *apae* eulogize the chief's good qualities. Of course, no one chief personifies all possible laudable traits. And one chief frequently embodies a trait that another does not possess, and vice versa. In light of this observation, Afua Kuma's almost inexhaustible list of *apae* in praise of Jesus accentuates his place as Chief among chiefs.[25] Jesus is the Chief among chiefs because he exemplifies at least four special qualities, which Africans, especially West Africans, associate with chiefs: regal splendor, gentle astuteness, disinterested liberality, and intercessory expertise.

Jesus is Chief among chiefs because, first, he exudes ceremonial elegance and noble assurance:

> Mere chiefs and kings are not his equals,
> though filled with glory and power,
> wealth and blessings, and royalty
> in the greatest abundance.
> But of them all, he is the leader,
> and the chiefs with all their glory follow after him.
>
> He is the one for whom
> women lay down their cloths on the path,
> and pour sweet-smelling oil on his feet.

23. Kuma, *Jesus of the Deep Forest*, 11.
24. Laryea, "Mother Tongue Theology," 53.
25. Ibid., 54.

> They run to and fro amidst shouts of praise before him.
> It is true: Jesus is a Chief![26]

This last stanza recalls the day Jesus of Nazareth rode into Jerusalem on a donkey. Here his disciples and the crowds welcomed him with branches, mainly from palm trees, and proclaimed his lordship. Notice, though, how Afua Kuma Africanizes Palm Sunday. She does this by replacing the traditional "Hosanna" shout with an emphatic cry, "Jesus is a Chief!"

According to her, however, it is not enough simply to describe Jesus as *a* chief. Jesus, she says, is Chief among chiefs. A little later in her prayers and praises, therefore, she reinforces Jesus's distinctive majesty by associating him with objects and rituals linked to the *asantehene*, the Ashanti's paramount chief, such as the sacred stools and the talking drums.[27] Anthropologist Robert B. Fisher tells us that missionaries once dismissed the sacred royal drums as "symbols of satanic forces."[28] With this next extract, though, Afua Kuma clearly defies such missionary misunderstanding. Here the talking drums announce Jesus as the paramount Chief as well as the African *Christus Victor*:

> Horns and instruments sound all night till sunrise.
> And what is the reason?
> Jesus has come!
> Priests go before him playing stringed instruments,
> And young men shout praises behind.
> All the chiefs have set up their chairs
> and wait for him.
> That's why his heavenly guitars are playing;
> the earth trembles and the thunder roars.
>
> The sun's halo and the rainbow
> are the signs of his coming,
> while all of the chiefs
> beat the gong-gongs, the *nnawuta* and *adawuru*,
> mightily and gloriously.
> We say, "All quiet!" for Jesus will speak.
> The chiefs encourage him with drumming.
> Women come from the grave-side and shout happily,
> "Jesus is victorious!"[29]

26. Kuma, *Jesus of the Deep Forest*, 20.
27. Fisher, *West African Religious Traditions*, 34–35, 54–58.
28. Ibid., 34.
29. Kuma, *Jesus of the Deep Forest*, 31.

At this point, I may briefly note the thoughts of those who question an African appeal to the victorious Jesus. Several scholars, including theologian Volker Küster, dispute the usefulness of the chief analogy. They say it centers around an image that suggests dominance and power. And, as I have noted, such authority notions sustain the *Christus Victor* model. Since dominance and power are seldom part of Africans' daily lives, several scholars view the *Christus Victor* model ambivalently. It appears only to underscore Jesus's imperial rule (*theologia gloriae*) without fully appreciating his passionate suffering (*theologia crucis*).[30]

Jesus is Chief among chiefs because, second, he models gentle astuteness. Blessed with great spiritual perception, he transmits much-needed moral and religious advice by sprinkling his speech with trickster tales and proverbs: "For he is greater than the greatest chiefs," Afua Kuma decrees, "but not in silver or gold; / with wisdom and grace he builds his throne, / and with knowledge he moulds a kingdom."[31]

Jesus is Chief among chiefs because, third, he practices disinterested liberality. He gives the needy many good things, ranging from plentiful *fufu* to abundant *kente*, and he does so without ulterior motive.[32] "If Jesus should call you, smile," Afua Kuma advises, because "he gives gifts freely. / We must make a head-pad to carry away his gifts," so generous is he.[33]

Jesus is Chief among chiefs because, fourth, he epitomizes intercessory expertise. He mediates between individuals and groups in disagreement, effecting at-one-ment where once division prevailed:

> *Amansanhene*: Jesus the Arbitrator,
> He who brings nations together.
> Milk and honey flow in his veins.
> Children rush to meet him;
> crowds of young people
> rush about to make him welcome
> Chief of young women:
> they have strung a necklace of gold nuggets and beads,

---

30. See Bediako, *Jesus in Africa*, 22; Küster, *Many Faces of Jesus Christ*, 67, 76; and Laryea, "Mother Tongue Theology," 54.

31. Kuma, *Jesus of the Deep Forest*, 23.

32. *Fufu* is a starch-based product, made from mashed-up cassava plant. Incidentally, *fufu* has pride of place in a rather amusing creation story that the Ashanti tell about God's (*Onyame's*) separation from the world. See Mbiti, *African Religions and Philosophy*, 94–95.

33. Kuma, *Jesus of the Deep Forest*, 23.

>   and hung it around your neck.
>   So we go before you,
>   shouting our praises, "Ose, Ose!"[34]

Jesus is Chief among chiefs, then, because of his reconciling activity. He is *Amansanhene*, the great chief who assembles all his sub-chiefs and resolves conflicts. I should add that the final words, "'Ose, Ose,'" are an impressive cry of jubilant praise, often shouted by those leading a chief in procession, and thus they précis our second African Jesus-image.

Jesus and Divination

Having spent some time discussing our first two African Jesus-images, I now move to our third and fourth. There is less of Afua Kuma's verse to work with here, as we will see, but, in the end, I think we shall need to admit that these final two African Jesus-images combine with the first two to create an overall vision that illustrates the Africanization of Christianity.

Since a lively sense of the spiritual world pervades Akan traditional society, the Akan must be viewed as a deeply, fundamentally religious people. They believe special powers saturate everything in existence. And they hold that God, other spirits, or the ancestors (the so-called living dead) inhabit or influence particular people, mountains, trees, and streams. Accordingly, every Akan community houses one or more specialists in the area of engaging sacred powers. Such specialists are like distinctive vehicles or vessels for the holy, ferrying back and forth between dissimilar yet connected realms of meaning. In Africa, then, and especially among the Akan, religious specialists are intermediaries.[35]

Diviners are African religious specialists. They are "agents of the unveiling mysteries of human life," to cite Kenyan theologian John S. Mbiti, and they are, by and large, "friends of the communities" they serve.[36] They employ natural bits and pieces, sixth sense, mediums, foreshadowing, hypnotism, even possession, to acquire and then transmit hitherto undisclosed wisdom. And apart from a few instances, this wisdom either pacifies or galvanizes society. Among the Akan, then, people

---

34. Ibid., 23.

35. Fisher, *West African Religious Traditions*, 92, 102, 114–16; Mbiti, *African Religions and Philosophy*, 1–3, 162–88.

36. Mbiti, *African Religions and Philosophy*, 172.

both consult and esteem diviners for their power in relation to God on the one hand, and to the community on the other.

One of Afua Kuma's dominant images for Jesus comes from the divination system. She intones:

> O great and powerful Jesus, incomparable Diviner,
> the sun and moon are your *batakari*.
> It sparkles like the morning star.
> *Sekyere Buruku*, the tall mountain,
> all the nations see your glory.[37]

Now, I suspect this extract's multifaceted symbolism belies Afua Kuma's extraordinarily rich experience of Jesus. Consider her first line. Even though she knows, and perhaps even reveres, diviners as sacred go-betweens, not to mention community builders, she implies that Jesus's acts of divination are pre-eminent. Appearing very early in her prayers and praises, this avowal heralds her high Christology. Here Jesus's superiority lies in his unparalleled ability to manipulate time by working with the past as well as the *near* future to calm fretfulness and stimulate trust.[38] Her second line is also revealing. If the sun and moon serve as Jesus's *batakari*, which is the long sinuous robe that prominent northern Ghanaians wear, especially when they wish to indicate their boldness and readiness to serve others, then her trope further underscores Jesus's unarguable authority.[39]

Diviners often function like seers. They isolate the cause of an individual or community malady by looking into it, paying attention to all possible explanatory factors, and then they secure its remedy by manipulating various objects in order to acquire some kind of life-affirming oracular knowledge. They see into the past and near future, in other words, and then advise people accordingly. For Afua Kuma, Jesus excels in this act of divination. She cries out: "Jesus, the Seer among prophets / who always speaks the truth. / Wisest of soothsayers, the resurrected

---

37. Kuma, *Jesus of the Deep Forest*, 6.
38. Bediako, *Jesus in Africa*, 15; Mbiti, *African Religions and Philosophy*, 15–28.
39. The *batakari* is also a war robe, since it is often associated with Ashanti chiefs, like King Osei Tutu, when leading his army into battle. Connecting the *batakari* to Jesus suggests Afua Kuma's Jesus has a military function. Also, with respect to the quoted stanza, its final two lines link Jesus to *Sekyere Buruku*, one of the divinized forested mountains associated with Ghana's Eastern Region. While Afua Kuma therefore recognizes the existence of provincial deities and forces, like *Buruku*, she nonetheless proclaims that Jesus, as the tall mountain, towers above them.

body, / Who raised himself from three days in the grave."[40] Here Jesus's bodily resurrection both authenticates his wisdom and accentuates his power. It may even hint at Afua Kuma's hopeful sense that Jesus helps her and her community overcome death—and death, at least for Africans, is an ever-present, never-distant malady.

Since death opposes life, African Independent Churches tend to view Jesus as the "giver of life" and "the healer." Some of the most popular types of Independent Churches are the "prophet healing" churches.[41] Here people call on Jesus to confront malevolent forces, together with their human accomplices, like unscrupulous diviners, and compel them no more to cause illness, adversity, or death. This observation brings me to our final African Jesus-image in Afua Kuma's prayers and praises.

Jesus as the Healer

Africans feel constantly threatened by death. They live in some of our poorest countries, of course, and many suffer from a horrifying lack of food (either the right amount or the right kind), of clean, safe drinking water, of access to organized health care, and of adequate housing. Without these basic needs, many Africans never enjoy the opportunity to realize their full human potential. In this context of too-scarce resources, not to mention misery and premature death, the image of Jesus as Healer prevails, as described in one of Afua Kuma's verses:

> The famine has become severe;
> let us go and tell Jesus!
> He is the one who,
> when he raises his hands,
> gives even our enemies their share,
> and our brothers bring head-pads
> to carry the food away.[42]

Here Afua Kuma views Jesus as the Healer, because he continues in Africa what he initiated in Palestine—he performs signs and wonders, such as feeding and nature miracles. "*Ntafowayifo*: Wonder-worker! /

---

40. Kuma, *Jesus of the Deep Forest*, 29.

41. For details, see Benjamin C. Ray, *African Religions: Symbol, Ritual, and Community* (Upper Saddle River, NJ: Prentice Hall, 2000) 172-95.

42. Kuma, *Jesus of the Deep Forest*, 39.

The streets flow with water though there's no rain! / Indeed, Jesus, you are amazing!"[43]

In a public lecture, John S. Mbiti explores the African belief in Jesus as the Healer. Besides acknowledging Jesus's capacity for signs and wonders, he claims that Jesus also heals by fighting the devil, "which on the African scene means witches, sorcerers, evil eye, and unwanted spirits."[44] Afua Kuma agrees. Jesus has "killed the evil spirit," she asserts confidently, "and cut off its head!"[45] And as "the Lion of the grasslands," Jesus takes his sharp claws and tears out Satan's entrails, leaving "them on the ground / for the flies to eat."[46]

Jesus is the healer, because he fortifies fragile people, inspiring in them the courage to face what Mbiti sees as common African maladies: namely, "childlessness, diseases, famine and malicious persons or mystical powers."[47] Afua Kuma unites to Mbiti in this respect:

> Doctor of the sick!
> Helper of traders and craftsmen!
> Chief of farmers;
> who gives us our produce!
> When we are thirsty and there are no streams,
> he gives us fruit to quench our thirst,
> There are oranges and mangoes,
> pineapple, and sugar cane, too.
>
> You are the fruitful beans
> Which burst and spring from the pod.
> You let the barren bear twins!
> Lion of the grasslands!
> We call to you, "Come!"[48]

Jesus also reassures sick and dying people. According to Mbiti, "that means, He is Lord over death and life. He gives perfect rest, which means health in this life and peace in heaven when one dies. Persons are safe

---

43. Ibid., 14.

44. John S. Mbiti, "'And He Vanished Out of Their Sight': Emerging Images of Jesus Christ in African Christianity," Brite Divinity School, Fort Worth, TX, February 20, 2003. I thank Professor Mbiti for providing me with a copy of his remarks.

45. Kuma, *Jesus of the Deep Forest*, 7.

46. Ibid., 46.

47. Mbiti, "'He Vanished Out of Their Sight,'" 7.

48. Kuma, *Jesus of the Deep Forest*, 28.

in the hands of Jesus, even when they are sick and die."⁴⁹ As the Healer, Jesus is therefore *Christus praesens*, wholly present in the Spirit in others' suffering. Afua Kuma concurs:

> Jesus is the one
> who fills his basket with sickness,
> and dumps it into the depths of the sea.
> He has been here already and taken sickness away.
> He stands on the sea with outstretched arms,
> while the devil walks the forest in agony.⁵⁰

Later, she reiterates her point:

> When we met with Jesus
> he had tied together both sickness and death,
> and cast them into the sea.
> This is the reason why the nations rejoice
> and the people are happy.⁵¹

Africans "encounter Jesus Christ concretely," Mbiti says, "in His work as Healer of sicknesses and related problems."⁵² And as part of the healing process, Jesus the Healer inspires others to come together around the common purpose of eradicating sickness:

> An important outcome of the healing practice in Independent Churches is that Jesus Christ makes the Church into a healing community (fellowship). In many places in West Africa, for example, groups made up of the sick and those who look after them, develop around healing prayer houses. They then experience Jesus Christ, not only as One Who heals, but also as One Who brings people together and cements them into a fellowship, a community.⁵³

As someone involved in the Independent Churches in Africa, Afua Kuma speaks a mother tongue theology, one that inscribes her community's history in Jesus's own healing history:

> Our ancestors didn't know of *Onyankopon*: the great God.
> They served lesser gods and spirits, and became tired.

49. Mbiti, "'He Vanished Out of Their Sight,'" 8.
50. Kuma, *Jesus of the Deep Forest*, 32.
51. Ibid., 45.
52. Mbiti, "'He Vanished Out of Their Sight,'" 8.
53. Ibid., 8.

> But as for us, we have seen holy men, and prophets.
> We have gone to tell the angels
> how Jehovah helped us reach this place.
> Jehovah has helped us come this far;
> with great gratitude we come before Jesus,
> the one who gives everlasting life.[54]

With her Africanization of the Christian mythos, Afua Kuma shows how African faith and hope may be grounded in Jesus Christ who, far from being alien to Akan culture, has a very definite role to play within its religious universe.

Conclusion: Grassroots Religion

As with other traditional cultures, most African languages have no word for "religion." The spiritual suffuses Africans' everyday world so that the Western compartmentalization that defines "religion" simply does not hold in African societies and culture. Broad, fluid definitions of religion work better here, because they honor the moveable meanings, or shall I say "spirits," that permeate African life. Religion, then, is that which gives multifaceted activities and thoughts ultimate significance and fosters individual as well as community flourishing. Whatever else it is, religion, as I am defining it here, involves constructing meaning from the material of everyday life.[55] It is an ongoing process and creative enterprise. Accordingly, Afua Kuma's prayers and praises disclose how she herself participates in this process in the midst of Ghana's forested hills.

I have never met Afua Kuma, yet I suspect her religious poetry gives shape and meaning to her world. It reflects her deep-seated hopes, fears, joys, and sorrows. But her verse does not simply reflect her own private petitions; in Africa, the individual exists in relation to her community. Religion emerges out of, and is formed by, an intricate web of complex relationships, each responsible for, and dependent upon, the

---

54. Kuma, *Jesus of the Deep Forest*, 30. This quotation's first line needs some attention. As Mbiti implies, it is contrary to the Akan understanding of the Supreme Being (*Nyankopon*). Mbiti says, "God is no stranger to African peoples, and in traditional life there are no atheists. This is summarized in an Ashanti proverb that 'No one shows a child the Supreme Being.' This means that everybody knows of God's existence almost by instinct, and even children know Him" (Mbiti, *African Religions and Philosophy*, 29).

55. This approach to religion in Africa finds support in Evan Zuesse, *Ritual Cosmos: The Sanctification of Life in African Religions* (Athens: Ohio University Press, 1985).

other. Not surprisingly, Afua Kuma's Obo Kwahu community views her prayers and praises as somehow their own. Her words are their words, words requesting at the basic level, food, clothing, shelter, and health, as well as the strength to harness powers to solve the many problems that continue to plague them in life.

Certain Christian theologians might want to ask of Afua Kuma's work, "How is it Christian?" While this is not necessarily an insignificant question, it does not reflect my purpose or even my understanding. In my opinion, we are not so much witnessing the Christianization of Africa as the Africanization of Christianity.[56] In a sense this is inevitable, for Christianity, like any religion, exists first and foremost at the everyday, grassroots level. Whether or not they see themselves as part of a postcolonial reclamation project, Africans, like Afua Kuma, draw upon their own cultural resources—using the vernacular and stressing all things local—to create their distinct Christian self-understanding. Contemporary Africans thereby demonstrate their own agency over and above Western colonizers, missionaries, and theologians. In truth, though, this initiative-taking is really nothing new.[57] Whatever else scholars of religion and popular journalists tell us about new developments in Africa, Christianity's history in Africa has always been a history of largely African initiatives, and, as such, Afua Kuma's *Jesus of the Deep Forest* offers a modest but not unimportant contribution to this unfolding narrative.

---

56. This is the thesis of numerous recent books on the topic of Global South Christianity. See Joel A. Carpenter and Lamin Sanneh, editors, *The Changing Face of Christianity: Africa, the West, and the World* (Oxford: Oxford University Press, 2005); Philip Jenkins, *The New Faces of Christianity: Believing the Bible in the Global South* (Oxford: Oxford University Press, 2008); Mercy Amba Oduyoye, *Beads and Strands: Reflections of an African Woman on Christianity in Africa* (Maryknoll, NY: Orbis, 2004); and Lamin Sanneh, *Whose Religion Is Christianity?: The Gospel Beyond the West* (Grand Rapids: Eerdmans, 2003).

57. Philip Jenkins makes this point quite clear in *The Lost History of Christianity: The Thousand-Year Golden Age of the Church in the Middle East, Africa, and Asia* (New York: Lion, 2009).

SIX

Essential Being

Reflections of Christianity and Human Survival in Caribbean Literature

Mozella G. Mitchell

> Some few watch too.
> In voices low,
> They talk
> of great ebors
> When Nezer of Moruga
> walked
> this earth.
> Mighty Babalorisa,
> Papa Nezer,
> father to them all,
> And still remembered
>
> They talk too,
> of drummers,
> And those ebors,
> when Montelo
> master drummer,
> would summon up,
> the ancestors;
> and chant
> the ancient songs
> and dance
> the ancient dance
>
> . . . . .

> Iya sits
> within their midst.
>
> The quiet comes,
> All wait.
> The air is heavy
> with the smell
> of incense burnt,
> and sweet oil poured
> and candles lit.
>
> The quiet comes,
> all wait.
> Now the tales will start;
> Tales,
> of the mighty doing,
> of the Orishas;
> Tales,
> of Oludumare,
> Great, wise and
> just.
>
> And the sacredness,
> of her trust.
> The grey/white sky,
> brightens,
> Into morning
> Eshu, stands guard,
> at another
> dawning.[1]

Introduction: Interiority and Struggle

PEARL EINTOU SPRINGER'S POEM reflects the spirit of religiosity in her Caribbean setting and the determination to maintain the distinctive

---

1. Pearl Eintou Springer, "The Yard (for Iya Lorisa Melvina Rodney)," in *At the Crossroads: African Caribbean Religion and Christianity*, edited by Burton Sankeralli (St. James, Trinidad and Tobago, West Indies: Caribbean Conference of Churches, 1995) 199, 201. I should add that *Babalorisha* is the title of the priest of the religion referred to in earlier times as Shango and as Orisa Religion. *Iya* is short for *Iyalorisha*, which is the title for a priestess of the religion. Oludumare is the supreme being of the religion, and Eshu is one of the tutelary deities of the Yoruba pantheon of Orishas from which this religion is revived, along with other such African-derived religions of the Caribbean and Latin America as Santeria of Cuba and Puerto Rico, Candomblé of Brazil, and Vodun of Haiti.

human dignity and cultural rootedness necessary for a people with a wholesome and healthy sense of self. This spirit is retained and thrives in the face of centuries of struggles, conflicts, and suffering that Springer's people have undergone in the diverse mixtures of peoples, cultures, circumstances, and conditions common to the relatively short history of this region's development. Because her poem typifies what I characterize as essential being, I begin my discussion by examining both her character as a literary artist/political activist and how this specific poem reflects what I see as a theme in at least two other works of literature from the English Caribbean: V. S. Reid's novel *New Day* (1949) and Earl Lovelace's novel *The Wine of Astonishment* (1982).

Before going further, I want to state briefly what I mean by "essential being." I certainly have been influenced by some writers who have discussed the notions of being and essence, human meaning and genuine existence, such as existentialist theologians and philosophers (Paul Tillich, Jean-Paul Sartre, Martin Heidegger, and the like) and psychological thinkers (such as Carl Jung, later Jungian thinkers, and others). However, I do not intend to entertain or engage any philosophical or theological arguments by posing abstract concepts regarding reality. I simply refer to what is defined as basic, necessary, indispensable, and vital to any human being, howsoever human beings themselves in their most fundamental understanding see such qualities. Everyone of necessity sees her- or himself as basically human from certain common standpoints, and as living either authentically or inauthentically under particular conditions and circumstances. Without arguing the point, then, I assert that essential being comes from within the person or persons and is not imposed from without. Generally, this is what the struggle is about in the works included in this chapter. This principle comes out clearly in the experiences, actions, reactions, resistance, and vocal expressions of the persons in the literary creations that depict the religious and social realities of individuals and groups living under Western Christian dominance, mainly British, in areas referred to as the Global South.

Pearl Eintou Springer: Life and Literary Art

Pearl Eintou Springer is a highly accomplished author/activist from Trinidad and Tobago. Her life and writings offer instructive revelations of religious and spiritual meaning from a comparative perspective—

between Christianity as seen from the viewpoints of both the Global North and the Global South. Springer's unique character has been shaped by her life experiences as social activist, poet, dramatist, and librarian (founder of the National Heritage Library of Trinidad and Tobago), mother, and priestess of the Orisa religion, the African-derived Yoruba religion of Trinidad and Tobago. "Her religious experience growing up in Santa Cruz (Trinidad and Tobago), a heavily Catholic town, was of a strong Catholic nature; but her mother was from mixed African and Black Carib Indian stock, and her maternal grandfather was a Congolese African, son of a slave on a plantation on the Island of St. Vincent."[2] Her spirituality was formed through the juncture of her neo-African religious background and her Catholic upbringing. By way of her maternal grandfather (who lived to be 108 years old) she was exposed to African-derived methods of healing, slave songs of the plantation, and similar cultural and spiritual influences. "Her Catholic religious background was challenged when she as a young woman spent time in England in the Black Panthers movement of the 1960's and came back to Trinidad and Tobago and was very intensely involved in the Black Power Movement of 1969 and 1970."[3] This is when she came to a crucial spiritual realization influenced by Afro-centricity: "You cannot be liberated at all if you serve the God of another."[4]

The poem "The Yard," a part of which was quoted above, reveals much when looked at from the perspective of Springer's spiritual journey from the Catholic faith back to and grounding in her native African and Afro-Caribbean religious roots. Iyalorisha Melvina Rodney, her spiritual mother and the head of the Iyalorishas (priestesses of the Orisa religion) of Trinidad and Tobago, to whom this poem is dedicated, guided her journey:

> Through divination it was determined that Ogun, the [Yoruba] Orisha [deity] of iron, war, strength, etc., had claimed her, and she was advised to go to Nigeria to be initiated. She did, and later questioning of the validity of her initiation and receiving assurance only made her realize the depth to which Christianity had

---

2. Interview with Pearl Eintou Springer, San Juan, Trinidad and Tobago, December 2, 2004; cited in Mozella G. Mitchell, *Crucial Issues in Caribbean Religions* (New York: Peter Lang, 2006) 192.

3. Ibid., 192–93.

4. Ibid.

misguided her. She was also claimed by Shango the [Yoruba] deity of fire and lightning, war, etc., and Oya, the [Yoruba] mother deity of the sea, guardian of cemeteries, etc., and she was initiated [in these], becoming even stronger in her religious commitments.[5]

This pilgrimage led her to play a leadership role in organizing the Orisa religious groups in the country and engage in strong and intense political battles to gain equal recognition and legitimate social status for Orisa among the other world religions (Hindu, Islamic, Christian, etc.) in the country.[6] The Yard (also called *palais*) is the sacred place of gathering and celebration of the Orisa faith, where the event of the great *ebo*—an annual week-long religious festival involving priests, priestesses, and other practitioners in sacred dances, singing, drumming, divination, sacrifices, other rituals, and feasting in honor of all the gods, as well as the ancestors—takes place. Springer's poem is a song (similar to a ballad) to the Orishas (such as Eshu of the crossroads who opens the way to the sacred, Ogun, Oya, Omele, Osayin) in which she describes some of the Orisha and their traits as depicted in the *ebo* procession of deities, the activities going on in the Yard, and she especially honors historical roots as seen in her references to Papa Neezer ("Mighty Babalorisa, Papa Nezer, father to them all, . . . still remembered") and other ancestors, and tales of the mighty doings of the Orisha. One stanza in the poem expresses the notion of essential being as experiencing restoration and acceptance in the context of the warm and receptive Yard experience:

> Syncretized veil
> > of christian prayers
> > and saints,
> are abrupted,
> in welcome
> renaissance,
> of self.[7]

5. Ibid., 193.
6. Ibid.
7. Springer, "The Yard," 200. As in other African-derived religions of the Caribbean and Latin America, African-derived Yoruba religious practices such as Orisa in Trinidad and Tobago historically were veiled or disguised by use of Catholic prayers, artifacts, rituals, and saints, since the open practices of these religions were legally proscribed during African slavery in these areas and for many years afterwards. Besides my own work, see Frances Henry, *Reclaiming African Religions in Trinidad: The Socio-Political Legitimation of the Orisha and Spiritual Baptist Faiths* (Kingston, Jamaica, West Indies: University of the West Indies Press, 2003); Roger Bastide, *African Civilizations in the New World*

Such lines acknowledge the process of what we may call the unveiling of African-derived religions in the Caribbean, especially Trinidad and Tobago, where many are shedding the Christian (especially Roman Catholic) practices and elements previously blended (syncretized) with their African-derived religions as a means of concealing the actual practices within them. Now that a greater sense of religious freedom is experienced or demanded by some practitioners, they no longer feel the need to disguise their practices with Christian elements due to legal prohibitions against open practices, as was historically typical of this and other Yoruba religions brought to the New World context by slaves from West Africa. Instead of concealing their spirituality, they can now experience and embrace in full their religious and cultural roots and become more genuinely their true selves. This was not the case, however, prior to the last quarter of the previous century.

Human Dignity and Self-Worth

If we look at Lovelace's and Reid's novels, we find writers depicting and recreating their conceptions of the real worlds of Caribbean peoples within the Western Christian-dominated societies of Trinidad and Tobago as well as Jamaica. We see how such peoples managed to survive and maintain their humanity under very difficult circumstances only a few decades back. Their portrayals of the religious, political, and social realities and of the character and actions of religious and political leaders of the times are instructive for an understanding of both Western and non-Western Christianity today. Though the settings of these two novels are separated by space and time, Lovelace's work having as its setting the island nation of Trinidad and Tobago from the period of 1917 to 1951, and Reid's work having its setting decades earlier on the island of Jamaica between 1865 and 1944 (beginning earlier and overlapping parts of the time of Lovelace's work), the works have much in common— a commonality that enables us to secure a comparative picture of the religious realities of the two areas as well as the nature and character of their struggles and experiences. Two main similarities are that both

(New York: Harper and Row, 1971); Dale Bisnauth, *History of Religions in the Caribbean* (Kingston, Jamaica, West Indies: Kingston, 1989); and, Leslie G. Desmangles, *The Faces of the Gods: Vodou and Roman Catholicism in Haiti* (Chapel Hill: University of North Carolina Press, 1992). Today, some of the proponents of these religions are eliminating the Christian disguises in so far as possible and embracing their "pure" religious roots.

nations exist under British colonial rule and so are subject to the joint political/religious authority of the Church of England and the British crown, and both have populations of predominantly African origin and culture, whose basic spirituality and religiosity are similar. Additionally, this spirituality and religiosity are essential to their authentic social and political existence whether they are members of the Church of England, as in the case of the Campbell family in *New Day*, or members of the Spiritual Baptist faith, as in the case of Bee and his community of believers of the Bonasse area of Trinidad. Yet, revealing differences do exist in the intents and purposes of the two novels and how the writers present the situations facing the characters within their historical/political and geographical settings, as well as their portrayals of how the characters deal with their particular issues and realities. We will begin with the later novel, Lovelace's *The Wine of Astonishment*.

Lovelace's *The Wine of Astonishment*

Lovelace tells the story of the congregation of Spiritual Baptists in Bonasse, Trinidad and Tobago, led by the pastor referred to as Bee, and their struggle to worship in their own way, retaining the religious and spiritual elements that combine both Christianity and the African Traditional Religion of Yoruba, in the face of strong opposition from the Church of England and the Roman Catholic Church, which, with the backing of the legal authorities, manage to outlaw the Spiritual Baptist practices and attempt to impose on the congregants what the congregants consider to be the rather dry and lifeless Catholic or Anglican way.[8]

The story is told through the first-person narration of Eva, Bee's wife, who is not only the mother of her own family but also the symbolic mother figure of the entire community, and who voices the individual and group struggles from before and after the passing of the severely restrictive Shouters Prohibition Ordinance of 1917 until its lifting in 1951. Eva vividly describes the situation facing the community, of which the church is the core meaning. In conveying this meaning and its significance of ownership and freedom, she states:

---

8. Earl Lovelace, *The Wine of Astonishment* (London: Heinemann, 1982) 64. See also Eudora Thomas, *A History of the Shouter Baptists in Trinidad and Tobago* (New York: Calaloux, 1987). Finally, see Springer, "Orisa and the Spiritual Baptist Religion in Trinidad and Tobago," in Sankeralli, *At the Crossroads*, 99–103.

> We have this church in the village. We have this church. The walls make out of mud, the roof covered with carrat leaves: a simple hut with no steeple or cross or acolytes or white priests or latin ceremonies. But is our own. Black people own it. Government ain't spent one cent helping us to build it or to put bench in it or anything; the bell that we ring when we call to the Spirit is our money that pay for it.[9]

Eva goes on to describe Spiritual Baptist worship practices: singing hymns and ringing the bell, shouting hallelujahs, speaking in tongues when the Holy Spirit comes, preaching the Word to the "downtrodden and the lame and the beaten" and touching "black people soul."[10] Very generally, she characterizes the vitality of the church in relating meaningfully to the community socially, economically, physically, politically, as well as spiritually. Yet the schools and other components of the larger community saw their church and its practices as a threat and began to characterize them as uncivilized and barbarous, satanic. Their children were encouraged to "give up the church and turn Catholic or Anglican" in order to have a better chance at material success. When such inducements did not entirely destroy the church, the authorities found another plan to make them surrender. All manner of harassments were leveled against them, such as building codes and other restrictions, complaints, until the government finally passed the law prohibiting specific practices other than those of the "official" or "established" Anglican or Catholic Churches. Afterwards, they either followed the prescribed worship formats or worshipped secretly. Police raids and mass arrests were carried out against those who disobeyed the ordinance, however.[11]

We witness here a truly engrossing narrative work of fiction depicting the clash of socio-religious values, principles, actions, and responses, both group and individual, as well as societal. Clearly, the oppressive nature of the official church and colonial government is seen as the cause of the hardships and troubles of the families, and the in-group struggles that lead to the deterioration of community structure of those of the Spiritual Baptist faith, which otherwise appears to be a genuine spiritual reality. In contrast to the more staid and externally constructed official, established churches, this Spiritual Baptist faith has such vital significance for its

---

9. Lovelace, *Wine of Astonishment*, 32.
10. Ibid., 32.
11. Ibid., 33–35.

adherents that they do not hesitate to risk their lives to maintain it. The seriousness and depth of meanings produced by the author's portrayals of characters, action, and outcome of plot can have great impact on our understanding of the relations between the religiosity and spirituality of two groups of Christian adherents, Western traditional or orthodox and the non-Western, African-derived or Afro-Christian groups.

Among the Bonasse community and the Spiritual Baptist believers are the usual heroes, villains, and ordinary citizens that one may find in any novel. The usual themes found in colonial societies are also found here: the people who suffer from oppressive practices of the occupying government; the political figures who for the sake of their own self-aggrandizement betray the people of their own ethnic group who help elect them to administrative office in hopes of having in them a voice of justice and fair representation in the halls of government; and those among the populace who press for justice and equity through their elected representatives and, even when such treatment is not immediately forthcoming, are patient and wait for changes to come about. The latter tend to retain a sense of hope. Others, however, may not be as patient and enduring, but take a more militant stance and attempt to force change and justice one way or another. Prototypes of all of these characters appear in the novel and in the Bonasse community. Ivan Morton is the betraying official who, even though he grew up with Eva and Bee and others in the community and depended heavily on their support in getting elected to office, thought little of turning almost a deaf ear to their pleas for justice in helping maintain their church and assisting with other dire needs of the community. The Spiritual Baptist pastor, Bee, is the true leader of the people, in contrast to Morton, as Bee remains strong and faithful and a stalwart promoter of the people in terms of looking after both their spiritual and material/cultural needs. He stands up for his community and speaks out for their rights and privileges, and leads them in actions of resistance to the unjust legal restrictions. He and his family suffer for their resistance, but he and they bear with the situations and retain hope for the changes that he encourages them will have to take place.

The crucial turning point of the plot revolves around Bolo, the champion stickfighter, though Prince, the crude as well as heartless police officer and traitor of his own people, plays a significant part in bringing the action to a head when he preys upon the religious community to arrest and torment them into compliance with the harsh restrictions. Lovelace has in Bolo somewhat of a unique character who comes close to being a hero of the people. He embodies the religious and cultural values of the people, the principles and goals so precious to the group. And he has the courage of his convictions, strong enough to stand up to the authorities, even though he spends time in prison for his actions. The peculiarity is that he uses his courage to attack the people, as well, in some twisted way so as to call attention to their "cowardliness" in allowing their rights to be trampled upon. He turns himself into a sort of gadfly to sting the people into a realization of their own self-destructiveness. Indeed, he becomes even more than a gadfly when he for months terrorizes the town and has everyone afraid to correct him in his wrongdoings. It would take Bolo and his destructive actions against both himself and others to bring about a crisis that would cause him to lose his own life and cause the death of one of the young daughters of another townsman, as well as to shock the town into seeing the depth of its oppressive status in not being able even to worship as they desired. Yet Bolo is not the hero, and may even be an anti-hero; for Bee is the true hero, who is left to ponder the reality of the situation and agonize over what has really happened to the dignity and humanity of himself and his people.

After the tragedy of Bolo and others and the coming of the new political campaign and election, the church comes back and the ordinance is lifted. Amazingly, the people are able to worship in their usual way with all the traditional bell-ringing, hand-clapping, singing, dancing; but the Spirit does not come, not even with the spirited preaching of Bee. They do not know why the Spirit will not come. But the author concludes the novel in a rather suggestive way, as Bee and Eva leave the church and walk past a somewhat dilapidated house and yard—with bamboo for posts and coconut branches for a roof, with a steel band tent, with steel pans, with young barebacked men playing the pans, and dancing going on—and suddenly the Spirit returns in their hearts the same as they had previously felt it in the church. Eva declares:

> I listening to the music; for the music that those boys playing on the steelband have in it that same Spirit that we miss in our church: the same Spirit; and listening to them, my heart swell and it is like resurrection morning. I watch Bee, Bee watch me. I don't say nothing to him and he don't say nothing to me, the both of us

bow, nod, as if, yes, God is great, and like if we passing in front of something holy.[12]

Here Lovelace reminds us of the crucial spiritual role of the steel band in Trinidad and Tobago, a part of the African cultural/religious atmosphere that pervades the country. In her introduction to the novel, critic Marjorie Thorpe reveals the value to be gleaned from the clash of these two Western and non-Western Christian religious cultures and the tenacity of the adherents of the latter to hold on to their beliefs in the midst of harsh persecutions:

> As a syncretistic religion, born out of Africa's encounter with Europe in the New World, Lovelace sees in the Spiritual Baptist system of faith and worship, in their "Africanization of Christianity," a living example of the creative and regenerative impulses inherent in the black creole cultural tradition. The conflict between the Bonasse Spiritual Baptists and the established authorities is therefore conceived as only one other episode in the centuries-old struggle between Prospero and Caliban; and it is this which accounts for the symbolic significance of the church in the world of the novel. In tracing the history of this particular community, Lovelace is reflecting on the more general experience of the black man in the Caribbean.[13]

Thorpe correctly surmises that in concentrating on the familiar theme of the experiences of deprivation and oppression, Lovelace does not portray the black West Indian as "courageous victim" but rather as an "authentic hero-figure."[14] Such an emphasis makes a world of difference in the impression the story has on its readers. For instance, this approach allows us to witness the courage and endurance that the religious and cultural rootedness of the characters provides in their struggle for survival. Their heroic stance in clinging to the principles and practices of their faith against all odds proves the validity of them.

Reid's *New Day*

We find some similarities in this regard in Reid's novel, which has as its setting the British colony of Jamaica. Although the society may be

---

12. Ibid., 146.
13. Marjorie Thorpe, "Introduction," in ibid., viii–ix.
14. Ibid., ix.

composed of various religious groups that include Africanized Christians such as Native Baptists, Revival Zion, and Pocomania, the main characters and families that constitute the focus of this historical novel are mainly worshippers in the Church of England. Their religious, cultural, political, and social stance is grounded in what may be considered an African worldview, and it is this that shines through their reactions and responses to the experiences they encounter in the British-dominated world they inhabit. Their religious orientation even as Anglicans has a certain character all its own, as we shall see, in the socio-political and religious saga Reid presents of one family—the Campbells—and its descendants and their impact on the circumstances and socio-economic and political developments of their times.

Published in 1949, the novel covers the period of eighty years from 1865, when Jamaica was ruled by a governor appointed by the Crown, to 1944, when Jamaica was granted a constitution that permitted self-rule under Crown supervision, the "new day" suggested by the novel's title. As Reid states in the preface, his emphasis is not on a recount of the history of the period but rather on the fictional Campbell family, in an attempt to "transfer to paper some of the beauty, kindliness, and humor" of his people, "weaving characters into the wider framework of these eighty years and creating a tale that will offer as true an impression as fiction can of the way by which Jamaica and its people came to today."[15] This he does and much more, as the members of the family are always intricately involved in the religious, political, social, and cultural struggles of the various periods, and their actions convey to the reader an acute sense of the Afro-Jamaican religious and cultural distinctiveness in contrast to the religious and cultural nature of the Church and society that exercises control over them, which is portrayed as caught up in political and social corruption.[16]

The patriarch of the family, John Campbell, is a devoutly religious adherent of the Christian faith and as well as its biblical teachings, and he raises his children according to such dictates and principles. He has given all his children biblical names: Emmanuel, Ruth, David, Ezekiel, Samuel, Naomi, and John; and his wife's name is Tamah. Everything John Campbell does is put in biblical and religious perspective, interpreted by means of Christian teaching and through recitation of Scripture such as

---

15. V. S. Reid, "Author's Note," in Reid, *New Day* (New York: Knopf, 1949) viii.
16. Reid, *New Day*, 132–33.

the Psalms or the singing of hymns of faith. He is well-respected and often feared as he exercises his religious and spiritual authority both in his family and in the community.[17] Although John Campbell is a member of the middle class, specifically the landowning mulatto black populace, he identifies with the poor in their fight for justice. And this identification is a major theme of the novel—a struggle for justice that John Campbell sees as grounded in his biblical faith. But rather than launch an outright rebellion, he urges waiting on God to bring about their justice.[18] The pivotal point of the action is the three-year drought in which much suffering is endured by all, both the well-to-do and the poor, who cry for relief from the government but are unheard. Eventually the Morant Bay Rebellion takes place in 1865, bringing about extensive violence and Governor Eyre's mass execution of any of the people who were thought to have approved of the rebellion. And though there are other circumstances in which religious character and significance stand out in the novel, John Campbell himself and the manner in which he bears with the situation of the fomenting rebellion and its aftermath, which ultimately costs him his life, exemplifies the theme of essential being, and the struggle for human survival.

Even though John Campbell did not favor the fomenting rebellion, which was taking place both within and without the Church of England and led by brave black churchmen like Deacon Paul Bogle, and strongly forbade his children to take part in it, he found himself tied to it by the mere fact that he had signed the petition to the Queen demanding representative government. Consequently, the message was brought to him that he was on the governor's hit list and that he and his family must escape into the mountains. It was hard to convince him of this, but he finally gave in and packed up his family and escaped to the mountains for a spell, declaring, "I will hide in caves like mountain boar. I will flee from the mighty King Saul till his wrath subsides."[19] And so he did for sometime, but events would not allow him to remain there.

After a time, discovering that many of the brave ones had been slaughtered, even though some had not joined the rebellion as such, John Campbell was reluctant to stay away, because of his strong faith that justice would be served. So many of the people had been hanged, shot,

17. Ibid., 11–19.
18. Ibid., 13–14.
19. Ibid., 154.

slaughtered, whole families killed, untold horrors perpetrated—Deacon Bogle hanged, Aaron Dacres and his son Moses killed, Mr. Abram killed, Mr. Gordon hanged—that John Campbell was resolved to leave the mountain caves and go to the governor and plead for mercy, thinking that his spiritual character and honesty would place him in good stead and that the English possessed Christian charity: "I will ask to see Governor Eyre. I am no' Stoney Gut man. The English will not make war on Christians."[20] He had resolved to sacrifice himself, answering Davie, who had declared that his father did not understand:

> You it is who do not understand, Davie. My navel-string is buried at Morant Bay, and it is my own people who are hanging down there—innocent blood is being shed. If only the death o' me can help, then die I will. Perhaps they keep killing because they can no' find the guilty.[21]

And so Father Campbell marches down from the mountain with his family to meet the rival British soldiers gunning for them and other rebels, all the family singing "Onward Christian Soldiers." In this tragic trek, the father and the family are mercilessly attacked by the soldiers, and Father John Campbell and his son Emmanuel are killed, as Johnny and Davie escape into the mountains to become the continuation of the family line that will go on for generations. Later, as Davie gives a vivid account of the injustices and the bloody put-down of the rebellion before the British commissioners sent to investigate the incident, he mentions the ironic fact that the Anglican pastors did not pray over the bodies of his father and brother.[22]

After Davie is pardoned and restored, he and his younger brother Johnny, the story's narrator, both make their residence at one of the Cays in land not under the Queen's dominion, along with Lucille, who escaped the tragic circumstances with them and serves as a mother figure for Johnny, as Davie does so as a father.[23] In this stage of the story, Davie loses a lot of his original rather free-flowing, rebellious character and

20. Ibid., 163–66.
21. Ibid., 166–67.
22. Ibid., 169–71, 208–14.

23. Johnny narrates the story from various vantage points—as an old man looking back on the events, as a boy of eight looking up to and admiring his older brother (more or less as a father figure), as well as at other ages.

takes on the religious character the father had possessed.[24] The family line of descendants continue through the political and social changes that take place, and the new generations carry on the family traditions of the struggles for justice and equality as necessary for survival and prosperity: Davie died in the hurricane on the Cay that was his home; Lucile died in the Great Fire of 1882; James Cleary, son of Lucile and Davie, was a good business manager who carried on the business of his deceased father Davie, but he and his English wife died in the small pox epidemic; their son Garth, along with Davie and Johnny's brother Ezekiel's son Carlos Fernandez, played major roles in the new political, social, and economic development of the twentieth century, such as unionizing and supporting the oppressed Jamaican workers.

New Day brought the reader through the struggles of generations for justice and human dignity, and the stories were told not with grimness and defeat but with hope and humor as the author intended. The ending is one of celebration of the "new day" that has long been desired, stated in the speech of Garth before the governmental powers:

> "Full self-government within the orbit of the British Commonwealth!—Universal Adult Suffrage—Give us a chance to shape our own destinies!—Let us stand beside you, Mother England, but free and self-respecting—not as whining children but adults, with full respect to the obligation we owe our parent!—Get rid of imperialism!—Let us have no decline and fall, but a permanent institution that will stand as long as free men live!"[25]

It should be clear that it is the strong religious commitment and genuine spiritual character that sustain the characters in their continuing struggles for justice and equality. They maintain their loyalty and faith even though they witness the failure of the established church to live up to its biblical faith.

Conclusion: Established Church Failure

We have considered the spiritual character and religious faith and commitment of Pearl Eintou Springer, especially her role in the Orisa religion of Trinidad and Tobago and in fighting for justice in her society. We have witnessed the religious and social commitment of Bee

24. Reid, *New Day*, 221, 222.
25. Ibid., 367.

and other members of the Bonasse-based Spiritual Baptist faith. And we have examined the spiritual rootedness of the John Campbell family, transmitted through at least three generations of struggles of their descendants for justice and equality under British colonial rule in Jamaica. All three examples attest to the depth of meaning and genuineness of the religious faith of these persons in particular Global South contexts.[26] In each case, the contrasts to the established church traditions leave much to be desired of these traditions in their failure to possess the strength of their faith convictions.

---

26. For an extended discussion of Lovelace's novel in the context of Christianity's expansion in the Global South, see Darren J. N. Middleton, *Theology after Reading: Christian Imagination and the Power of Fiction* (Waco, TX: Baylor University Press, 2008) 111–47.

PART THREE

Christianity in Central and South America

SEVEN

"They Come Smiling Out of the Morgue"

Historical Resurrections in Ernesto Cardenal's Nicaragua (1934–70)

Ellin Sterne Jimmerson

Introduction

ERNESTO CARDENAL WAS BORN in Granada, Nicaragua to an upper-middle-class family in 1925. In 1947 he went to Columbia University, where he studied Ezra Pound's poems, and then returned to Nicaragua and began writing what he called *exteriorista* (exteriorist) poetry characterized by concrete imagery, specific language, montage-like organization, zigzagging time, historical subject matter, and biblical interpretive filters. He became one of the most widely read poets in the Spanish language.

In 1954, Cardenal participated in a plot to assassinate Nicaragua's president Anastasio Somoza García, one of Latin America's greediest and most brutal dictators and the United States' primary Latin American client. After converting to Roman Catholicism, Cardenal became committed to strict non-violence, entered the priesthood, and became one of Latin America's most idiosyncratic liberation theologians, interpreting the Bible, the church, and culture through the lens of military dictatorship, torture, and poverty. Cardenal scandalized many followers of philosophical non-violence when, beginning in the 1970s, he concluded that priestly calls for non-violent change would prolong the intense suffering of the Nicaraguan people. He began to publicly support the guerrilla Sandinistas, occasionally going to the front for Bible study with the soldiers.

The Sandinistas miraculously overthrew Somoza and his Mafia-like National Guard on July 17, 1979. Cardenal became Minister of Culture in the Nicaraguan Government of Reconstruction, serving until 1987. The government lasted until 1990 when it succumbed to illegal U.S.-sponsored *contra* attacks. He continues to write in Nicaragua and is rumored to have been nominated for the Nobel Prize in Literature in 2005.

This chapter's purpose is to investigate selected works of Ernesto Cardenal. Combining the techniques and interests of literary criticism, history writing, and theology, it shows how Cardenal's poems work literarily, asks what happened in Nicaragua between 1934 and 1970, and, by utilizing reflections on key men scattered in a number of his poems, explores his theology of resurrection. My work is organized chronologically by the dates on which these men in Nicaraguan revolutionary history died and, as Cardenal understands it, were resurrected. The dates correspond to the forty-year period between the first and second Sandinista guerrilla movements.

Blurring the Line between Fiction and Non-Fiction

One of the purposes of *Mother Tongue Theologies* is to examine non-Western and post-Western fiction in order to reflect on Christianities from the Global South. Because, from the perspective of the West, Cardenal blurs the line between fiction and non-fiction in his poetry and his theology, one needs to consider in what sense they are fiction. If by fiction one means that which is a wholesale invention, Cardenal's poems and theology would not properly be described as fiction. They deal with events and people who not only actually existed—they deal with events and people who held Nicaragua's life in the balance. However, if by fiction one means that which creates verisimilitude, one can properly refer to Cardenal's poems and theology, as well as all history writing, autobiographical essays, and journalism, for example, as fiction. Primarily that is because one can never re-create the past. All one can do is pick and choose from among facts as one understands them to create entirely new documents and experiences. Furthermore, the task is not only to get to the bottom of the past, it often is to deal with the present for the purpose of influencing the future. So we historians raise questions and then imaginatively create relationships between them and carefully selected sources.

This is what Cardenal does. For him the issue is the total reality of things, peoples, and events. For him, an image of senators as bats hanging upside down is not a metaphor—it is reality in its totality. Similarly, resurrection is a reality that deliberately bypasses the West's absorption with whether the body has begun to decompose. For Cardenal, the bigger issue is whether life is only for the wealthy and powerful. To conclude that resurrection, or life triumphing over violent death, is not a theological-historical reality for Nicaraguans is a dangerous conclusion. By the same token, poetry for him is the form for exposing reality and for provoking definite rearrangements of reality. In other words, *exteriorista* poetry for Cardenal is a means by which the resurrection of Nicaragua can be accelerated.

Augusto César Sandino (r. February 16, 1934)

Augusto César Sandino was the Nicaraguan "General of Free Men" who waged a successful six-year guerrilla war against U.S. Marines and their Nicaraguan allies beginning in 1927. On February 16, 1934, Somoza's National Guardsmen ambushed and murdered Sandino on his way to a peace conference with the president of Nicaragua, and hid his body. In "Zero Hour," "National Canto," "Lights," and in *Cosmic Canticle*'s "Birth of Venus," "The Empty Grave," and "Omega," Cardenal creates documentation of Sandino's resurrection by constructing conceptual and factual evidence. Of primary significance, which Cardenal documents by creating a headline-like wire to America, is the undeniable fact that Sandino refused to surrender.[1] Second, Sandino was ambushed and murdered by Somoza and the Nicaraguan National Guard.[2] Third, the reality of the Sandinista guerrilla movement was powerful testimony to Sandino's resurrection, a resurrection that was in no way metaphorical. It was material and could be witnessed in the bonfires of the guerrillas in

---

1. Ernesto Cardenal, "Zero Hour," in Cardenal, *Zero Hour and Other Documentary Poems*, edited by Donald D. Walsh, translated by Paul W. Borgeson Jr. et al. (New York: New Directions, 1980) 5.

2. Ibid., 9.

the far-off, northern mountains.³ The issue for Cardenal is not whether Sandino's resurrection did or did not happen in the Western, scientific sense. The issue is that Sandino refused to surrender to the United States and its Nicaraguan agents, that he was murdered, and that Nicaragua kept him alive in the guerrilla movement. The issue is not past facticity; the issue is present and future reality.

Unlike most Western theologians or historians, Cardenal does not develop an argument about resurrection. Instead, in allusive language Cardenal provokes elliptical, historical-theological associations between Sandino and Jesus Christ. For example, he constructs a run-on list of mines, lumber companies, and businesses like America's Magnavox, and then juxtaposes them to references to the U.S. Marines and rape to make it clear that the context of Sandino's death and resurrection was an economically, militarily, and sexually predatory system.⁴ Cardenal matches Sandino's birthplace to conquered Nazareth and its conquered indigenous people, teases out an association between Sandino's last assemblage of his men and Jesus Christ's Last Supper, and, with an off-hand reference to the number thirty, he promotes an association between the betrayals of both.⁵ He makes the allusion explicit by saying that anyone who sets out to save a people ends up being crucified. Borrowing language from the Gospel of John—"in my Father's house are many mansions (14:2 KJV)"—Cardenal ironically allows the economics of Jesus's farewell discourse to bleed through. Sandino, Cardenal writes, mortgaged his father-in-law's house to free Nicaragua, while in the presidential mansion Nicaragua had been mortgaged.⁶ Hinting at the Apostle Paul's designation of Jesus as "the firstborn from the dead (Col 1:18 KJV)," Cardenal makes explicit his conclusion that Sandino's murder relates to Jesus Christ's crucifixion by calling Sandino the "firstborn of murder victims."⁷

For Cardenal, Sandino's death and resurrection have loosely connected layers of meaning. He was murdered because he implied

---

3. Ibid., 7.

4. Ibid., 29.

5. Ibid., 5. Also see Ernesto Cardenal, "National Canto," in *Zero Hour*, 20.

6. Cardenal, "Zero Hour," 6.

7. Ernesto Cardenal, "Birth of Venus," in Cardenal, *Cosmic Canticle*, translated by John Lyons (Managua, Nicaragua: Editorial Nueva, 1989; Willimantic, CT: Curbstone, 1993) 95.

communion—or, to cast communion as a political issue, unity. Furthermore, Cardenal suggests Sandino was murdered because he and the communion he implied were light. Therefore, he was resurrected as light in 1970s Sandinista bonfires in the desolate northern mountains. In "Lights" the bonfires have a cosmic dimension. They are reminiscent of the future-oriented, movement-oriented Milky Way—a sweep of stars that in the book of Revelation implies a future, apocalyptic rearrangement of reality.[8] In a non-rational manner Cardenal urges an intuitive comprehension that resurrection takes place where light meets the absence of light. It occurs in the space of shadows and evolutionary, revolutionary movement. Resurrection, he suggests, is the flickering shadow of a guerrilla sitting motionless next to a revolutionary bonfire.[9]

Cardenal emphasizes empire's paranoiac obsession with news that contradicts its purposes. It suppresses good news such as the arrival of Sandino in Managua and silences true news.[10] Resurrection, he makes clear, is good news—news which consists of truth and truth-telling. He continues to tease out the implications for indigenous peoples of Sandino's resurrection by deconstructing a Guarani word for resurrection. It is, he says, the same word as that for "making truth-telling flow."[11]

Cardenal does not mean to imply that Sandino's resurrection was metaphorical or anything other than real. It clearly had historical and material dimensions with implications for the body, the tomb, and the power of resistance. In an associative manner, Cardenal suggests that resurrection has an explicit contex: it originates in oppression, implies revolutionary refusal to surrender to military and economic predators, is associated with betrayal, murder, and suppression of truth, and contradicts the oppressor's reflexive urge to mutilate and hide the body. He is arguing in an elliptical, non-rational, non-Western way that not only is resurrection a theological reality, it is a historical reality in that it has to do with the body. Most significantly, it applies to victims of oppression the evidence of which is found in the empty sepulcher and

---

8. Ernesto Cardenal, "Lights," in Cardenal, *Flights of Victory* [*Vuelos de Victoria*]: *Songs in Celebration of the Nicaraguan Revolution*, edited and translated by Marc Zimmerman (Maryknoll, NY: Orbis, 1985) 32–33. See also Cardenal, "Zero Hour," 7.

9. Cardenal, "Zero Hour," 7.

10. Ibid., 8–9.

11. Cardenal, "National Canto," 29.

the absence of the corpse.[12] In an imaginatively constructed farewell discourse, Cardenal brings together several elements characteristic of his poems—his un-Western nonchalance when it comes to theological pronouncements, his conclusion that God is on the side of Nicaragua, and a sardonic footnote so dear to Westerners seeking to prove a point: "'We'll come out of this all right God willing'" / (THE LIVING THOUGHTS OF SANDINO, Ed. 1961, p. 139.)," he writes, off-handedly insisting that Sandino's life, death, and resurrection were part of a God-driven historical process.[13]

Adolfo Báez Bone (r. April 1954)

The Nicaraguan National Guard captured, tortured, and killed Adolfo Báez Bone, one of the leaders of the 1954 April Rebellion plot to assassinate Somoza, and tried to dispose of his body. The Guard tortured Báez Bone not only because he attempted to assassinate Somoza, but because he and his fellow revolutionaries, of whom Cardenal was one, had attempted to bring Good News to Nicaragua. In "Zero Hour," the motif of news is conveyed elliptically in documentation about Pablo Leal, whose tongue the Guard cut out, and about Cardenal's classmate, Luis Gabuardi, whom the Guard burned alive while he shouted *"Death to Somoza!"*[14] It is suggested in a report of a sixteen-year-old telegraph clerk, whose name no one knew, who sent secret messages at night, and who, when he was caught, was murdered. It is conveyed in a report of a kid, caught at night sticking up posters which read, "SOMOZA IS A THIEF," whom laughing guards dragged off into the woods.[15] Good News, Cardenal is suggesting, is not pleasant news. Good News is news that is reliable, urgent, courageous, and defiant.

In a montage of concepts in *Cosmic Canticle*'s "Latin American Documentary," Cardenal subtly suggests that any concept of Good News must deal with the motif of ethnic crucifixion in a predatory empire. He alludes parenthetically to Jesus Christ's precarious ethnicity by inserting an aside about the silencing/torture of one of Nicaragua's Miskito Indians: "(The Miskito with his tongue cut out and his mouth sewed

12. Ernesto Cardenal, "The Empty Grave," in *Cosmic Canticle*, 294–96.
13. Ernesto Cardenal, "Omega," in *Cosmic Canticle*, 474.
14. Cardenal, "Zero Hour," 15.
15. Ibid.

up with wire.)"[16] He immediately connects the Miskito's death to the silencing/torture of Jesus Christ. The 3 o'clock hour, the suspension of the Miskito's naked body in the air, and the pleas for relief from thirst are details reminiscent of the crucifixion. Cardenal offhandedly makes the implication more explicit: "they put him through you could almost say Christ's passion."[17]

He emphasizes the connection between the silencing/torture of crucifixion and the predatory nature of empire by typologically matching psychotic Somoza, who may personally have castrated Báez-Bone and who had an obsession with washing his hands, to the murderous Pontius Pilate who, when he turned Jesus over to the mob, also washed his hands.[18] The Guard tried to permanently silence the Good News tongues, mouths, and shouts, Cardenal implies, by refusing to speak about the location of the body.[19] National Guard silence was an effort to permanently erase Báez Bone from the Nicaraguan Good News resistance narrative.

By defying the tomb as the place of the permanently dead, Báez Bone defied the Guard. In "Epitaph for the Tomb of Adolfo Báez Bone," Cardenal insists that the hero's tomb was Nicaragua, a place of resurrected life. Báez Bone's resurrection was material, in Nicaragua, and in the ongoing revolution. His resurrection was temporal in that he was murdered in April and had been resurrected by May, ecological in that he was resurrected in Nicaragua, and mythic in that when he was killed a Nicaraguan hero was born. Báez-Bone's resurrection was good, true news for the people of Nicaragua. The Good News of his resurrection contradicted the National Guard's false news that mutilating, killing, and disposing of Báez Bone's body erased him from Nicaragua's resurrection-oriented resistance narrative.[20] His revolutionary resurrection was not metaphorical. It was material in the imaginations and decisions

---

16. Ernesto Cardenal, "Latin American Documentary," in *Cosmic Canticle*, 237.

17. Ibid., 237.

18. Ibid.

19. Ernesto Cardenal, "Epitaph for the Tomb of Adolfo Báez Bone," in Cardenal, *Apocalypse and Other Poems*, edited by Robert Pring-Mill and Donald D. Walsh, translated by Thomas Merton et al. (Buenos Aires: Carlos Lohlé, 1969; New York: New Directions, 1977) 14.

20. Ibid., 14. See also Cardenal, "Zero Hour," 11–12, 15.

of successive revolutionaries, undermining the death-claims of Somoza and his National Guard.

Rigoberto López Pérez (r. September 21, 1956)

On the afternoon of September 21, 1956, poet Rigoberto López Pérez infiltrated a party for Anastasio Somoza García and shot him in the chest. National Guardsmen immediately killed López in a barrage of machine gunfire. Somoza died in a Panama hospital three days later. His sons continued his murderous dynasty.

In the short, verb-structured poem "The Pork Rigoberto Didn't Eat," Cardenal emphasizes López's self-propelled insertion into Nicaraguan history.[21] Combining elements of oral history and theology, Cardenal begins with a legend-evidenced theological conclusion that López was resurrected in the Nicaraguan revolutionary narrative. He subtly emphasizes the motif of underground witnessing to truth. To underscore the reliability of the witnesses, he passes along concrete details about López's decision to assassinate Somoza—he joined friends in León's Central Park on September 21, 1956, and bought some fried pork in a banana leaf, but when he saw a drunken worker and a beggar he could not eat.[22]

Cardenal emphasizes movement: López "arrived," "saw," "bought," "set about eating," "threw the pork with yucca to the ground," and announced the Good News that the crucifixion of Nicaragua was going to come to an end.[23] Cardenal elliptically suggests that the theological event began with the decision to alter the course of Nicaraguan history. In light of the drunken worker and the beggar, López's resurrection became historical the moment he decided to effect their transformation from sub-existence to full human existence.

Cardenal concludes that López's transformation was a sacred event implying sacrificial death and resurrection. In "Landing with Epitaph," he meditates on the deaths of Sandino, López, Leonel Rugama, and other specific Nicaraguan heroes.[24] Using the image of a microphone on an airplane which is about to touch down on the sacred soil of a

---

21. Ernesto Cardenal, "The Pork Rigoberto Didn't Eat," in *Flights of Victory*, 103.
22. Ibid., 103.
23. Ibid.
24. Ernesto Cardenal, "Landing with Epitaph," in *Flights of Victory*, 39.

tomb of martyrs, his time-and-space-specific Good News motif bleeds through.[25] In his understated manner, Cardenal makes his point clear: revolution and resurrection in part consist of meaningfully changing reality in time and space.

Camilo Torres (r. February, 1966)

Camilo Torres was a Colombian priest and sociologist who left Bogotá's National University to join the National Liberation Army guerrillas. He died in combat four months later, in February, 1966. Although most Latin American liberation theologians and "radical priests" did not join guerrillas, Torres's example influenced a movement to the left among mainstream Catholic clergy. It dramatically affected Cardenal. In 1970, he visited Torres's fragile, grieving mother, Doña Isabelita Restrepo, in Cuba. In her apartment he noticed a snapshot of Torres as a child, wearing a mischievous smile and a sailor suit. The photograph had a label not unlike a newspaper headline: "Souvenir of My First Communion."[26]

In his poetic meditations on the death and resurrection of Torres in *Cosmic Canticle*'s "Towards the New Man" and "Latin American Documentary," and in his poem "Epistle for Monsignor Casaldáliga," Cardenal constructs a montage of images and thoughts about their theological meanings. He does not flesh out a Western-style theological argument, proceeding carefully from one point to the next. Instead, he sets up porous associations.

Cardenal suggests that, in part, Torres's death and resurrection were about the urgency of religious and physical communion and the implacability of material existence. He draws on his memory of the snapshot of Torres in his mother's home in Cuba: "SOUVENIR OF MY FIRST COMMUNION / *Camilo Torres Restrepo* / (in his sailor's suit)."[27] He shifts to lines that connect Torres's first communion to his death in combat, then shifts again to connect Torres's first communion and death in combat to the more than one hundred references to the kingdom of God in the Bible, ninety by Jesus Christ.[28] Cardenal's theology of resurrection is about the communal movement of humankind

25. Ibid.

26. Ernesto Cardenal, *In Cuba*, translated by Donald D. Walsh (Buenos Aires: Carlos Lohlé, 1972; New York: New Directions, 1974) 175.

27. Ernesto Cardenal, "Towards the New Man," in *Cosmic Canticle*, 177.

28. Ibid., 178.

into full material existence in time and space. Saying that "we" are the future-oriented ones who will make up mankind, Cardenal alludes both to Jesus Christ and to the revolutionaries—Sandino, Báez Bone, Torres—who urged on communion, transformation, and metamorphosis of a humanity not yet fully in existence.[29]

Cardenal emphasizes the theological meaning of news in the context of oppression. He observes that Torres's death had become a Colombian newspaper's false headline: "CAMILO TORRES DEAD / enormous black letters / and he's more alive than ever defying *El Tiempo*."[30] The upper case type of "CAMILO TORRES DEAD" visually references a prior line about the Roman Empire's multi-lingual, headline-like label for Jesus on the cross: "SUBVERSIVE."[31] Cardenal is developing a conclusion that resurrection in part is about Good News defiance: to say that Jesus Christ was the "King of the Jews" was to admit that Jesus Christ was a subversive of whom the Roman Empire was mortally afraid. Good News, then, is not opposed by bad news. Good News is opposed by false news of permanent erasure, permanent death, permanent poverty, and permanent oppression. Cardenal is also making another point: it was Jesus Christ, the tortured and executed political subversive, who was bodily resurrected in defiance of the Roman Empire's effort to permanently erase him from Jewish reality.

Cardenal counters Bogotá's false news by constructing his own headline about the truth of death and oppression in the continent: "THE OPEN VEINS OF LATIN AMERICA."[32] The headline obliquely contradicts the false news proclaimed in the newspapers of Colombia, Chile, Nicaragua, Costa Rica, Peru, and Brazil: "EXTRA! CAMILO TORRES DEAD."[33] It was false news, which, according to Cardenal, was nonetheless toasted with the blood of the poor as though it were champagne.[34]

Torres died because one hundred children were dying every day of hunger in the pretty Colombian countryside and because Jesus Christ had admitted, "I was hungry."[35] Hoping to permanently erase Camilo

29. Ibid.
30. Ernesto Cardenal, "Epistle for Monsignor Casaldáliga," in *Zero Hour*, 89.
31. Ibid., 88.
32. Cardenal, "Latin American Documentary," 219.
33. Ibid., 226.
34. Ibid.
35. Ibid., 226–27.

Torres from Colombian reality, his enemies secretly disposed of his body in a forest. Cardenal ends the stanza by reiterating his conviction that the Good News of the kingdom of God is that it exposes the false news of Pilate, capitalism, and military dictatorship, which would have Colombians believe that permanent death was Colombia's eternal fate.[36]

Ernesto "Che" Guevara (r. October 9, 1967)

It is almost beyond dispute that the single most important event of the twentieth century in Latin America was the Cuban Revolution. More than any other event, it gave the people of Latin America a context for hope. Without doubt the iconic figure of hope was neither Fidel Castro nor Camilo Cienfuegos, it was Argentina-born doctor Ernesto "Che" Guevara, who died trying to export the revolution to Bolivia. There are two famous photographs Cardenal refers to in his meditations in *Cosmic Canticle* on the death and resurrection of "el Che" in 1967. His Bolivian assassins took one of the photos shortly after they ambushed, killed, and then mutilated Guevara's body; it unintentionally projects a cruciform, double entendre, Christ-like image. Meditating on the image, Cardenal elliptically concludes that because he implied the natural law struggle toward a unified humanity, a unity which implies a communal economy, Guevara is a marker on the planet's long evolutionary timeline: "The first fish / died of suffocation. The first fish that leaped to the land was like el Che."[37]

The other photograph of Guevara that Cardenal references still appears prolifically in Latin America as a red and black poster of the bereted revolutionary gazing into the right horizon. In a montage of associations, Cardenal suggests that Che can be understood as one can understand Jesus Christ, as a freedom-seeking natural phenomenon: "Like the insect longing to break out to the sunlight / colliding again and again: / until the window is drawn back for it / and it flies out to freedom. / The kingdom of heaven in the planets."[38]

For Cardenal, Guevara, revolution, and a communal economy imply a movement-oriented, evolutionary step towards life in a universe

---

36. Ibid., 227.

37. Cardenal, "Towards the New Man," 180; idem, "Condensations and Vision of San José de Costa Rica," in *Cosmic Canticle*, 62.

38. Cardenal, "Latin American Documentary," 239.

that by definition is not static. Faith, he says, in part consists of understanding this.[39] Cardenal intuitively associates Guevara and the Cuban Revolution with Old Testament prophets of a new economy. In 1959, he muses, Fidel Castro spoke out like the Deuteronomists against usury, and Guevara, as head of the Bank of Cuba, signed his name simply as "che" in the lower case.[40] He layers onto his montage of intuitive associations a theological understanding that Guevara died because he was part of the economic evolution of the kingdom of heaven. As he did for Sandino, Cardenal constructs a farewell discourse for Guevara to Castro, which alludes to Jesus Christ: "Farewell letter from el Che to Fidel."[41] Because Guevara died a movement-oriented, hope-supplying, evolutionary death in the context of massive oppression, his body-mutilating Bolivian assassins did not have the last word. Guevara was resurrected, and his resurrection is still proclaimed in that red-and-black poster one sees all over Latin America.

Leonel Rugama (r. January 15, 1970)

A twenty-year-old poet, ex-seminarian, and leader of the urban guerrillas, Leonel Rugama died in a shootout with National Guardsmen in a Managua barrio. He died inevitably and defiantly, famously insulting the Guard, which ordered him to surrender, by shouting, "Surrender your mother!" From the day the Guard carried his bullet-riddled body to a city morgue while the Nicaraguan newspaper *La Prensa* photographed his grieving mother, until the Sandinistas declared a miraculous victory over the Somoza-National Guard dictatorship on July 17, 1979, Sandinista guerrillas painted lines from Rugama's "The Earth Is a Satellite of the Moon" on barrio walls all over Nicaragua.

In his poem, the last line of which is "Blessed are the poor for they shall inherit the moon," Rugama had castigated the United States' pope-blessed, increasingly exorbitant Apollo moon flights, which he linked to the increasingly deadly hunger of the people living in Managua's Acahualinca slum. Cardenal retrieves Rugama's insight and positions it as a motif in his lengthy and complex "Oracle Concerning Managua." In the poem he addresses Rugama while analyzing the theological

---

39. Ernesto Cardenal, "Assaults on Heaven from the Earth," in *Cosmic Canticle*, 390.
40. Ibid., 395.
41. Ibid.

meaning of an earthquake that devastated Managua three years later, killing as many as fifteen thousand people on the morning of December 23, 1972.

He contradicts Sinatra-like "moon over Miami" images of tropical Central American delights. In Managua, he writes, "the moonlight shimmers on the shit" of Acahualinca where old women scare off the buzzards when they pounce on guts thrown out by slaughterhouses.[42] Segueing, Cardenal retains the motif of light, inserts the elements of pre-light time and lack of knowledge, and patches in throw-away documentation of torture. At dawn, he says, one could hear the roaring of the hungry lions in Somoza's zoo, but "we didn't know the prisoners were in with the animals."[43]

Rugama died a substitutionary death for consumptives and whores, Cardenal concludes simply. His life and death contradicted official false news, the endless lies which came over the teletype on the battlefield of language, lies which made the ugly seem beautiful and the beautiful ugly.[44] The purveyors of official news created headlines on January 15, 1970: "SANDINO NEST DESTROYED WITH MACHINE GUN AND CANNON FIRE."[45]

Cardenal fast-forwards to the earthquake, references the National Seminary in Managua which Rugama challenged by leaving, and issues an apocalyptic announcement: "Now from the seminary you can see another Managua: block after block after block, leveled flat!"[46] Cutting and pasting, Cardenal creates an intuitive association between the natural catastrophe and the catastrophe of capitalism and the Somoza-National Guard dictatorship, which had been structurally supported in part by a system of false news including advertisements, glossy magazines, and censorship. Focusing his literary sight, he writes like a reporter about the rubble of a nightclub and the remains of a business's false promises, then shifts to apocalyptic announcements of the torture chambers sliding into a lagoon, then shifts again to Somoza's destroyed wedding-cake-like presidential palace surrounded by the dictator's wind-blown

---

42. Ernesto Cardenal, "Oracle Concerning Managua," in *Zero Hour*, 44.
43. Ibid., 46.
44. Ibid., 57.
45. Ibid., 59.
46. Ibid., 62.

false messages.[47] Cardenal offhandedly concludes that the earthquake was "a geological midwife or whatever you want to call it / that night the Sandinistas went free," casually alluding to the biblical creation motif of the earth groaning as if in labor and to the earthquake that threw open the prison doors of Christ's apostles Paul and Silas.[48]

Via his associative method, Cardenal suggests that Rugama's death, because it was—in the context of massive poverty, terror, and torture—substitutionary and defiant, was indicative of Easter. Dying for others was an act of Easter "praxis," by which he means analysis and action in light of Jesus Christ's crucifixion and resurrection.[49] As it had been for Christ, the context of Rugama's historical resurrection was a death-dealing, movement-arresting, history-stopping, lies-telling, humanity-dividing system of oppression. He died and was resurrected because of a profound desire for authentic, holistic communion. Humanity, Rugama understood, had not been animated by the corporations, Somoza, or the National Guard. The species with whom Rugama sought communion and on whose behalf he died were the God-animated people who are "immortal."[50] His death and resurrection in Nicaragua in 1970 had implications for all the Nicaraguans dead because of a system that sought to stop Nicaraguan history. Because only those who have died can be reborn, according to Ernesto Cardenal's non-Western, liberationist theology, the immortal Nicaraguan people "come smiling out of the morgue."[51] They testify not only to the historical resurrection of Jesus Christ but to the historical resurrections of Augusto César Sandino, Adolfo Báez Bone, Rigoberto López Pérez, Camilo Torres, Ernesto "Che" Guevara, and Leonel Rugama.

Conclusion

Cardenal's theology of resurrection as a historical event relies upon a redefinition of "history," whereby he is able to undermine prevailing Western doctrines of resurrection. Westerners generally associate resurrection with belief, apply it to an unspecified future time prior to

47. Ibid., 62–63.
48. Ibid., 64.
49. Ibid., 55.
50. Ibid., 67.
51. Ibid.

the final judgment, think it involves a thoroughly spiritualized state, and believe that it happens in an eternal place beyond that which is here. Cardenal's concern is related to the Western preoccupation with whether Jesus Christ's resurrection was a "historical" event. There are two general Western theological conclusions: One is that resurrection is the consequence of a simple article of faith that Jesus Christ is Lord; it is true religiously but is unrelated to other conclusions about history or science. The other conclusion is that resurrection must be reconciled with history, understood as the discipline of excavating the past, and with science. Concluding that resurrection cannot pass the tests of history and science, many Western theologians reject it as a historical event. The practical outcome is that the historical Jesus of Nazareth, who was a particular, crucified victim of empire, must be separated from the spiritual Christ of faith who is timeless and universal.

For Cardenal, this split is a disaster for people suffering economic oppression and military dictatorship. He urges the reunion of history and faith. He does this in part by keeping the aforementioned cast of Nicaraguan revolutionary characters—and their historical contexts of torture, repression, poverty, and death—on the pages of his theological inquiries at all times. He does it by calling attention to the parallels between Jesus' historical trajectory—his birth from the womb of the oppressed in an economically and militarily predatory empire, his resistance, his betrayal, his farewell discourse, his torture, his mutilated body, his death, and his grieving mother—and the historical trajectories of Nicaraguan revolutionary heroes. He also does this through the motif of news. The Good News of Jesus Christ's resurrection was news that contradicted the empire's false news that time would stand still for the people it oppressed. It was news that was good because it was defiant, urgent, and reliable.

Thus, in his elliptical, run-on, bleed-through fashion, Cardenal articulates a new definition of "historical" as that which is a transformative, future-oriented insertion into the reality of oppression on behalf of fully realized existence here and now. Resurrection is historical because it originates in oppression that is defied by insertions into reality on behalf of the oppressed, insertions that attempt to interrupt a crucifying status quo.

EIGHT

The Syncretism of Candomblé and Feminism in Helena Parente Cunha's *Woman between Mirrors*[1]

Isabel Asensio-Sierra

> *Dobrem os joelhos para a mulher,*
> *A mulher nos pôs no mundo;*
> *Por isso nós somos seres humanos.*
> *A mulher é a inteligência da terra.*
> *Dobrem os joelhos para a mulher.*[2]

Introduction: Candomblé and Women

THE FORMATION OF THE Afro-Brazilian religions goes back to the period of slavery and is uniquely related to the social division of slaves. From the sixteenth to the nineteenth centuries, the Portuguese divided the African slaves that had been brought to Brazil into *nações*

---

1. Helena Parente Cunha, *Woman between Mirrors*, translated by Fred P. Ellison and Naomi Lindstrom (Austin: University of Texas Press, 1999). The Portuguese title is *Mulher no espelho*, which literally means "woman in the mirror." The translators probably chose the title *Woman between Mirrors* because the main character stands between mirrors in order to see different reflections of herself. For our purposes, all quotations from the novel belong to the translated edition.

2. This is Obarixá's song. Obarixá is a male deity who makes all things that exist. He sings in honor of Odu, a female goddess. The song translates: "Kneel yourselves before the woman, / the woman puts us on this world; / because of her we are human beings. / The woman is the intelligence of the earth. / Kneel yourselves before the woman" See Cristina Abdon Cury and Sueli Carneiro, "O poder feminino no culto aos orixás," *Vozes* 84:2 (March–April 1990) 157–79.

(nations).³ These nations granted the slave population the possibility of staying close to other ethnic members among whom it was likely to find former religious leaders from Africa. This factor, together with speaking their mother tongue, helped slaves maintain their traditions and, therefore, continue their religious practices. The practice of such religions in a different context, the New World, together with the influence of the dominant religion that the Portuguese were imposing, Roman Catholicism, would shape the former into today's Afro-Brazilian religions, the most traditional of these being Candomblé.[4]

Candomblé was never a rigid and fixed religion; in fact, it could not afford being so because, as Afro-Brazilian religions were prohibited by the Catholic Church and were criminalized by Brazilian governments, practitioners became aware of the need to include Catholic elements in their movement as a sort of veil.[5] Since its emergence in Brazil, Candomblé's interactions with other religions, especially Catholicism, have been very active, and syncretization with Catholicism was definitely, in Tina Gudrun Jensen's words, "a survival strategy."[6] Some of the Catholic elements that one may observe are the altars, statuettes of saints, and crucifixes that are usually exhibited in Candomblé temples, also known as *terreiros*. As part of the process of syncretization, even Candomblé's *orixás* (gods) underwent a transformation. The *orixás*

---

3. With this term the Portuguese referred to "an ethnic group's local geographical area and their cultural traditions" Tina Gudrun Jensen, "Discourses on Afro-Brazilian Religion: From De-Africanization to Re-Africanization," in *Latin American Religion in Motion*, edited by Christian Smith and Joshua Prokopy (New York: Routledge, 1999) 275–94. Then, the idea of *nação* (nation) came to play an essential role in the process of maintaining the various African ethnic identities and the transmission of their respective traditions. In addition, Jensen affirms that "As the Afro-Brazilian religions began to appear, the concept of nation was reinforced . . . as a symbol of transmission of local religious traditions, . . . an ethnic identity marker" (ibid., 276–77). The nations distinguished among each other depending on the group of venerated gods, and the type of sacred music (*atabaque*, a traditional musical instrument) and language utilized in rituals.

4. Clarence Bernard Henry offers this definition: "Candomblé is a monotheistic religion that is based on the worship of a supreme being known as Olódùmarè who rules through several lesser deities known as *orixás*" ("Music and Female Imagery in the Candomblé Religion of Salvador, Bahia, Brazil," *Journal of Latin American Lore*, 22:1 [Winter 2004] 109–36).

5. Candomblé was prohibited and persecuted until 1888, when emancipation began in Brazil. Thereafter, the practice of Candomblé spread throughout the country and the number of practitioners increases every year.

6. Jensen, "Discourses on Afro-Brazilian Religion" 277.

started to have a Catholic appearance in the sense that they were juxtaposed with Catholic saints, although these deities originally represented the various elements of nature.

Candomblé is certainly a matriarchal religion, with well-defined female and male roles in its basic structure: women are reproductive and belong to the inside of the *terreiro*; men, on the other hand, can go outside the temple to the streets. It is common of many religions that females are conceptualized as mothers, nurturers, and protectors; besides, the female is often construed around a myth of creation and origin of life. Candomblé is no exception: female roles resemble those of women from West African communities, where they were considered a major source of life and sustainers of the community, and for that were solemnly respected. As women reached old age, they were believed to be intellectual carriers of positive energy. Women were considered to be equal, or superior, to deities, so they were preferred as priestesses and mediums instead of men. Although men have played a noteworthy role in the organizational structure of Brazilian Candomblé since the nineteenth century, women still maintain a higher rank. In fact, the first *terreiro* was founded by women in approximately 1830 and today most traditional *terreiros* are directed by *mães-de-santo*, a supreme priestess with absolute power.[7]

In his book, Paul Christopher Johnson affirms, "The terreiro's metaphysical objective is to generate religious power, axé . . ."[8] He continues that "[a]xé is not only transforming force, that which can change one's personal life, it is also a lineage one enters, a line across time into the past."[9] One of the most attractive features of Candomblé is that it offers a change to its devotees, a renovation of their lives. For this reason, Candomblé has shifted from being a religion associated with lower-class Afro-Brazilians to one that embraces more middle- and upper-class white practitioners. Candomblé is particularly appealing to women because it gives them the opportunity of engaging in roles of power

---

7. See Malgorzata Oleszkiewicz, "El papel de la mujer en el candomblé," in *Religion and Latin America in the Twenty-first Century: Libraries Reacting to Social Change: Papers of the Forty-second Annual Meeting of the Seminar on the Acquisition of Latin American Library Materials, Rockville, Maryland, May 17–21, 1997*, edited by Mark L. Grover (Austin: University of Texas at Austin, 1999) 193–200.

8. Paul Christopher Johnson, *Secrets, Gossip, and Gods: The Transformation of Brazilian Candomblé* (New York: Oxford University Press, 2002) 44.

9. Ibid., 48.

that were traditionally associated with men. As leaders of the house, *mães-de-santo* are strong and courageous and, through the initiation ritual, help other women face the problems of life. In their article, scholars Cristina Abdon Cury and Sueli Carneiro state that being in contact with the *orixás* provides "*uma mudança significativa na vivência*" (a significant change in life)[10] to those women who initiate in Candomblé. In an interview with a Candomblé woman by the same authors about what a Candomblé woman is, the interviewee responded: "*O candomblé traz apoio à mulher, traz igualdade. Pelo menos no candomblé, nós, as mulheres, estamos numa boa. O orixá é aquilo que está lá bem no fundo da gente e que o candomblé traz pra fora*" (candomblé brings support to the woman, it brings equality. At least in Candomblé, we, women, are at ease. The *orixá* is the goodness one has deep inside and Candomblé lets it out).[11]

Trance and the Reaffirmation of Female Identity

The main character of Helena Parente Cunha's novel, *Woman between Mirrors*, needs such strength and courage, and a transformation in her monotonous daily life.[12] Thus, the protagonist engages in a search for her inner self that will eventually lead her to Candomblé initiation. Cury and Carneiro pay special attention to the experience of trance because "*Diante do transe, da inter-relação pessoa-entidade, elas adquirem nova postura frente ao mundo. . . . elas demonstram uma sensação de segurança e maior força para se defrontar com os problemas da sociedade envolvente*" (Through the trance, through the person-entity interrelation, they acquire a new attitude towards the world. They demonstrate a sense of security, and a larger force to confront the problems of the surrounding society).[13] After much reflection and several trance experiences, Parente Cunha's protagonist reaches the maturity and self-affirmation as a woman that she was lacking at the beginning of the novel. Cury and Carneiro

10. Cury and Carneiro, "*O poder feminino*," 168.

11. Ibid., 169.

12. Parente Cunha does not name the main character, but, rather, uses a circumlocution: "the woman who talks." Parente Cunha also employs the phrase "the woman who writes" to refer to the main character's alter ego who appears from the reflections in the mirror. For our purposes, I will refer to "the woman who talks" as the main character, the protagonist, or simply, the woman.

13. Cury and Carneiro, "*O poder feminino*," 168–69.

affirm that "*o transe expressa a reação da mulher à condição de marginalização, pode-se considerá-lo do ponto de vista mítico como a reafirmação da condição feminina, pois a possessão se associa além disso à fertilidade, fecundidade e a sexualidade*" (the trance expresses a woman's reaction to marginalization, it could be considered, from the mythical point of view, as a reaffirmation of the feminine condition, because possession is also associated with fertility, fecundity, and sexuality).[14] The main character seeks the trance experience because it represents the reaffirmation of her female identity, which is denied to her by the patriarchal environment that surrounds her life.

Narrative and the Construction of Self

Woman between Mirrors begins with a bold and direct statement: a woman is going to tell the narrative of her life. The motivation to narrate emerges only when she stands facing her reflection in the mirror. Parente Cunha utilizes a well-known metaphor and commonplace in literature written by women, that is, one's self-image in the mirror as the sign of another, hidden identity. It is a vision that the woman failed to see because of the fog that blurred her eyes, a fog that was symbolically formed by social conventionality. As for the main character, such awareness occurs at the time of a mid-life crisis. Among the infinite number of mirror reflections, an alter ego emerges claiming authority over her, and so, the process of narrating becomes even more challenging because the main character now needs to find her real self and the true script of her life. The multiple layers of identity are confusing for the reader as well. The protagonist asks herself and the reader a series of rhetorical questions: ". . . when I say I, I'm not the woman who is writing this very page. When I say I, I'm merely imagining myself. She is the one who is writing. And my face in the mirror? Who is it? Who is the woman who writes me? I know, because I made her up."[15] As the novel proceeds, both the protagonist and the readers reach their own conclusions. *Woman between Mirrors* is a narrative that creates itself at the same time that the main character searches for an identity of her own.

For the main character, discovering her identity takes time and reflection, and she does it in retrospective, by tracing back her memory

14. Ibid., 175.
15. Cunha, *Woman between Mirrors*, 2.

into her childhood. Through this digression into the past, the readers grasp a better understanding of the woman who talks and her alter ego, known as the woman who writes. The latter represents the type of female novelist who tries in any way to depict the former as a defenseless woman repressed by a sexist society. The words of the woman who writes graphically differentiate with italic letters from the rest of the text; they attempt to define the protagonist and her problems using a Freudian jargon with the intention of psychoanalyzing her. However, the protagonist refuses to be controlled by this sort of discourse. She does not want to be told how she feels but, rather, she desires to be the vehicle of expression of her own feelings.

It is obvious that the two women, or more precisely, the two voices, do not understand each other because each of them represents a different type of woman in contemporary society. On the one hand, the woman who talks is submissive and obedient to the order established by the institution of marriage; she is also willing to make sacrifices for those around her, that is, her husband and children.[16] On the other hand, the woman who writes is an intellectual, nonconformist, fervent proponent of feminist ideology. There exists a gap between the two voices that needs to be bridged. The woman who writes employs a hyperbolic feminist discourse that neglects the individualism of the main character whose search goes beyond ideological discourses. At the same time, the novel strategically satirizes the male-oriented sexual jargon characteristic of psychoanalysis that the alter ego utilizes when interpreting the birth of the younger brother as the abrupt end of the main character's childhood. According to her alter ego, the woman who talks was forced to leave childhood suddenly only to become a premature adolescent. In a period of life such as adolescence, when the individual needs to experience the world and find a model from whom to learn, the female protagonist confronts a father who totally ignores her or, if he addresses her, does so only to criticize and diminish her.

These negative memories of her childhood contrast with those of her childhood's nanny, and her reminiscence of sea images. Here appears, for the first time in the novel, the nurturer figure of the older Afro-Brazilian woman with whom the main character establishes loving maternal-filial bonds. The main character refers to her nanny as the

16. This submissive and obedient attitude is about to change as she embarks on a journey into her inner self.

only person who provides warmth in her coldest nights, and calm in her deepest sufferings. In addition, she describes her nanny as the typical Candomblé *mãe*: "My nanna's crinkly hair is parted in the middle with two little braids fastened at the back of her head. Her medals were tinkling under her white starched dress."[17] The comments about her black nanny are also accompanied by references to the ocean and its smells, sounds, and waves that come to the shore from distant lands, beautiful images that repeat constantly throughout the novel. The text subtly alludes to various female *orixás* from Candomblé, such as Oxum and Yemanjá, both goddesses of waters.[18] With this, the novel also reveals a fundamental idea: the setting aside of Anglo and European feminism in order to find other forms of feminism that will focus more on the individual and the spiritual.[19] Thus, the writer turns to Candomblé and the relation person-god-entity. The main character's past memories are unconscious desires to return to her most intimate self. In other words, in her search for identity, the main character needs to revisit the origins of her culture in order to achieve a total understanding of both her individuality as a woman and her Brazilian identity.[20]

The female protagonist belongs to a conservative, white, upper-middle class family that had always been concerned about keeping up with society's expectations, among them, having black servants to work around the house, from whom they maintain certain social distance. For example, the father never allows his daughter to play with the cook's son. Another bourgeois convention is private education. The woman who talks explains that she went to a Catholic school where she received an education centered on traditional gender roles. She has definitely been raised in a tyrannical environment, solely exposed to an authoritarian father's volition. When she most needs models to follow, she does not know where to find them. Would she find one in the oppressive figure of the father? Or would she find it in the virtually absent figure of the mother? The mother, although physically present, is practically invisible

17. Cunha, *Woman between Mirrors*, 19. Mothers of Candomblé traditionally wear white dresses, turbans in their heads, and crosses and other jewelry around their necks.

18. While Oxum is the female *orixá* of fresh waters, Yemanjá is the female *orixá* of the seas.

19. Here I mean "second wave" feminism, which mainly focuses on practical issues concerning the political, social, and cultural roles of women in contemporary societies.

20. Although the main character emphasizes her race towards the novel's end, she does not detail it; rather, she leaves it to the reader's interpretation.

because the domineering presence of the father always minimizes her role in the house. The sole task of the mother is to teach her to perpetuate the submissive and sacrificial role that women have traditionally fulfilled. The main character remembers:

> My mother used to repeat certain phrases. Rules for living. In the first place, her husband, second, her husband, third, her husband. After that, the children. Yes, she was quite happy. Sweet-smelling, she waited for my father to come home from work. She used to wait for him. Perfumes, silences, whisperings. Her tiny smile.[21]

In contrast, her Afro-Brazilian nanny used to tell bedtime stories of her African descendants, stories that dealt with the values of these ancient societies and the stronger role women played in them. Because of her close relationship with her nanny, she became familiarized with Afro-Brazilian culture at a very young age. For example, she recalls the Mother of the Waters festival: "Right in front of the gate, I could see the black Bahian women going by, all in white, starched petticoats, necklaces of many-colored beads, on their heads shawls wound into turbans. They carried flowers and presents."[22] The recurrent references to the Afro-Brazilian tradition are the protagonist's attempts to identify her cultural identity in a country that is characteristically multi-cultural at the same time that she searches for her female individuality.

As a result of a rigorous, traditional education, the main character has become a compliant model woman. Indeed, she sacrifices herself for those around her in all circumstances and confirms it when she states, "I accepted my father's liking my brother better. I accepted my husband's not letting me go out alone. I accepted living at the beck and call of my three children. I accepted, I accepted, the risk and the loss, and alone with myself came out the better for it."[23] She ponders whether rebelling against such oppression would have been meaningful, asking, "Which is more authentic? To cry out no, and make a big thing of it? To whisper yes, very softly?"[24] The dilemma of rebellion versus submission is articulated by the confrontation between the protagonist and her alter ego, the woman who writes. Until now, the protagonist has fallen into

---

21. Cunha, *Woman between Mirrors*, 12.
22. Ibid., 44.
23. Ibid., 7.
24. Ibid.

the category of the submissive woman, while her alter ego represents a more liberal type of woman. The two types of women are in ceaseless conflict because women who do not conform to the traditional feminine position find themselves at odds with society. The main character comments on this fact: "The free life she [the woman who writes] chose didn't shake her loose from her phantoms. She may be a free spirit but she ends up paying for it."[25] In other words, a patriarchal society dissents when women do not choose a life focused on the institution of family.

Nevertheless, the disagreement between these women is necessary to achieve a state of self-awareness and ultimate emancipation from their long-established social roles. On the one hand, the woman who talks struggles to realize her distressing reality because she feels happy. On the other hand, the woman who writes seeks to open the main character's eyes and accuses her of committing a sin of omission. Throughout the novel, the main character comes to the realization that she is happy only because she was taught to feel so, and that she must learn to experience emotions of her own, not imposed ones. Despite her alter ego's attempts to unveil the reality to her, the main character rejects the Anglo and European feminism and chooses to search for another form of coping with her mid-life crisis, a form that is not prescriptive but, rather, spiritual, which she finds in Candomblé.

Candomblé and Female Liberation

By means of self-reflection, the novel shows how the female protagonist reaches a conscious, peaceful, and confident state of mind that will positively affect the rest of her life. Every time the woman goes back in time, there is a return to the origins and sounds of Afro-Brazilian songs and drums. Since childhood, the main character has associated nature and nurture with her Afro-Brazilian surroundings. White upper-middle-class people have separated her from that comfortable world of her youth and now, as an adult, she returns to it at the same time she searches for her inner self. Everything that is connected to this Afro-Brazilian world appeases her: her nanny, the chants, and drums of Xangô. During the first half of the novel, the references to Candomblé take place when she evades her modern life reality and lets nostalgia take her to her past. During the second half of the novel, however, the

25. Ibid., 24.

protagonist experiences the rituals of Candomblé through trance to ultimately discover her inner identity. The woman also finds serenity in her solitude, or rather, in the "desperation of her solitude."[26] During those moments of privacy, she enjoys simple things for which her husband and sons had criticized her, such as music of her taste. Only when she is alone does she not feel inhibited or restrained. She regains liberation with Afro-Brazilian music and dance. Music and dance are associated in *terreiro* ceremonies with trance and possession by the *orixá* of the devotee's body. Clarence B. Henry states that "Music is one of the most important vehicles of religious expression in Candomblé. It is the mode through which people communicate with the *orixás* associated with the religion."[27] For the woman, the trance is a moment of surfacing what is most repressed inside her. Only when the *orixá* has descended into the devotee's body, can the devotee completely free himself or herself. This spiritual and physical possession serves to channel peacefulness and to release daily pressures. Then, when she is alone at home, all the emotions that had previously been hidden inside emerge to the surface.

One more thing the woman enjoys in her solitude is sexual pleasure. The conservative Catholic ideology imbedded in Brazilian white upper-middle-class society taught her that sex and pleasure are taboo, particularly for decent girls. She remembers, then, her first kiss on the mouth, which, for a naïve girl like her, meant sin and even the possibility of getting pregnant. The rhythm of music provides her with both spiritual and physical pleasure, a pleasure that she induces in herself. This experience resembles Candomblé ceremonies during which the *orixá*'s possession of the devotee's body functions as metaphor of sexual possession. In her case, her body is sexually seized by orgasm:

> In the throbbing rhythm, I claim my quota of freedom, enjoy a sensuality I never knew, take pleasure in a physical beauty that brings me back up. When I turn off the record-player, I go into the shower and let the water run all over my satisfied body, after the orgasm that I gave myself. The water rids me of so many fears, sloughs off so much dead skin, divests me of so many fears. For a few minutes that I stretch out as much as I can, I live my nakedness which comes out even more in the flowing water; the more the water runs over me, the more naked I feel.[28]

26. Ibid., 27.
27. Henry, "Music and Female Imagery," 110.
28. Cunha, *Woman between Mirrors*, 26.

She has not previously felt such sexual satisfaction because she has been taught that woman-man sexual relations conventionally focus on the male satisfaction bestowed by the woman.

As the novel develops, the woman becomes more aware of the sort of life she has had and the need to discover her authentic identity as an independent woman. She asks herself questions such as, "What did I do with my life? What did I do with my death? When was it I died?"[29] She has finally realized that her marital life and maternal-filial relationships never fulfilled her. She recognizes that she disregarded everything that made her happy for the sake of her family, including her passion for writing, and that they never offered her anything in return. She decides, then, that she deserves to give herself a second opportunity to start a new life. As she liberated herself from her father's house, the woman must liberate herself from her husband's. She uses the metaphor of the window as a channel to exit oppressive spaces, and she affirms: "This window is not the window of my room, in my father's house. It's the window of my corner, in my husband's apartment. This window opens me onto what's closing in. Like the other one. They're the same window."[30] After leaving her husband, the woman begins talking about a young man who seems to emerge from her imagination. She lets herself fall into his arms and be seduced by him. She describes his seduction as if it were a trance, joining together into one single body: "I'm falling into his arms. He pulls me close in against him. I melt into that embrace.... His skin goes clear through my skin."[31] She uses the language of fairy tales to talk about their relationship; she dreams of an African kingdom and of a prince who will take her to African shores. She uses the Afro-Brazilian oral tradition as a channel of reflection and liberation. Thus, she employs the same discourse that oppressed her in the past, but this time to free herself from it.[32]

As already mentioned above, Parente Cunha utilizes the metaphor of the mirror as source of self-discovery. After leaving her husband, she looks at her naked body reflected in the mirror. Alone, she touches herself to be certain that her body is hers. The gaze leads to masturbation

---

29. Ibid., 64.
30. Ibid., 69.
31. Ibid.

32. The fairy tale discourse is structured around well-defined gender roles where the woman is typically a damsel in distress saved by a prince.

and to total acknowledgement of herself. To start her independence, she decides to have a love affair with one of her husband's friends. The whispers of the wind, the breeze of the sea, the distant drum sounds, and the dark night create an erotic atmosphere for the first night that she spends with another man. For the first time, the woman feels desirable and learns about the pleasure that a woman can feel. In moments of freedom, pleasure, and harmony with her body, the woman experiences a rebirth and returns to a primitive nature that carries her to the origins of the Afro-Brazilian, to the shores of African lands and their drums. After such an eye-opening experience, one in which she discovers the pleasure that bourgeois morality has denied her, the main character talks now with her body:

> My meetings with my husband's friend took place in my apartment. Every day. Getting naked is teaching me mysteries my body knew nothing about. I never supposed my skin held so many violent and delicate sensations. The dark recesses of my depths open up rare, new dimensions every day. In learning to know my lands and my seas, I'm beginning to feel a strong drive to leave these walls behind, get out of the streets, discover places I've never been.[33]

Feeling self-confident and self-sustainable, she decides to continue with her writing and to look for a publisher who may be interested in publishing her novel.

Having regained her freedom, the main character goes out to the streets to visit one of the oldest black neighborhoods of Bahia. Sitting in a café, she can see four hundred years of Bahia's history: peddlers, prostitutes, older men dressed in white conversing among themselves, the cantinas' rhythms and music; blacks, mulattos, and whites all together; the new is old, and the old is new. The sight of these people and their daily lives makes her ponder her Brazilian identity and African roots in Brazilian culture. Not only does she need to encounter her sexual female self, but also she needs to determine her cultural identity. She evokes again her childhood and recalls listening to the sounds and rhythms of Candomblé *terreiros* from her room. With the curiosity of a child, she would innocently question her father about those ceremonies, who

---

33. Cunha, *Woman between Mirrors*, 87–88. French feminist Hélène Cixous initially introduced the idea of a woman writing with her body in Cixous, "The Laugh of The Medusa," *Signs* 1:4 (Summer 1976) 875–93.

would angrily ask her to shut up: "In those days, at my father's house, it was nasty to talk about, nasty to think about candomblé, something a white person should steer clear of. But Daddy, I'm not all that white, I'm dark. Hush up, girl."[34]

In short, the main character expresses a desire to return to her Afro-Brazilian origins and reexamines her cultural self: "Where is my place? . . . What about my great-great-grandparents? Where did I get my dark skin? From a whitening of the colors from Nigeria? From the hot winds breathed out of Guinea? What drums were beating when my blood first started flowing?"[35] Outside her husband's house, she searches for her place: she walks along the streets of Bahia, streets that have Afro-Brazilian smells and flavors. An attractive young black man enters the bar where she is at and she feels inevitably attracted to him. He wears the signs of Xangô, the god of lightning and thunderbolts, one of the main gods of Candomblé. Later that night, the woman cannot stop thinking about him; she opens the window to let the rhythms of the distant drums and the ocean's breeze enter into her body. Everything invades the pores of her body and senses while she thinks of the handsome young black man. During these minutes of closeness with nature, the main character feels strong and self-confident with her identity and her body.

Conclusion: Choice and Destiny

Now that the main character has acknowledged her body, she rejects her alter ego again, only to reclaim authority over both her body and her life's narrative. She starts attending Candomblé ceremonies, during which she goes into trance. Visiting *terreiros* and experiencing trance are ultimately subversive actions against her father's expectations and those of the white upper-middle social class in which she was raised. During trance, she is transported to the other shores of the Atlantic where Xangô takes possession of her body.[36] She feels the need of making contact with

---

34. Cunha, *Woman between Mirrors*, 110. This is the only reference to the main character's race. Whether she is white, mulatto, or black is left to the reader's interpretation.

35. Ibid., 109–10.

36. During the trance experience, the *orixás* are called into the *terreiro* through music and dance. Then, the *orixás* descend into the devotee's body and possess it. Henry states that a major belief in Candomblé is that music and dance are inseparable because only they "can summon a deity from the spiritual realm, who is then manifested in the bodies of special devotees" (Henry, "Music and Female Imagery," 111–12).

nature and she plunges into the ocean, towards its deepest tempests. The trance experience is equated with sexual intercourse, the highest moment of trance being the orgasm. Such spiritual, and sexual, experience completes her, and she feels "filled to the full . . . A fresh encounter, plunging to the utmost depths of my waters, my night, my storm, my roots."[37]

The main character states that she does not believe in powerful gods controlling her destiny. She believes, however, that her destiny is her choice and her choice is her destiny. Then, her decision is to write with her own body, to liberate herself from scripts that tried to define her. During her arduous attempt to work through her existential dilemmas, she rediscovers the Candomblé religion, which is uniquely rooted to the Brazilian national and cultural identity. Through Candomblé, then, she locates her own sense of personal significance and self-worth; this mother tongue theology shapes her identity immeasurably. In addition, as Candomblé gives women a chance of engaging in roles of power that were traditionally associated with men, so does Parente Cunha by providing her female main character with the opportunity to write. Both Candomblé and writing's inherent transforming force grant Parente Cunha's character a reaffirmation of her female identity. Through the caring and loving relations women are able to develop and enjoy among each other in Candomblé (female goddesses, mothers of Candomblé), Helena Parente Cunha ultimately suggests a bonding relationship among the community of other women writers.

---

37. Cunha, *Woman between Mirrors*, 129.

PART FOUR

Christianity in Asia and the Pacific Islands

NINE

The Pilgrim's Progress

Ayemenem House and the Syrian Christian Church in Kerala, India

Mini Chandran

Introduction

ARUNDHATI ROY'S *THE GOD of Small Things* highlights Ayemenem, a remote village in Kerala, the southwestern state of India. Ayemenem is in the Kottayam district, which has a high literacy rate and is also home to the oldest newspaper in Kerala's regional language, Malayalam. By focusing on the Syrian Christian community of Kottayam, Roy's novel also serves as a sociological commentary on what is arguably the oldest Christian community in the world. In this chapter I view Ayemenem House as a metaphor for how the Syrian Christian church braved the political storm sown by the winds of caste and class in Kerala. Even as the intense and sad tale unfolds retrospectively, the novel is premised on Kerala's socio-cultural reality, where religion and Marxism co-exist peacefully in an oddly symbiotic relationship. Kerala has a composite religious culture with a population that is almost evenly divided among Christians, Muslims, and Hindus. A Benedictine monk who established a Christian monastery in Kerala on the lines of a Hindu ashram, Bede Griffiths observes: "Kerala has the distinction of being the most Christian state in India. Christians are said to number about one fourth of the population, and their influence is even more considerable as they are one of the wealthiest communities."[1]

The state has also the distinction of having a pragmatic Marxist party that grew and flourished at an enviable pace. In Roy's words, "The Marxists worked from within the communal divides, never challenging them, never appearing not to. They offered a cocktail revolution. A heady mix of Eastern Marxism and orthodox Hinduism, spiked with a shot of democracy."[2] Griffiths, however, points to the "combination of wealth and poverty, of a high level of education with much unemployment, which largely account for the growth of communism in Kerala."[3] The Christian community today, despite being a minority, is considered to be wealthy and influential in the state; and of the Christian denominations, the Syrian Christians are the aristocrats.

Syrian Christians in Kerala

The Syrian Christians of Kerala are considered to be the earliest Christian community in India. It is believed that the community was founded by the evangelical efforts of Saint Thomas, who is believed to have arrived on the Malabar coast in 52 CE. The Syrian Christians of today consider themselves the descendants of the high-caste Nambudiri Brahmin converts of Saint Thomas.[4] The Syrian Christians gradually came to occupy a high status in the society of Kerala, in return for military and mercantile services rendered to regional rulers. However, this inclusion within the upper echelons of society was not in complete negation of existing religious and caste codes of the native state. Robinson states, "They [the Syrian Christians] negotiated their position through alliance with the local rulers and maintained their status by adhering strictly to the purity-pollution codes of regional Hindu society."[5]

Sociologists have noted that the Syrian Christians were accorded a respect that was on par with high-ranking Hindu communities like the Nairs, and that the church partook of many distinctions and exclusive

---

1. Bede Griffiths, *Christ in India: Essays Towards a Hindu-Christian Dialogue* (New York: Scribner's, 1966) 48–49.
2. Arundhati Roy, *The God of Small Things* (New Delhi: India Ink, 1997) 67.
3. Griffiths, *Christ in India*, 48.
4. Rowena Robinson, *Christians of India* (New Delhi: Sage, 2003) 39.
5. Ibid., 41.

practices on the basis of caste. Robinson notes that the low-caste Pulaya and Paraya Christians had separate churches and were prohibited from worshipping along with the Syrians until the twentieth century.[6] The "high-caste" Syrian Christians will not tolerate the thought of a marital relationship with a low-caste Pulaya convert even today. Framed against this socio-ethnic background, Ammu's and Velutha's declaration of independence from the love laws that "lay down who should be loved and how much" gains in significance.[7]

Ayemenem House

The stance that the Syrian Christian church adopted with regard to social and communal issues in Kerala is reflected in the happenings of Ayemenem House. The House epitomizes the ambivalence that characterized the relations of the church with other communities and political groups in Kerala. The breaking away of John Ipe from the patrimony of the Syrian Christian legacy to found the Mar Thoma church is a case in point. "Around 1800 one of the Syrian Christian Bishops, Mathew Athanasius, influenced by one Abraham Malppan made a move to the Protestant side and this was the beginning of the Kerala Mar Thoma Church," writes P. K. John.[8] The splintering of faith is reflective of the schisms that the church was subject to, maybe in a past that is older than Rev. John Ipe. It is intriguing that Roy refers to the Ipe family as Syrian Christians when this would actually have made them Mar Thoma Syrians, who have a different church and liturgical practices.

The religious zeal of John Ipe apparently runs awry with his two children Benaan and Navomi. Better known as Pappachi in the novel, the Imperial entomologist Benaan John Ipe is two-faced and sinister, burning his peculiar brand of male chauvinism and groveling admiration for white-skinned people into his daughter Ammu's memory. It is difficult for her to shut out the Jekyll and Hyde personality of her father. In the public domain his image was that of "a sophisticated, generous, moral man," but in the domestic realm "he turned into a monstrous, suspicious bully, with a streak of vicious cunning," and took a perverse

---

6. Ibid., 75.
7. Roy, *God of Small Things*, 180.
8. "Christians of Kerala," Kerala History Series, Ananthapuri.com, n.d., online: http://www.ananthapuri.com/kerala-history.asp?page=christian.

pleasure in physically penalizing his wife and children.[9] Perhaps Roy is underscoring the essential hypocritical approach of Christian clergymen and nuns who apparently undertake philanthropic projects while nurturing personal cruelty. The Unsafe Edge in Ammu, which leads her into an abusive marriage with a man she hardly knows and later into a tempestuous affair with an untouchable, can perhaps be linked to the traumatic childhood that was inflicted on her. Pappachi, however, being ruled over by the God of Big Things, like the Christian church, apparently is blessed with a successful worldly life and death. The fact that his death finds a mention in no less than an English newspaper like the *Indian Express* can be seen as an index of his social acceptance. Even after death he dominates the living room of Ayemenem House in the form of a photograph that lends an "underlying chill" to the atmosphere.[10] It is also significant that of the legacy of expensive suits and cuff links and Anglophilism that he bequeaths to his children, it is only the Anglophilism that survives. The church in Kerala, incidentally, has been wrongly or rightly associated with a certain pro-Western or pro-English attitude. "The Syrian Christians, who populate the region in large numbers, found quite an unlikely ally in their quest—the English language and the Empire. Geographically insulated from the larger context of the national movement, the community tried to master the language and send its children to proper English colleges in Chennai—like the characters in the book. In that sense, they were living proof of the success of Macaulay's civilising mission," observe Binoo K. John and Arthur J. Pais.[11]

Pappachi is the whited sepulcher, but Navomi's (Baby Kochamma) renunciation of her church for the Roman Catholic faith is a much worse act of hypocrisy, done as it is for misplaced sexual desire. Baby Kochamma initially attempts to win over the handsome Irish monk Father Mulligan by uncharacteristic demonstrations of charity—forcibly bathing a poor child and articulating theological doubts. The Bible mediates this unspoken passion that sparks between them, but it is an emotion that they dare not name. The only reason that motivates Baby Kochamma to venture out of the folds of Ayemenem House to adopt

9. Roy, *God of Small Things*, 180.
10. Ibid., 51.
11. "The New Deity of Prose," *India Today*, n.d., online: http://www.india-today.com/itoday/27101997/cov.html.

the Catholic faith is that she foolishly hoped that this would give her greater chances to be with Father Mulligan. Frustrated in her aims, she is forced to return to Ayemenem, but remains a Catholic. The duplicity and cruelty that we discern in Pappachi is more than evident in Baby Kochamma, whose Christian façade harbors the demons of jealousy and spite. The schism that had become apparent with Rev. John Ipe has now gained an alarming overtone in its Machiavellian tendencies. It is the ruthless and scheming Baby Kochamma who choreographs the tragic opera of Velutha, Ammu, and her children. Ironically, even after having achieved her aims, she sits like a malevolent spider in the middle of the spiteful web she has spun around her.

The Church and Marxism

Baby Kochamma's hatred for Marxism is a trait that is generally shared by the Christians of Kerala, as Roy herself notes: ". . . in Kerala the Syrian Christians were, by and large, the wealthy, estate-owning (pickle-factory-running) feudal lords, for whom communism represented a fate worse than death."[12] Significantly, Baby Kochamma's nephew Chacko, who is the representative of the next generation that grew up with the Marxist movement in Kerala, likes to believe that he is a Communist at heart. However, his Marxist predilection is confined to superficialities, and sometimes acts as a convenient cover for his philandering ways: "He would call pretty women who worked in the factory to his room, and on the pretext of lecturing them on labour rights and trade union law, flirt with them outrageously. He would call them Comrade, and insist that they call him Comrade back (which made them giggle)."[13] Ammu sees through his act, and thinks he is the "Oxford avatar" of the old feudal landlords who forced their attentions on the women workers who depended upon them for livelihood.[14]

Such conflicting attitudes are crystallized in the tense moments that they spend in the blue Plymouth that waits at the railway gate for the Communist marchers to go by. The car becomes an island of Christianity battered by hostile red flags; the anger and suspicion in the atmosphere is palpable. While Baby Kochamma retreats into her fear,

12. Roy, *God of Small Things*, 66.
13. Ibid., 65.
14. Ibid.

Chacko tries to be at ease and Ammu is openly mocking. The twins are like two waifs waiting for the march to go by so that they can continue with their lives, little realizing the magnitude of the momentous event that is taking place. Nobody is quite at home in this unfamiliar atmosphere. That said, the successful Communist party did have its share of Christian supporters, and Roy attempts to explain it thus: "Structurally. . . Marxism was a simple substitute for Christianity. Replace God with Marx, Satan with the bourgeoisie, Heaven with a classless society, the Church with the Party, and the form and purpose of the journey remained similar."[15] Perhaps this explains why Chacko adapts to the new faith with more ease than Baby Kochamma to her Catholic faith.

Chacko's stance, however, cannot be conflated with the ecumenical position of contemporary Kerala. The march that isolates the blue Plymouth happens in 1969, the year of *The Sound of Music* in Kerala and the American war in distant Vietnam. It also marks the rise of the militant breed of Marxism called Naxalism, which was to sweep Bengal forcefully and Kerala on a much lesser scale. The Communists are in power once again under the chief ministership of E. M. S. Namboodiripad, but they have undergone changes. Their confidence has been somewhat dented by the church-led "*vimochana samaram*" (liberation struggle) that eventually culminated in the dismissal of the democratically elected Communist government in 1959. The *vimochana samaram* witnessed the harnessing of communal forces on an unprecedented scale, a coming together of various faiths, such as the Hindu Nairs and Christians of all denominations, to topple a government that was run by people who professed no faith in religion. The success of the movement in overthrowing a democratically elected government was to influence political equations in the state subsequently, by making future governments of all political hues extraordinarily wary of vexing communal issues. Moreover, the vertical split in the Communist Party of India in 1964 into the Communist Party of India, with its Russian sympathies, and the Communist Party of India (Marxist), with its pro-China sympathies, undermined the party's credibility considerably. The whimsical voters of Kerala, who tend to vote for the Congress party at the national level and the Communist party at the state level, were only complicating matters further, for this forced the party at the helm of the state to rule and protest against the Central government simultaneously. Hence the Marxist

15. Ibid., 66.

government of 1969 is not the confident and united Communist party that came to power initially in 1957.

This complex political commotion can perhaps explain the rather piquant situation at the railway gate where a group of workers who belong to the ruling party take out a demonstration in protest against the government. However, it is rather puzzling as to why Velutha would want to conceal the fact of his membership in the Marxist party, considering his employer's leftist leanings. The lower-caste Velutha is a contradiction in terms, being a Christian as well as a Marxist. Velutha's approach is more agnostic than godless Marxist; he does not seem to share his comrades' inherent distrust of the bourgeoisie. He willingly expends his skill in carpentry, making furniture for Mammachi and toys for Ammukutty, and later embraces the forlorn twins in a love that is undemanding and unconditional.

The Church and Caste

The House's treatment of Velutha and his family becomes a modern socio-religious index, given the fact that Christianity was originally perceived as an empowering discourse in Kerala. In fact, the early novels in Malayalam are Christian narratives written by "original" Christians and low-caste converts, such as Mrs. Collins's *Ghatakavadham* (1877), Potheri Kunhambu's *Saraswathivijayam* (1893), and Joseph Muliyil's *Sukumari* (1897). Of these authors, Mrs. Collins, the wife of a Christian missionary in central Travancore whose express purpose was to extol the virtues of Protestantism as opposed to Syrian Christianity, also dealt with the caste issue. Potheri Kunhambu, a lower-caste Hindu in north Malabar, worked extensively for the uplift of the untouchables and posited conversion to casteless Christianity as the solution to problems of discrimination. Joseph Muliyil, himself a lower-caste Christian convert, had a similar polemical narrative in *Sukumari*. Dilip Menon points out: "In Kerala, in particular, Christianity was the interface through which lower castes experienced modernity. And it was Christianity that allowed their entry into a public sphere generated by inter-religious discussions."[16]

16. Dilip Menon, "A Place Elsewhere: Lower-Caste Malayalam Novels of the Nineteenth Century," in *India's Literary History: Essays on the Nineteenth Century*, edited by Stuart Blackburn and Vasudha Dalmia (New Delhi: Permanent Black, 2004) 439.

It is interesting to observe the happenings in Ayemenem House almost a century after Kunhambu's novel. Velutha is needed by the House, but the untouchable Paravan cannot hope to enter the house. The high-caste Syrian Christians will eat off the table he has made for them, but will refuse to eat anything that he has defiled by touch. Here I must stress the non-proselytizing nature of the Syrian Christian church in Kerala. K. C. Zachariah records: "As a consequence of their position in society, St. Thomas Christians never attempted to bring the lower caste non-Christian neighbours into the knowledge of Christ and to the Christian church. They clung too much to the caste system and did not bother themselves with any attempt to convert their neighbours belonging to other castes to their religion."[17] Hence Velutha receives his basic education in the school for untouchables that was established by Rev. John Ipe, and his carpentry skills from a Christian missionary, but never becomes an accepted member of the community. For all his Christian views regarding caste and equality, Rev. Ipe appears unable or unwilling to admit Velutha to a school where all castes can come together. The education he acquires makes Velutha something like an upper caste, but not quite; he is in-between.

Life is crystal clear for Velutha's father, Vellya Pappen, who knows his place, which is outside the steps leading to Ayemenem House. His caste of Paravans, who attempted to escape from the humiliation of untouchability by converting to Christianity, had realized by then that caste was a cross they would have to bear. In *Saraswathivijayam* we witness a high caste Nair attempting to capture the essence of the "new religion" of Christianity:

> They do not have a particular caste. In fact, they do not have castes at all. Many people of different castes have joined them. They join and become one, like the sea. In my estimate alone, they consist of high caste *embrandiris* and lower castes like *thiyyas*, *sudras*, *kaniyans*, *asaris* and untouchables like *pulayas*. . . . All of them, men and women alike, can read and write. There are good orators and scholars among them. They have English education too. . . . They do all sorts of work.[18]

---

17. K. C. Zachariah, *The Syrian Christians of Kerala* (New Delhi: Orient Longman, 2006) 74.

18. Potheri Kunjambu, *Saraswathivijayam* (Kottayam, India: DC Books, 2004) 59–60; translation mine. The caste names mentioned in this extract indicate Kerala's stratified society in the nineteenth century, ranging from the Brahmin upper caste of *embrandiris*

However, the dream of an egalitarian society that was offered by the Christian church soured as the children of the converts faced daily reality; the stigma was not a superficial skin that they could slough off. After independence, the government refused to give them the benefits allowed to other lower castes—reservations in educational institutions and government jobs. Neither did they gain the social acceptability that Christians had. What conversion had effectively done was take away the benefits without bestowing social prestige. That this is indeed the plight of Dalit (which is the new nomenclature for lower castes) Christians is borne out by hard sociological data:

> Though Catholics of the lower castes and tribes form 60 percent of the Church membership they have no place in decision-making. Scheduled caste converts are treated as low caste not only by high-caste Hindus but by high-caste Christians too. In rural areas, they cannot own or rent houses, however well placed they may be. Separate places are marked out for them in parish churches and burial grounds. Inter-caste marriages are frowned upon and caste tags are still appended to the Christian names of high caste people. Casteism is rampant among the clergy and the religious.[19]

Even Kochu Maria, the cook in Ayemenem House, wants people to recognize her as a Syrian Christian, a Mar Thomite and not a Pelaya, Pulaya, or a Paravan. It is into this world that Velutha strides with a nonchalance that scares his father, annoys his touchable employers, and endears himself to Ammu and her children. However, Velutha is also suitably docile in maintaining his distance from Mammachi and concealing his party membership from Chacko. He might be a carpenter by profession and a Christian by faith, but it is his caste identity as Paravan that Velutha also takes into consideration. Perhaps the only adult who accepts Velutha the individual is Ammu. Here again, it is the "unsafe" Ammu who combines "the infinite tenderness of motherhood and the reckless rage of a suicide bomber" and goes on "to love by night the man her children loved by day."[20] Ammu can set aside the caste and class laws only under cover of

---

to intermediary castes such as *thiyyas* as well as *sudras*, and lower ones such as *kaniyans* and *asaris*. The untouchable *pulaya* was at the lowest rung of the social ladder.

19. S. M. Michael, "With Respect to Caste and Creed," *The Little Magazine*, 6:4–5 (2006) 73.

20. Roy, *God of Small Things*, 44.

night at the History house, where time apparently stops and a neutral ground can be prepared for the lovers.

Ammu flouts caste laws before by marrying a Bengali Brahmin, and Baby Kochamma's attitude sums up the average Syrian Christian mindset. She hates the twins because they were "Half-Hindu Hybrids whom no self-respecting Syrian Christian would ever marry," and is very upset about Ammu being a divorced daughter "from a intercommunity love marriage."[21] Needless to say, the average upper-caste Hindu would also refuse to marry the Half-Hindu Hybrids. George Isaac, Roy's uncle and the real-life model for Chacko, conceded in an interview that Ammu has close parallels with his sister, Mary Roy, Arundhati's mother. He asks, "Ammu panics and enters into a sexual relationship with somebody outside the area of acceptability. She does something unspeakable by Indian standards. How would you feel if your sister panics and has an affair on the banks of the Meenachil river with a Pulaya?"[22] With such words, Isaac recalls Mammachi, who becomes angry when she first hears of the affair from Vellya Pappen.

The Church and Gender

Isaac's remarks also point to another concern within Ayemenem House, and by extension, the church—that of gender. How does the House treat its women? While Benaan John Ipe is educated to become an entomologist, his sister Navomi's academic background is left vague. What the novel tells us is that she is confined within the four walls of the House, "marked" for marriage and thus an easy prey for any suitable boy that might come her way. Her passion for Father Mulligan is the normal and healthy sexual desire that any young girl of her age would feel for an attractive man, but given her social condition, she has to resort to subterfuges to be able to express it. The repression that she has internalized and exercises on herself is what changes her into the bitter individual who begrudges others their innocent pleasures. After her abortive attempt to become a nun, the other "education" Navomi receives is one in ornamental gardening, underscoring the fact that women are, at best, only decorative.

21. Ibid., 45–46.
22. Venu Menon, "Who's Ammu?" Rediff on the Net, n.d., online: http://www.rediff.com/news/oct/18booker.htm.

The plight of Benaan's wife, Shoshamma, is worse. Life with the duplicitous and jealously possessive Pappachi is hell on earth, but not once does Mammachi give vent to her feelings. Ironically, this Christian woman seems to embody the conventional Hindu concept of a good wife who has the Pati Parmeswar (one's husband is God) concept. She accepts whatever comes her way, hiding the "raised, crescent-shaped ridges," the "scars of old beatings from an old marriage" underneath her scanty silver hair.[23] Mammachi's personality is consistently undermined by her husband and her son. Her husband's sneer when she initially establishes the pickle factory is the patriarchal contempt for feminine innovation. However, once the factory becomes a success solely due to her hard work, male desire for control takes over, and her son Chacko becomes its exclusive owner. A woman's productivity that is dismissed contemptuously is accepted later, but only on male terms. It is significant that it is the church that is instrumental in initiating Mammachi into business, as she starts making tender mango pickle and banana jam for the Kottayam Bible Society. But the church apparently does not give her any notion of self-respect as woman, for at no point does she question the justice of the physical abuse that she has to tolerate or the hijacking of the business enterprise that she has set up. In fact, Mammachi can survive only in a male-dominated world. Witness how the thwarted love for her husband is redirected toward her son, who stops Pappachi from beating her: "The day that Chacko prevented Pappachi from beating her, Mammachi packed her wifely luggage and committed it to Chacko's care. From then onwards he became the repository of all her womanly feelings. Her Man. Her only Love."[24] The reverent love she has for Chacko enables her to overlook his philandering, but she is never able to forgive Margaret for marrying him. Significantly, all the humiliation that she is subject to as woman and wife does not sensitize her to her daughter's trauma. Apparently, there is no space in this society for female bonding.

It is indeed a society that does not need its females. They are not acknowledged in any position of authority. Ammu has no right to be in Ayemenem House or in the pickle factory. "Though Ammu did as much work in the factory as Chacko, whenever he was dealing with food inspectors or sanitary engineers, he always referred to it as *my* factory, *my* pineapples, *my* pickles. Legally, this was the case because Ammu, as a

23. Roy, *God of Small Things*, 166.
24. Ibid., 168.

daughter, had no claim to the property."[25] Robinson notes: "Even today, daughters customarily sign off their rights to ancestral property before they marry. Immovable property is retained in the male line. In the absence of male heirs, the propertied groups devise various means to ensure that property is retained in the patriline."[26] We can definitely discern an autobiographical element here; indeed, Mary Roy, Arundhati's mother, is famous for challenging the Christian Succession Act in court. Until the Supreme Court of India decision in the Mary Roy case in 1986, daughters of a Christian family were entitled only to a quarter of the son's share if the father died without drawing up his will. Mary Roy's victory was received with dismay, as this was seen as a potential weapon in the hands of daughters who might use it legally to wrest property rights from their brothers. It was perceived to be a fundamental threat to amicable relationships in a Christian family and a dilution of the rights of the Christian male. The retrospective nature of the verdict further vexed the issue. The church brought pressure upon the government of Kerala to submit a writ petition seeking to eliminate the retrospective nature of the verdict, but the Supreme Court dismissed this petition. In his conversation with Ammu, Chacko summarizes the position of a son in respect to a daughter in a Christian family prior to the Mary Roy decision of 1986: "What's yours is mine and what's mine is also mine."[27] Ironically, the House is eventually inherited by Rev. John Ipe's daughter, Baby Kochamma, who, like Ammu, has no legal right to the House. This is the final disintegration of the House as it falls into a state of disrepair and abandonment.

The Church and Hinduism

The House shares an uneasy relationship with the other dominant religious faith of the region, Hinduism. This troubled alliance is exemplified in the "friendship" of Chacko and Comrade Pillai. Although faith does not play an extensive role, it is evident that the fraternity of Communism that they profess is inadequate to bridge the divide between them. Chacko is guilty of coveting Kalyani, his comrade's wife. By not coming to the aid of Velutha in his hour of need and denouncing him to inspector Thomas Mathew, Pillai is culpable of bearing false witness to a

25. Ibid., 57.
26. Robinson, *Christians of India*, 146.
27. Roy, *God of Small Things*, 57.

neighbor. He is also eventually responsible for the Marxist party siege of Paradise Pickles that leads to its closure and the near-total bankruptcy of Ayemenem House.

But Pillai initiates Rahel and Estha into the joys of the temple art of Kathakali, and Hindu mythology, thus making the characters real and lifelike for the twins reared on another faith. That they can watch and identify with the emotional nuances that the dance drama unravels is proof of the cultural and religious osmosis. But perhaps this is also not very surprising considering the fact that they are half-Hindus themselves.

Conclusion: The House Later

When Rahel returns to Ayemenem House after twenty-three years, it is quite different from the one originally founded by Rev. John Ipe, the Punyan Kunju blessed by the Patriarch of Antioch. Treacherous love laws and the inevitable forward course of history have turned this House into the ghost of its former self, condemning its inmates to an utter loneliness that surrounds them like a benighted blanket. The House has turned secretive, drawing down its roof about it like a hat, hunching alone in the middle of Baby Kochamma's vicious garden at the top of the hill. The garden itself "had grown knotted and wild, like a circus whose animals had forgotten their tricks. The weed that people call communist patcha (because it flourished in Kerala like communism) smothered the more exotic plants. Only the vines kept growing, like toe-nails on a corpse."[28]

Such an atmosphere of desolation is indicative of an eroding faith. After the horror of the drama that was jointly orchestrated by faith and political ideology, the House has gradually sunk into torpor from which there seems to be no exit. Faith recedes into the background, as Baby Kochamma and Kochu Maria become willing captives of the neo-colonization that creeps into their living room through the dish antenna. The red flag outside Comrade Pillai's printing press has bled away. Communism has struck up a compromise with capitalism. Comrade Pillai's son Lenin has changed his name to Levin to facilitate his work in the embassies of capitalist countries in Delhi. The transformation everywhere is insidious but apparent, and the power that rules is the god of globalization and liberalization.

28. Ibid., 28.

Converting the Idolatrous Heathens

British Missionaries in the South Sea Islands and India in Children's Fiction

Ymitri Mathison

Introduction

CONCEALED BENEATH A FAÇADE of discursive innocence, children's evangelical tract fiction contributed and sustained the belief of the native as a child, a tabula rasa, or in Rudyard Kipling's words, a "half devil and half child," to be taught Christianity and conmittantly British culture and civilization.[1] These novels underscored the importance of educating natives to insure their loyalty to the empire and a Christian way of life. However, the proselytizing idealism of missionaries was tempered by colonial policy, and children's fiction of the nineteenth and early twentieth centuries reflected adult worldviews of the problematic relationship between colonialism and "missionaries [who] often—necessarily—combined evangelism and exploration: they had to find the heathens before they could convert them."[2] Although wary of Britain's expanding colonial rule, secular persuasion, and commercial ambitions, missionaries were at the forefront in India and the South Sea Island territories opening them up for trade by "arriv[ing] in regions barely

---

1. Rudyard Kipling, "The White Man's Burden," in *The Norton Anthology of English Literature: The Major Authors*, edited by Stephen Greenblatt and M. H. Abrams (8th ed.; New York: Norton, 2006) 2289–90.

2. M. Daphne Kutzer, *Empire's Children: Empire and Imperialism in Classic British Children's Books* (New York: Garland, 2000) xix.

touched by Western influences, preaching the superiority of Western religion, technology, and cultural practices."[3] Written for readers living in England, children's as well as adult evangelical tract fiction, like commercial secular romance and adventure fiction of the empire, titillated their readers with the exoticism of the empire, especially through "cheap missionary biographies which dwelt on the more sensational aspects" of missionary work, for example, cannibalism in the South Sea Islands or suttee in India, with British readers vicariously enjoying their moral and cultural superiority.[4]

Superficially a children's novel, but actually a Christian tract, Mary Martha Sherwood's *Little Henry and His Bearer* (1814) essentially begins the genre of didactic children's evangelical tract literature. Incorporating British fantasies of the tractable native, it involves eight-year-old Henry's attempts at converting his devoted Hindu servant into Christianity. Marguerite L. Butler's *Tulsi, the Story of an Indian School Girl* (1934), published by the London Missionary Society, shows us how a century later missionary conversion and education has been consolidated and institutionalized. The novel focuses on a young Indian girl and her education into British culture and Christianity in a Christian boarding school in India. In contrast to religious tract fiction, commercial, secular boy's adventure fiction of the empire incorporated Christianity and missionaries but only to the extent that they developed the plot, which frequently involved young boys experiencing danger in the far corners of the empire. In R. M. Ballantyne's *The Coral Island* (1857) three young boys stranded on a deserted island encounter pirates, missionaries, and cannibalistic natives, and in Rudyard Kipling's *Kim* (1901) a young Irish boy is apprenticed as a spy for the British while he and his Lama search for the river of life (salvation).

---

3. Norman Etherington, "Introduction," in *Missions and Empire*, edited by Norman Etherington (Oxford: Oxford University Press, 2005) 4. The Charter Renewal Act of 1813 revoked the ban on missionaries evangelizing in British-controlled areas of India through pressure from the Evangelical movement. The British government also pursued a policy of religious neutrality in other parts of the empire. "Colonial administrators barred Christian missionaries from parts of Nigeria and Sudan. Elsewhere missionaries worked for decades in lands that never came under imperial control. They pointedly resisted colonization schemes for New Zealand, South Africa, Malawi, and other regions" (ibid., 2).

4. Ian Bradley, *The Call to Seriousness: The Evangelical Impact on the Victorians* (New York: Macmillan, 1976) 77.

In this chapter, I aim to show that in both children's evangelical tract fiction and boy's adventure fiction native conversions were a process of indoctrination into British cultural, educational, and religious values, and that both types of literature made concrete to their readers Britain's religious mission, which was subsumed under the larger imperial enterprise. That boy's adventure fiction frequently included evangelical endeavors suggest their close integration and importance into the imperial project, not just culturally but also economically. Significantly, readers of both evangelical tract fiction and boy's adventure fiction were British children and adults, not natives, so evangelical tract fiction's purpose was actually to convert the British audience. Since the ultimate purposes of boy's adventure fiction were secular and commercial, they incorporated more of the ambiguity and problematic nature of native conversions and the missionary enterprise.

Fiction as Propaganda

Believing literature to be "an adjunct of civilization, whose advance was thoroughly congruent with the concerns of religion," the evangelical movement used tract fiction as propaganda to collect donations, to encourage more recruits, and also influence children into becoming servants of the empire.[5] Evangelical Christian societies such as the Society for the Propagation of Christian Knowledge (SPCK) and Religious Tract Society (RTS) published "tracts, penny histories, little books of heroes, children's stories, and Sunday magazines in order to control the much-feared spread of insubordinate, irreligious and revolutionary activity" not by the natives in the empire but by the lower classes at home.[6] They seized on the new genre of children's literature to influence, instruct, and preach to a hitherto untapped demographic: children, especially working class children, whom they feared would be overly influenced by the new, very affordable mass market literature, the penny dreadful, aimed at both working class adults and children.[7] This new genre of fiction became a vehicle for the indoctrination of British children into evangelical Christian

---

5. Doreen Rosman, *Evangelicals and Culture* (London: Croom Helm, 1984) 194.

6. John M. MacKenzie, *Propaganda and Empire: The Manipulation of British Public Opinion, 1880–1960* (Manchester: Manchester University Press, 1984) 201.

7. The penny dreadful enjoyed its heyday during the years 1830–80. See MacKenzie, *Propaganda and Empire*, 201.

beliefs. The urgency of their mission was reinforced by the belief that "[t]he message of the cross was more than an arid theological truth—it was a living truth of power and experience"—and that an innocent child not saved was eternally condemned to hell.[8] Although children's literature, especially evangelical tract fiction, "invoke[d] the old typological universe of good and evil," the novels in spite of themselves presented the ambiguity and complexity of the imperial enterprise, "what might be called the spirit of adventure or thrill of transgressing norms."[9]

The expansionist imperial mission infused the Victorian evangelical movement with the belief of a divinely ordained, providential role for Britain in which it had the Christian responsibility to convert the indigenous population[10] because early Victorians believed in "the expansive wonders of their industrial revolution, their special forms of religious, political, and economic grace, and their bourgeois-heroic values of self-help and upward mobility."[11] When the ban on evangelical missionary activity in East India Company-ruled territories of India was lifted in 1813, "inflows of overseas missionaries grew from a trickle to a flood." However, their "principal importance lay in their provision of institutional support in the form of seminaries, schools, and hospitals."[12] For most schools begun by missionary societies, "a balance between preaching, proslytisation, different modes of religious instruction and

---

8. Brian Stanley, *The Bible and the Flag: Protestant Missions and British Imperialism in the Nineteenth and Twentieth Centuries* (Leicester, England: Apollos, 1990) 62.

9. Nancy Armstrong, "Preface: Victorian Children's Literature as Political Foreplay," in Fiona McCulloch, *The Fictional Role of Childhood in Victorian and Early Twentieth Century Children's Literature* (Lewiston, NY: Mellen, 2004) xv.

10. Independently funded through donations, missionaries were vociferous critics of the British government's colonial policies, even though "territorial conquest in India was a major precipitant of the missionary movement" (Ronald Hyam, *Britain's Imperial Century, 1815–1914: A Study of Empire and Expansion*, [2nd ed.; Lanham, MD: Barnes and Noble, 1993], 93).

11. Patrick Brantlinger, *Rule of Darkness: British Literature and Imperialism, 1830–1914* (Ithaca, NY: Cornell University Press, 1988) 32. One of the major impulses for the British Protestant missionary movement's many missionary societies, charities, and schools, was the abolition of slavery, which was accomplished in 1833. The evils of slavery and the conversion of slaves into Christianity in the West Indies and Africa were a major theme of children's evangelical tract literature. See Margaret Nancy Cutt, *Ministering Angels: A Study of Nineteenth-Century Evangelical Writing for Children* (Wormley, England: Five Owls, 1979) 25.

12. Robert Eric Frykenberg, "Christian Missions and the Raj," in Etherington, *Missions and Empire*, 117.

formal-language education, acceptable to missionary supporters at home, missions on the spot, British officials and Indians themselves was difficult to achieve."[13] Hampered by the British government's continued policy of religious neutrality, the evangelical missionary movement was responsible for Britain's expanding colonial rule, refurbishing British national identity, and ironically for its religious civilizing mission. English was formally instituted as the language of instruction in India with the English Education Act of 1835, and from 1838 teaching in the vernacular was emphasized. As a result, the secularization of British educational policy was greatly deplored by the missionary movement, which believed that classical humanistic studies "far from cultivating moral feelings . . . was more likely to cause [Indians] to question moral law more closely and perhaps even encourage [them] to deviate from its dictates."[14] This criticism was based on self-interest since secular education limited evangelical endeavor.

Mrs. Sherwood's *Little Henry and His Bearer*

Women missionaries' impact is figured within the protective confines of the domestic sphere, the home, and school. Secluded from the realities of the imperial enterprise, they recuperate a presumed unitary English self in what was an entirely male endeavor by upholding moral virtues epitomized by English womanhood. Their role was to be nurturing, motherly educators firmly bringing British or native children into the fold of Britishness through education and conversions, or rather, where education was *for* conversions. Frequently involved in social and medical work, they domesticated the imperial project.[15]

Published in 1814 and one of the first evangelical tract novels, Mrs. Sherwood's *Little Henry and His Bearer* looked ahead to secular Victorian children's fiction's exploration of childhood psychological development: "once religious feeling became important in the child's reading, other

---

13. Andrew Porter, *Religions Versus Empire?: British Protestant Missionaries and Overseas Expansion, 1700–1914* (Manchester: Manchester University Press, 2004) 177.

14. Gauri Viswanathan, *Masks of Conquest: Literary Study and British Rule in India* (New Delhi: Oxford University Press, 1998) 47.

15. Andrew Porter, "An Overview, 1700–1914," in Etherington, *Missions and Empire*, 57.

types of emotions quickly followed."[16] A forerunner to Rudyard Kipling's *Kim*, Little Henry is neglected by his English adopted mother and is in the sole care of his extremely loving Indian bearer, Boosy, who teaches him to speak Hindu and about the so-called heathen religions, Hindustani and Moslem. When a clergyman's missionary daughter, the houseguest of his adopted mother, befriends five-year-old Henry, she teaches him to speak and read English and also converts him to Christianity—and heathen Boosy's conversion is a postscript to the novel. She had brought from England "a box of Bibles, and some pretty children's books and pictures,"[17] presumably written in English, to be used to convert the adult native population, considered to be intellectually on par with children. Ironically, the heathen she converts to Christianity, Henry, is British and—like Kim, the protagonist in Rudyard Kipling's *Kim*—also not British, because he was born in India. "[H]e could not speak English,"[18] and he believed that "there were a great many Gods."[19] Language and religion, then, are essential for the formation of culture.

Probably not intended by Mrs. Sherwood, the novel locates an important anxiety of the expanding imperial mission about the empire's expatriates, its civil and military servants: the fear that they would degenerate into barbarism. Britishness had become a fragile identity, especially for their children who could become "native" because they were left in the care of native servants. Henry's conversion reads like a textbook case for missionaries. When the clergyman's missionary daughter teaches Henry to speak and read English and converts him to Christianity, she implicitly acculturates him into Britishness; for example, she teaches him what sin is and "right from wrong" because the native servants could not teach this to him.[20] Ironically, her conversion of the child Henry emphasizes how women were firmly ensconced within the domestic sphere, because she then directs Henry to convert Boosy.

Within the larger secular and somewhat hedonistic British expatriate society, the evangelical mission to convert natives had a grave urgency. "Many Christians were haunted by an acutely arithmetical vision of the

16. Cutt, *Ministering Angels*, 20.

17. Mrs. (Mary Martha) Sherwood, *Little Henry and His Bearer*, (15th ed.; London: F. Houlston and Son, 1820) 18.

18. Ibid., 20.

19. Ibid., 23.

20. Ibid., 30.

vast numbers of those who were being lost" to hell for eternity.[21] When Boosy objects to converting to Christianity because he would lose his position in his caste, Henry is taught to read Hindustani by Mr. Smith, an evangelical missionary whose house he and his adopted mother are visiting, so he can read to Boosy sections of the Bible that Mr. Smith had translated. He believes that "sometime or other, the whole Bible will be translated in this manner."[22] Although sustained and institutionalized native education is at this point several decades away, catechetical schools for teaching natives to read and write were necessary for conversions, for them to read the Bible. Mrs. Sherwood's experience with them is indicated by "appointing herself to organize" them in the early nineteenth century, even though women were fairly restricted to the domestic sphere.[23] Henry makes Boosy "copy [the Persian letters] as they sat together; and so, by degrees, he had [sic] taught them all to his *bearer*."[24] The expenses associated with teaching missionary candidates to speak, read, and write in the native language emphasize the importance of self-supporting vernacular training missions undertaken by most missionary societies, for example, the London Missionary Society in India.[25] When Mr. Smith presents Henry with a Hindustani translation of the Bible "bound together in red morocco,"[26] we can see that missionaries were also scholars saturated in the ethos and attitudes of empire.[27]

Missionary ambitions did not always coincide with imperial ambitions and policies since their mission of native conversions meant

---

21. Stanley, *The Bible and the Flag*, 65.

22. Sherwood, *Little Henry and His Bearer*, 98.

23. Patricia Demers, "Mrs. Sherwood and Hesba Stratton: The Letter and the Spirit of Evangelical Writing of and for Children," in *Romanticism and Children's Literature in Nineteenth-Century England*, edited by James Holt McGravran Jr. (Athens: University of Georgia Press, 1991) 131.

24. Sherwood, *Little Henry and His Bearer*, 103; author's italics.

25. When an applicant to the London Missionary Society desired to "become a Missionary to Heathens," he went through a thorough vetting process beginning with him having to answer in writing a series of questions focusing on his Christian beliefs, education, health, income, marital status, etc. See Stuart Piggin, *Making Evangelical Missionaries 1789–1858: The Social Background, Motives and Training of the British Protestant Missionaries to India* (Abingdon, Oxfordshire: Sutton Courtnay, 1984) 287–89.

26. Sherwood, *Little Henry and His Bearer*, 101.

27. In the late nineteenth century one of the first missionary chaplains to the East India Company, Henry Martyn, translated the New Testament into Urdu. See Bradley, *Call to Seriousness*, 76.

building relationships with the natives. When Mr. Smith suggests that Boosy's resistance is temporary, it crystallizes the evangelical missionaries' mission of education to facilitate religious conversions, which opposed the British imperial policy of secularizing institutional education in India. Mr. Smith remonstrates Henry of his impatience: "something tells me that I shall see Boosy a Christian before I die; or if I do not see that day, he that outlives me will."[28] As a colonial subject, Boosy is voiceless in spite of his objecting to conversion due to loss of caste at the beginning of the novel. Mr. Smith, the scholar-missionary, stands as guardian of the Western tradition, and his belief in the inevitable conversion of Boosy attests to the paternalistic doctrine for the justification of the empire. Although published in 1814, the novel implicitly propagates J. Farish's widely believed pronouncement in 1838 at the Bombay Presidency: "The Native must either be kept down by a sense of our power, or they must willingly submit from a conviction that we are more wise, more just, more humane, and more anxious to improve their condition than any other rulers they could possibly have."[29] Embedded within a colonial discourse legitimizing Western domination, missionary work reoriented the direct and brutal exercise of political and military power over the natives into a gentler, expansionist mission with the Christian responsibility to convert and educate the natives, essentially re-creating British culture within the empire.

Marguerite Butler's *Tulsi, the Story of an Indian Schoolgirl*

Although "domestic fiction [became] less overtly didactic and evangelical over the course of the [nineteenth] century," in the early twentieth century novels such as Marguerite Butler's *Tulsi, the Story of an Indian Schoolgirl* (1934) provided a continued supply of propaganda tools to reinforce the evangelical mission to bring light to the "dark places on earth."[30] The missionary movement in India had been institutionalized in its mission to educate, civilize, and assimilate the Other. Establishing a paradisal world of idealized upper-class, Westernized Indian childhood, *Tulsi* reproduces an image of complaisant Indian subjectivity, with the focus on Tulsi and her family, rather than on the traditional

---

28. Sherwood, *Little Henry and His Bearer*, 104.
29. Quoted in Viswanathan, *Masks of Conquest*, 2.
30. Kutzer, *Empire's Children*, 47.

British missionary-hero, the guardian of British cultural and Christian traditions. No longer voiceless due to the reproduction of the dominant imperial culture in India, the native heathen actively seeks to be educated into the discourses of the imperial ideologies, English language and Christianity, so he can participate within the political and economic structures of the imperium. Tulsi's father, an educated, professional middle-class Hindu, has had a Westernized upbringing, having gone briefly to a mission school but taken out of it by his father when he was introduced to "foreign religious books."[31] Missionaries founded schools "to train local people as ministers and missionaries to spread literacy so the Bible could be read and to form the minds of children when adults proved indifferent or hostile to the Christian message."[32] Frequently hostile to Christianity, many upper-class Indian parents sent their children to mission schools to gain a British education because this was perceived as a requirement to advance in British Raj society, for example, to receive better civil service positions. Unlike the traditional conversion plot, where the British missionary hero converts deserving natives, the conversion of Tulsi's father comes from within when he buys St. Matthew's Gospel at a railway station.[33] Nineteenth-century personal conversions of natives by British missionaries in distant, newly discovered territories had given way by the early twentieth century to the easy accessibility of Christian paraphernalia, in major cities as well as remote villages, due to the extensive road and railway system created by the British. It was increasingly believed that the "instrumentality of literature and schools was better designed to lead the uninitiated overseas heathen gently along the labyrinthine paths of Christian metaphysics" than personal conversions by missionaries; it was also more economically feasible given the prohibitive costs of training missionaries.[34]

By giving an Indian girl the subjectivity traditionally reserved for the British boy-hero of boy's adventure fiction, Marguerite Butler problematizes the Victorian public school concept of muscular Christianity

31. Marguerite L. Butler, *Tulsi: The Story of an Indian Schoolgirl* (London: London Missionary Society, 1934) 29.

32. Etherington, "Introduction," 11.

33. Butler, *Tulsi*, 29.

34. Piggin, *Making Evangelical Missionaries*, 101. Significantly, *Tulsi*, published by the London Missionary Society, was a propaganda tool for the Society and copies of the book were presented to school children as prizes for collecting donations for "The Society's Fleet" in Papua [New Guinea] (see the flyleaf of the 1934 edition).

reserved only for British boys and a source of British masculinist vigor, designed to "instill obedience, duty, piety and hard work" in British children,[35] by seeming to grant it to a native Indian girl. Tulsi's supposed subjectivity is tightly enclosed within British imperial domesticity. Her picture of her "guru," Jesus Christ, which she asks Miss Dean to affix into a locket, is intertwined with reading aloud the "Hop o' My Thumb" fairy tale, doing sums, and learning table manners. Miss Moore, one of the teachers, gently suggests to her, "The sooner you learn to eat with your mouth shut the better."[36] For the native, Britishness is a fetishized commodity s/he is encouraged to consume to become the ideal colonial subject. However, Tulsi instinctively believes that indigenous authority is hampered by skin color, and her desire to be a "Christian" is interconnected with her desire to become white. Although her teacher tries to assure her that her skin "is so much prettier for India than ours. English people here look washed out," she remains unconvinced, but the gentle tone of condescension throughout the novel assures British readers of their cultural benignity and racial superiority.[37]

Infused with the dominant ideology's belief that Indian women should not be cloistered in a *zenana*, the separate and private women's quarters in a Hindu household, Tulsi's father's desire for his daughter is to re-gender imperial discourses concerning native identity. "It is my dream that she should start a school for girls of our community and give herself to a life of service. The power of an educated woman is great, and under her inspiration our hindering purdah customs might break down."[38] When an enlightened native desires to change centuries-old restrictive Indian social practices for women, he essentially becomes the missionary circulating the commodity of Christianity as patrimony for his children. Tulsi's father seeks to racialize and ground the mission in a new frontier, the private sphere of domesticity—the traditional purview of British missionary wives—in which natives wearing the mantle of Britishness will teach themselves the colonist's culture, values, and religion. In the nineteenth century, missionary wives were expected to teach "local women and children the skills of European domesticity . . .

---

35. Jeffrey Richards, "Introduction," in *Imperialism and Juvenile Literature*, edited by Jeffrey Richards (Manchester: Manchester University Press, 1989) 3.
36. Butler, *Tulsi*, 67.
37. Ibid., 102.
38. Ibid., 41.

and to teach reading, infused, of course, by spiritual truth."[39] By the early twentieth century, young unmarried British missionary women continued to serve in the domestic sphere as nurturing missionary teachers of native school children. Miss Dean, one of the teachers, is a foster mother to Tulsi, in training to take over sometime in the future.

R. M. Ballantyne's *The Coral Island*

Secular boy's adventure fiction of the empire presented grand narratives of the imperial experience, operating within a dominant hegemonic masculinity, endorsed by a celebration of violence, and influenced by missionary work. One of the first novels of boy's adventure, a child's robinsonade of three young boys marooned on a South Sea island, R. M. Ballantyne's *The Coral Island* (1857), incorporates two very important subjects: the claiming, mapping, and governing of new territories to bring them into the British Empire; and the importance of missionaries at the forefront of the imperial project to govern the natives by converting them into Christianity.[40] "'Savages' who did not 'develop' the land and its resources were often viewed as having no right of possession, and the task of 'civilizing' them—provided it was deemed possible—was defined in terms of their conversion both to Christianity and to 'productive labor' or 'industry.'"[41] Most writers of boy's adventure fiction focused on the paradigms of action and boyish heroism within the imperial enterprise, but Ballantyne, a Presbyterian elder, was "an author of conscience, a true believer, seeing the Christian position as both defensive and offensive," which, while denying "independence to subordinate races . . . [also] justified interventionism."[42] The novel reinforces Britain's moral duty to intervene by proving Ralph Rover, the narrator, beliefs that "[i]f [the island they are stranded on] should be inhabited, I [feel] certain, from all I had heard of South Sea Islanders, that we should be roasted

---

39. Patricia Grimshaw and Peter Sherlock, "Women and Cultural Exchanges," in Etherington, *Missions and Empire*, 180.

40. Daniel Defoe's *Robinson Crusoe* (1719) begins the sub-genre of the Robinsonade plot, especially in novels of the empire.

41. Brantlinger, *Rule of Darkness*, 25.

42. Stuart Hannabuss, "Ballantyne's Message of Empire," in Richards, *Imperialism and Juvenile Literature*, 60.

alive and eaten."[43] When the natives' warring against each other invades the boys' pristine island, they appear as childish, degenerative savages whom the boys teach, instructing them in the beginnings of civilization and forbidding cannibalism. They have no language because the boys must communicate by sign language, at best, although they do learn each other's names.

Missionaries were at the vanguard of the colonial process as they were essentially used to deploy the free trade ideology of imperialism, the practice of which amounted to piracy or illegitimate trade, frequently unofficially sanctioned by the state and often involving the exploitation and even destruction of natives in the name of progress. Kidnapped by pirates, Ralph Rover observes the pirate captain not plundering a trade ship because its captain is a native missionary. Bloody Bill, one of the ship hands, explains: "As for the missionaries, the captain favours them because they are useful to him. The South Sea Islanders are such incarnate fiends that they are the better off [sic] becoming tamed, and the missionaries are the only men who can do it."[44] Objectifying the natives as animalistic and godless permits the colonizer to justify his Christian duty to civilize him, to bring order to their society, to bring the light of Christianity to them, and de-emphasizes the political and economic motives for colonialism. Having been Christianized, the native missionary captain and his native crew have a vested interest in the British religious civilizing process and its cultural hegemony, and they are completely enclosed within the protective shield of the colonial state, which even the pirate ship respects. However, if native heathens obstruct the economic roadways of the imperial state, they are harshly dealt with. When the pirate ship anchors at an island to replenish its water supply, the natives obstruct their passage. The captain orders the ship to fire its cannon, killing five to six hundred natives. Until natives could be trained to be missionaries, the empire depended on British missionaries, who persisted in spite of death, deprivation, and hardship in newly discovered territories. They were the "most exceptional means [of] extending British interests, British influences, and the British empire."[45]

43. R. M. Ballantyne, *The Coral Island*, edited by J. S. Bratton (Oxford: Oxford University Press, 1990) 16.
44. Ibid., 214–15.
45. John Philip, quoted in Porter, in Etherington, *Missions and Empire*, 51. John Philip was the superintendent of the London Missionary Society in Cape Colony

When the boys leave their Coral Island in the schooner that Ralph inherits from the dead pirates, they discover that the other islands in the South Seas have been remade by the British in their image with a native missionary presiding over an "English" village: "The village was about a mile in length, and perfectly straight," and each house has "a little garden in front, tastily laid out and planted, while the walks were covered with black and white pebbles.... Each house had doors and Venetian blinds."[46] The Christianized natives' imitation of Britishness justifies the British missionary presence and proves its divinely ordained role.

One of Ballantyne's major sources, Michael Russell, suggests that "[t]he howl of superstitious fear has been succeeded by the language of prayer, and the shouts of ferocious war by the song of Christian praise."[47] In the village the boys are informed by the native missionary that a year ago they had been living "in the practice of the most bloody system of idolatry."[48] For the evangelical missionaries, the gravity of this issue was that "unless [the heathens] believed in Christ, they must be presumed lost for all eternity."[49] The missionary was a crusader against idolatry, which was "the master-sin of Heathenism" because it transgressed against the Ten Commandments.[50] Concealed beneath a façade of discursive approbation of Western civilization is the systematic destruction of native culture. The converted natives wear Western clothes, but both men's attire and women's dresses "were grotesque enough, being very bad imitations of the European garb."[51] The natives are educated and invested with cultural desire for Western civilization because of their conversion into Christianity. When Jack exclaims approvingly, "[w]hat a convincing proof that Christianity is of God," we see the dialectical relationship between Christianity and colonialism because converted natives are more compliant and willing to trade with the Europeans.[52]

(South Africa). His comments were in relation to Cape Colony in his book *Researches in South Africa* (1828).

46. Ballantyne, *The Coral Island*, 287–88.
47. Quoted in J. S. Bratton, "Introduction," in Ballantyne, *The Coral Island*, viii.
48. Ballantyne, *The Coral Island*, 288.
49. Stanley, *The Bible and the Flag*, 65.
50. Ibid., 64.
51. Ballantyne, *The Coral Island*, 289.
52. Ibid., 288.

Rudyard Kipling's *Kim*

Published in 1901, *Kim* serves as an emblem of the quintessential boy's adventure fiction of the empire, incorporating Victorian public school ideals. As controlling authoritarian figures, colonial religious authorities must be evaded so that, ironically, the child Kim can retain his innocence. In the nineteenth century childhood was conceived as "a cultural construction conforming to ideological desire in which any sense of 'real children' is erased/replaced by idealized innocence."[53] The three boys in *The Coral Island* retain their British identity in spite of being marooned on a deserted island, unlike Little Henry and Kim, who when left under the guardianship of natives relapse into a state of nativism and must be reclaimed into their imperial British raciality. Most imperialist writing "treat[s] the Empire as a 'dressing for dinner,' a temporary means of presenting Britain itself from relapsing into barbarism," and Kim's ambiguous and multiple identities figure between the imperial subject self-fashioning and the missionary imperative to civilize and assimilate the "other."[54] The two chaplains of the Maverick Regiment, Kim's father's regiment, at first believe they have caught a native thief because he looks Indian. By the early twentieth century, missionary activity in the empire has become insular, and so the mission of the regiment's two chaplains is only to minister to the regiment, not to convert natives. Insulated from the natives, Western cultural hegemony is upheld by seemingly empty religious rituals. Kim observes the "Sahibs pray[ing] to their God," a red-gold bull, but he does not realize the regimental officers are ritually toasting their mascot.[55]

When his father, O'Hara, keeps Kim away from the missionary authorities' powerful grasp, "[s]ocieties and chaplains anxious for the child, tried to catch him, but O'Hara drifted away. . ."[56] Their urgent imperative "to catch him" suggests that the idealized innocence of childhood is in danger of becoming contaminated by barbarism, which can only be prevented with a conscious commitment to transmitting British culture and values. Kim's eluding of the "missionaries and white men of serious aspect" shows the limits of evangelical endeavor and that

---

53. McCulloch, *Fictional Role of Childhood*, 3.
54. Brantlinger, *Rule of Darkness*, 230.
55. Rudyard Kipling, *Kim*, edited by Edward W. Said (London: Penguin, 1989) 131.
56. Ibid., 49.

the task of disseminating Christian cultural values was frequently and acutely challenged by the secular British culture and Indian society.[57] The Lama unwittingly insures that Kim is educated into Catholicism, his father's religion, by paying the school fees for St. Xavier School, a Catholic institution in Lucknow. The two chaplains' urgent mission to insure he is educated into his British raciality suggests that the world of childhood is infused or rather contaminated by the Other. As guardians of disseminating British cultural values, they insure the religious and moral well-being of the regiment and give themselves the task of educating Kim to follow in his father's footsteps of becoming a soldier, who unfortunately was not a respectable role model. "[T]he Regiment will take care of you and make you as good a man as your father—as good a man as can be."[58] Kim's conscious reasons for becoming a "sahib" are for the adventure, not for the traditional evangelical reason of converting to Christianity, and to participate in the Great Game, becoming in essence a young builder of imperial England. The imperial state was governed not by converting natives into Christianity, but "less by occupying it than by knowing it, classifying it, and rendering it visible. Faced with possession of imperial territories too vast to be directly and continuously controlled, the English state had little choice but to exercise its power in the production of knowledge."[59] Evangelistic work among the heathens in the nineteenth century helped shape the character of the empire, but by the early twentieth century the focus of the empire was in buttressing its authority, and the evangelical missions were least successful in India and had a better success rate in Africa where they placed more resources.

By the end of the nineteenth century, the colonial administration of India, having become institutionalized, could sustain a multiplicity of Christian religious values and missions. Although Father Victor tries to indoctrinate Kim before he is sent to St. Xavier, Kim ignores the priest's attempts to teach him "of a Goddess called Mary, who he gathered, was one with Bibi Miriam of Mahbub Ali's theology."[60] By conflating Christianity with Islam, Kipling acknowledges how the British are intertwined within Indian society in divergent and ambiguous ways.

57. Ibid., 50–51.
58. Ibid., 138.
59. Ian Baucom, *Out of Place: Englishness, Empire, and the Locations of Identity* (Princeton: Princeton University Press, 1999) 93.
60. Kipling, *Kim*, 165.

The traditional hierarchical structure that Mr. Smith, the missionary in *Little Henry and His Bearer*, took for granted gives way to an expansive relationship between the British and the Indians, in between rebellions and mutinies. Kim's integration of Christianity and Islam speaks to the British government's policy of religious neutrality, which created a space for religious dissent and freedom. Father Victor exhorts him to remember to say he is "Roman Cath'lic" at St. Xavier, but there is no indication that Kim converts into Catholicism.[61]

Evangelical tract fiction's doctrine of the power of Christianity to remake the native into its own imperial image is transmuted in *Kim* into an India containing incommensurable contradictions, which is emphasized by putting to the forefront the Lama's religion of Buddhism. The Lama's search for the river of life civilizes and assimilates the native into the imperial enterprise, and allows him and his religion to uphold the moral virtues traditionally epitomized by Western cultural hegemony and Christianity. When the Lama receives the salvation he had been seeking at the end of the novel—"Son of my Soul, I have wrenched my Soul back from the Threshold of Freedom to free thee from all sin—as I am free and sinless!"—imperial subject-fashioning gives way to an Indian arcadian or ordered life, a paradisal world that Christianity cannot compete with.[62]

Conclusion

When boy's adventure fiction of the empire incorporated missionaries converting natives and bringing stability to native society, it proved the interconnectedness between the secular British colonial government and the privately funded missionary enterprise. By the early twentieth century, missionaries were an inextricable part of colonial society, embodying the belief of a divinely ordained providential role for Britain and helping to justify its imperial enterprise. Unlike boy's adventure fiction, children's evangelical tract fiction, part of the propaganda arm of the various missionary societies, illustrated to the young reader the importance of converting natives to Christianity, which always involved indoctrinating natives into Britain's cultural values. However, the focus of most of the novels was not on native conversions, but rather on British children

61. Ibid., 165.
62. Ibid., 338.

and the task of reclaiming them from barbarism into civilized British citizens, which suggests an immense anxiety and fear that children, the most vulnerable members of society, might degenerate into barbarism. Rehearsing these fears, novels of both genres attempt to box the native into becoming a willing participant of British imperial society.

ELEVEN

Conflicts between Christianity and Korean Shamanism in Nora Okja Keller's *Comfort Woman*

J. Stephen Pearson

In her 1997 novel *Comfort Woman,* Nora Okja Keller foregrounds the interplay between Western Christianity and indigenous religion in Korean American experience. Christianity plays a major role in the life of title character Soon Hyo, who, having been forced into prostitution by the Japanese during World War II, escapes and finds refuge at a Christian mission in Pyongyang, where she marries American missionary Rick and moves with him to the United States, remaining there after his death to raise their daughter. However, because of Soon Hyo's continuation of her Korean tradition and Rick's Westernized inability to comprehend her past, Christianity functions as a central site for their marital conflicts.

This chapter examines Soon Hyo's experiences with Christianity, focusing on three issues: the role of Christianity in the Korean-Japanese conflict, syncretism between Korean indigenous religions and Christianity, and the conflicts that occur between the American and Korean characters due to differing cultural attitudes regarding both the human body and language. Before proceeding, however, it should be noted that Keller portrays Christianity solely through Soon Hyo's eyes; her husband Rick is never allowed to present his perspective. As a result, we know Rick's view of Soon Hyo only through her descriptions of their interactions. This scheme creates problems regarding how to interpret the Christian view of Korea: Since Soon Hyo and Rick are separated by gender, culture, class, and religion, the reader must constantly sort through the details to determine where the source of conflict lies.

Christianity in Korea

In describing the Christian mission in Pyongyang, Soon Hyo notes that it is disguised as a business because "the Japanese, . . . not trusting foreign influences, discouraged Christianity but encouraged businesses for the revenue that could be sent back to the Emperor."[1] Her description alludes to Christianity's role in the political conflicts that led her to the comfort camp, and it is important to understand that history.

Christianity took root in Korea in the eighteenth century when Catholicism was introduced by Korean intellectuals as part of Western scientific knowledge. In his overview of Korean Christian history, Wi Jo Kang notes that because these leaders introduced Christianity as a philosophical system, Koreans did not consider it a new or foreign religion, but referred to it simply as "Western learning."[2] Still, conflicts with Korean traditions did occur, often with bloody results, and Catholic priests could not openly serve without fear of persecution until an 1886 treaty with France.[3] By this time, Protestant missions were flourishing in the Korean-Chinese border region,[4] and by 1887 the New Testament was available in Korean.[5]

Concurrently, Korea's relations with Japan were degenerating. When the Koreans held off the Japanese at Kanghwa[6] Island in 1875, it not only angered the Japanese but provided them an opening for what Kang calls their "imperial ambitions."[7] The Kanghwa incident led to an 1876 treaty which Korea signed only when threatened with military force, thus marking their "gradual loss of independence."[8] Although many Western nations recognized Korean sovereignty,[9] the Korean government became increasingly influenced by Japan and by Westernization. The growth of

---

1. Nora Okja Keller, *Comfort Woman*, (New York: Penguin, 1998) 66.

2. Wi Jo Kang, *Christ and Caesar in Modern Korea: A History of Christianity and Politics* (SUNY Series in Korean Studies; Albany: SUNY Press, 1997) 2.

3. Ibid., 2, 7.

4. Ibid., 9.

5. Ibid., 12.

6. "Ganghwa" under the new South Korean romanization system. Because there are multiple Romanization systems in use, I have retained the spellings used by my sources.

7. Kang, *Christ and Caesar*, 12.

8. Ibid., 13.

9. Ibid., 13–14.

such influence led to an unsuccessful coup in 1884 in which the Korean Prince Min Yŏng Ik was wounded.[10] Interestingly, because the prince was treated with great care by a Presbyterian medical missionary, the failed coup became "the stepping stone for furthering Protestant mission work in Korea."[11]

When the Japanese finally gained control of Korea, their rule was welcomed by many of the Christian missionaries there.[12] Their support, however, did not allay Japanese suspicion of Korean Christian subversion: After an alleged assassination attempt on a Japanese official in 1911, the Japanese convicted 105 Christian men, although they released them in 1915 after international criticism.[13] And in 1919, they blamed the March First Independence movement on Christians and shut down churches, arrested and/or martyred numerous ministers and, in the worst incident, massacred all the Christian males of Cheamni village inside their own church building before setting fire to it.[14] International outcry regarding these events induced the Japanese to appoint a more tolerant governor over Korea, but after invading Manchuria in 1932, they renewed their efforts to control Korea.[15] This time, they imposed Shinto rituals on the Koreans, arguing that because the rituals were civil ceremonies rather than religious rites, they did not conflict with Christianity. Their arguments, however, were ineffective, and the majority of Korean Christians "refused to participate in the ceremonies."[16] The Japanese gained the cooperation of Methodists and Presbyterians only by threatening police harassment.[17] Still, by October of 1940 the situation had become unstable enough that the United States evacuated its citizens from Korea; by December, many Catholic and almost all Protestant missionaries had left, and by 1941, "the Christian churches in Korea were completely controlled by Japanese politics."[18]

10. Ibid., 14.
11. Ibid., 15.
12. Ibid., 43.
13. Ibid., 44–46.
14. Ibid., 51–54.
15. Ibid., 55–59, 61–62.
16. Ibid., 63.
17. Ibid., 65–66.
18. Ibid., 67. See also Donald N. Clark, *Christianity in Modern Korea*, (Lanham, MD: University Press of America; New York: Asia Society, 1986) 13.

As this historical survey shows, Christianity played a substantial role on both sides of the Korean-Japanese conflict. As David Chung notes, the Koreans' refusal to perform Shinto ceremonies led the Japanese "to check the dangerously growing Christian influence among Koreans. In this way Japanese colonialism very quickly found her bitter enemy to be the rapidly growing Christian church in Korea."[19] Meanwhile, in Korea, anti-Japanese sentiment was especially strong among converts with Confucian backgrounds, who had traditionally been "more or less contemptuous of everything that was Japanese."[20] Thus, Korean Christianity broadened the rift on both sides.

Keller's novel shows another level of complexity in the role of Christianity in the conflict. As most Western Christians had fled Korea before the United States entered the war, the continued presence of the Pyongyang mission four years later is impressive. Moreover, the fact that Christians shared the Koreans' tribulations suggests that the missionaries had experienced some of the same difficulties as Soon Hyo and were not sheltered from the troubles of the war; Keller implies this both when Soon Hyo compares her room at the mission to her room at the camps and when she continues to hear the noises from the camps while safe in the mission.

At the same time, Christians partly contributed to the conflict, insofar as their refusal to practice the Shinto rituals inspired Japan to crack down even harder. In fact, Korean Christian resistance reflects how successful missionaries were at spreading the "good news." As Chung-shin Park notes, "the biblical language and symbols offered by the Protestant church not only consoled frustrated, grief-stricken Koreans, but also gave them hope and a desire to be liberated from the colonial yoke."[21] This facet of Korean Christian worship appears in Keller's novel in her description of the "days of prayer," in which the missionaries connect the promises of God with Korea's troubles, leading Soon Hyo to imagine "heaven as a Korea liberated from domination, where the angels trod

---

19. David Chung, *Syncretism: The Religious Context of Christian Beginnings in Korea*, edited by Kang-nam Oh, (SUNY Series in Korean Studies; Albany: SUNY Press, 2001) 51.

20. Ibid., 126.

21. Chung-shin Park, *Protestantism and Politics in Korea*, (Korean Studies of the Henry M. Jackson School of International Studies; Seattle: University of Washington Press, 2003) 131.

over rivers littered with the charred bodies of the Japanese."[22] Visions like these encouraged Koreans to resist Japan. It is plausible, therefore, to say that the entire country, Christian and non-Christian alike, suffered because of the faith of a few. So while the missionaries underwent their share of trials from the occupation, plenty of non-Christians, including Soon Hyo, might have suffered less had the church been less faithful.

Syncretism

At the same time, the Christian presentation of the gospel led to syncretism. Keller demonstrates this phenomenon through Soon Hyo's own religious life, in which she retains her indigenous beliefs and spiritual gifts even after her baptism. During the mission's prayer time, she prays to her spirit-goddess, Induk, and after Rick dies, she supports herself and her daughter by practicing her gifts as a *mudang*, the ancient Korean tradition of female shamanism.[23] According to David Chung, a *mudang* is hereditarily "a medium, a diviner, but not a magician or a priest," whose duties include "general divination, diagnosis of sickness, and ghost chasing," for which "[she] summons spirits in the dark, sings and dances and channels."[24] In the novel, therefore, Christianity conflicts with Korean spirituality without eliminating its power.

Keller sets up this syncretism in Soon Hyo's first encounter with Christianity, which comes not via the missionaries, but via another syncretized *mudang*, Manshin[25] Ahjima, the "[o]ld lady of ten thousand spirits."[26] Manshin Ahjima's Christianity is complicated: she calls suicide "the devil's work"[27] and refers to "possession sickness,"[28] implying that she accepts a Christian worldview. Yet she continues to have *mudang* experiences, although she tries to explain them through a Christian

---

22. Keller, *Comfort Woman*, 92.
23. Ibid., 92.
24. Chung, *Syncretism*, 175.
25. "Manshin" is a term used to refer to shamans and is thus more of a title than a personal name. For a discussion of Keller's shamans in their Korean context, see Tina Chen, *Double Agency: Acts of Impersonation in Asian American Literature and Culture* (Stanford: Stanford University Press, 2005).
26. Keller, *Comfort Woman*, 38.
27. Ibid., 57.
28. Ibid., 58.

perspective. After having an episode in front of Soon Hyo, she laments, "Damn jealous, those men. The Satan General and the Jesus God fight over me.... I am the arena of their power contest. And in their battle to possess me, neither has any pity for me. I just can't take it sometimes."[29] Moreover, her excitement about Soon Hyo's vision of Korean independence calls into question how much she disapproves of spirit possession.[30] Interestingly, Soon Hyo is sent to Manshin Ahjima by Induk herself, who even speaks through the old woman during their meeting; these facts suggest that Induk knows about Ahjima's conversion but is not bothered by it.[31]

However, while it would be easy to claim that Soon Hyo never really converts, the novel reflects the historical reality of syncretism between the two traditions, for which the church was partly responsible, as some missionaries did not view the *mudang* tradition as substantially opposed to Christianity. L. O. Hartman's *Popular Aspects of Oriental Religions* (1917) suggested "that numerous points of contact between the indigenous Korean faith and Christianity existed when the Christian evangelism reached Korean shores."[32] These points of contact aided Protestant growth in Korea, as can be seen by the way Protestants preserved the name of the Korean deity *Hanŭnim*, which had been in use from the earliest days of Korean Christianity and was made official in 1912 due to what Chung describes as "public demand":

> Official adoption or accommodation of the *Hanŭnim* term was an important step taken by the Protestant churches to secure their permanent place in Korean society. And we suspect that this important step also gave rise to the "dangers" of inviting some of the essentially connected religious elements to the indigenous *Hanŭnim* belief, namely, the spiritual world structure which resembles very much that of the Mahayana-tinted shamanist heaven and hell; the souls, spirits, devils, as well as angels of syncretic lesser deities in the shamanist pantheon therein; the shamanist ecstasy with a cunning equation to the experience of the Holy Spirit and the ensuing healing power to the New Testament-like miracle.[33]

29. Ibid., 59.
30. Ibid., 60.
31. Ibid., 59.
32. Chung, *Syncretism*, 176.
33. Ibid., 177–78.

The comment about the Holy Spirit being connected to shamanist ecstasy calls to mind both Soon Hyo's reconnection with Induk, in which she gives herself to the deity and is offered salvation in return,[34] and to the sexual nature of their relationship[35]; both experiences have been explained in the Christian tradition as manifestations of the Holy Spirit. Thus the ease with which Soon Hyo maintains her spiritual traditions amidst her Christian surroundings is not necessarily hypocritical, but rather reflects both the similarities between the two traditions and the ways Christians translated Korean religion according to their own tradition.

Cultural Misunderstandings

Although Christianity played a substantial role in Korea's political landscape and adopted aspects of Korean religion, Keller shows that the two cultures never fully understood each other. For Soon Hyo, the American missionaries are so physically different from Koreans—"even the women were tall, with big hands and knuckles"[36]—that she can only distinguish the men from the women by their clothing (a nice joke on Westerners' lazy complaint that all Asians look alike). However, a more important reason for this difficulty comes from the fact that the Christians' attitudes toward gender equality made their behavior indistinguishable. As she narrates,

> Their actions, too, made it difficult to label them as men and women, for they did not behave as proper men and women.... At the mission house, I was embarrassed by the disrespect between the men and the women. Lives overlapping, men and women ate and worked together. They looked into each other's faces as they spoke, laughing with mouths open. Even while worshipping, they sat side by side, unseparated by a curtain or sheet, on the same bench, thighs and shoulders almost touching.[37]

This passage illustrates one difference between Christianity and Korea's long-established Confucian tradition, a difference which Christians knew about in the nineteenth century. For instance, in his 1898 essay

34. Keller, *Comfort Woman*, 96.
35. Ibid., 143–46.
36. Ibid., 67.
37. Ibid., 67–68.

"Open Korea and Its Methodist Mission," George H. Jones "clearly shows that early missionaries taught Korean Christians that all men and women were equal: 'The [Confucian] sages of Korea taught the nation that woman is inferior to man. Christianity flatly contradicts this, and there is a clash.'"[38] It should be noted that in some incidents, Keller prefers Western manners; for instance, a brief moment of eye-to-eye contact, improper within Soon Hyo's culture, brings temporary relief from her psychological pain.

Still, in spite of their beneficial results, the American missionaries do not understand Korean culture or politics. The most revealing example of this problem is the title of the speech Rick makes at churches around the United States, "Spreading the Light: My Experiences in the Obscure Orient."[39] The title itself exemplifies Keller's portrayal of the missionaries: "Orient" suggests orientalism and exoticism, while "obscure" recalls the stereotype of the inscrutable Asian. Moreover, by subtitling his talk "My Experiences," Keller suggests the kind of over-emphasis on personal subjectivity that allowed Westerners to see Asia as the "obscure Orient" in the first place.

Examples of this kind of cultural ignorance occur throughout the scenes in the mission. The missionary woman who prepares Soon Hyo for baptism naively assumes that she understands what baptism means; her comment that baptism and marriage are the two greatest moments of a woman's life shows her ignorance of the trauma Soon Hyo has undergone from having already had many "husbands."[40] Moreover, this woman does not realize that in Korean culture, white is the color of both death and purity. Hence, when Soon Hyo initially refuses the white baptismal dress, the woman both misinterprets her refusal as overly courteous ("Don't bother to thank me") and provides an unintentionally ironic response ("it must be a dream come true"): death, symbolized by the white dress, truly would be Soon Hyo's dream come true.[41] Once in the dress, Soon Hyo tries to "dissolve" herself in the river, not to find the new life promised in baptism but to use the dress as her burial shroud.[42]

38. Park, *Protestantism and Politics in Korea*, 56.
39. Keller, *Comfort Woman*, 107.
40. Ibid., 102.
41. Ibid., 103.
42. Ibid.

Rick also fails to understand Soon Hyo's trauma. Even though he has "heard rumors . . . about women being sent north of the Yalu [River—to the camps]," he never seems to realize that she did not go voluntarily[43]; he assumes that she was merely a common prostitute and never comprehends the horror of her experience. He even sees her suffering as a sign of God's favor and envies her difficulties. Therefore, his offers of forgiveness and solace sound as if he blames her for what has happened; he offers a God who convicts her, not a God who wants to heal her and relieve her suffering.[44] His willful ignorance shows itself especially strongly on their first night together, when he asks her if she knows what it is like to be with a man[45]—even after telling her God has cleansed her, he cannot accept what he knows to be true.

Body Issues

Rick's inability to accept his wife's sexual history exemplifies one of two main cultural conflicts in Keller's novel, namely, the proper use of the human body. In Rick and Soon Hyo's marriage, their differing views on the body come into irresolvable conflict when the erotic elements of Soon Hyo's possessions begin to manifest themselves.

Unsurprisingly, Soon Hyo's views of her body stem partly from cultural differences—Western clothes make her feel "naked"[46]—and partly from psychological issues: she over-indulges in ice cream because it reminds her of her childhood,[47] and cannot use public restrooms because the Japanese used that term to refer to the camps.[48] Her experience at the camps has also made her sexually dysfunctional. When she describes her wedding night, she says, "I let my mind fly away. For I knew then that my body was, and always would be, locked in a cubicle at the camps, trapped under the bodies of innumerable men."[49] Her body has been so abused that she will never enjoy intercourse again.

43. Ibid., 94.
44. Ibid.
45. Ibid., 106.
46. Ibid., 107.
47. Ibid., 152.
48. Ibid., 108.
49. Ibid., 106.

However, these issues are compounded by Rick's erotic tastes: although he says that Soon Hyo "seem[s] so mature" compared to the other girls, his sexual behaviors reveal that he thinks sexually only of girls.[50] He prefers Soon Hyo's hair down when they are in bed, but not during the day, for then she looks "like a little kid."[51] Moreover, their bedtime ritual is clearly that of an adult tucking a small child into bed.[52] It is hard to know whether Rick sees himself as her husband or her father.

This problem becomes important in understanding how Beccah (their daughter) is conceived. Soon Hyo, possessed by Induk, inadvertently wakes Rick, who is disturbed to find his wife masturbating in her bed.[53] Rick's solution to Soon Hyo's "sin"[54] is first to watch and then, after she realizes his presence, to enter her, explaining that "through a child will you be sanctified."[55] He hopes to improve her standing with God through a "productive" use of sex because he is so set in his religio-cultural notions of gender that he cannot condone sex for the sake of pleasure, much less think of sex in spiritual terms.[56] From Soon Hyo's perspective, however, Rick had joined both Soon Hyo and Induk in the bed, a fact that explains how Soon Hyo successfully conceives and that ironically supports Rick's concern for procreation. Yet at the same time, Soon Hyo realizes "that he would not use me again like that. I knew then that he could not."[57] The implication here is that Induk was in control of this episode, so that with Beccah's conception, Rick's role as sexual partner is over.

The conflict between their religious views on sexuality is soon brought into the open: what Rick views as no more than physical stimulation is to Soon Hyo a deeply moving spiritual experience. When he preaches to her the next morning against "self-fornication," she laughs, thinking, "How could he compare what went on between men's and

---

50. Ibid., 93.
51. Ibid., 107.
52. Ibid.
53. Ibid., 145.
54. Ibid., 146.
55. Ibid., 145.

56. However, this spiritualized concept was common in pre-Reformation Europe; Rick either lacks this historical knowledge or accepts a Protestant rejection of this more holistic view of the body's role within spirituality.

57. Keller, *Comfort Woman*, 148.

women's bodies with what happened spiritually?"[58] But when she tries to explain she was not in fact alone, Rick quotes Romans 1:26 and calls her "Succubus," implying that she is both a prostitute and a demon. Just as she cannot understand his comparison between physical and spiritual experience, he cannot understand the spiritual nature of her behavior and therefore cannot understand her explanation of that night.

However, Soon Hyo interprets Rick's reaction better than he can. She sees that the lust in his eyes is joined by "fear of death and disease... His fear that instead of saving me, he had damned himself. That he could not pass the test his God devised for him."[59] Although he had promised her on their first night together that she had been cleansed of her sin, he now realizes that he himself has not. As Soon Hyo understood after one of their early conversations, "This is his sin, the sin he fought against and still denies: that he wanted me—a young girl—not for his God but for himself."[60] His entire relationship with her has been the kind of battle that Manshin Ahjima experienced on their walk to Pyongyang; as she told Soon Hyo then, "The spirits are very jealous... They cannot stand it if you love someone more than them."[61] Rick had been testing/tempting himself with Soon Hyo, and only now does he realize the truth about himself.

Language

In addition to their differing views of the body, Soon Hyo and Rick also have differing views about language; this subject takes several forms in the novel, appearing variously as speech, names, deafness and music.

Soon Hyo's descriptions of Rick demonstrate that his view of language is conservative even by the standards of the 1940s: "A scholar who spends his life with the Bible, he thinks he is safe, that the words he reads, the meaning he gathers, will remain the same. Concrete. He is wrong."[62] Rick's naïveté towards the mutability of language may explain why he cannot perceive Soon Hyo's camp-related trauma: he thinks of prostitutes only as voluntary whores. Many of the problems he and Soon

58. Ibid., 146.
59. Ibid., 148.
60. Ibid., 95.
61. Ibid., 58.
62. Ibid., 21.

Hyo face stem from his application of this conservative hermeneutic to every aspect of their life.

For Soon Hyo, language is not concrete but powerful, and she worries both about how their differing views of language will effect Beccah—"the different sounds for the same object will confuse her"—and about how she can instill in Beccah a sense of bodily wholeness—"that she knows that all of what I touch is her and hers to name in her own mind, before language dissects her into pieces that can be swallowed and digested by others not herself."[63] Soon Hyo hopes that she will "balance her with language I know is true."[64]

One kind of word that Soon Hyo believes to be particularly powerful is the name. When Beccah is born, Soon Hyo asks Rick to pick a strong, protective name for her, as she is adamant that the name have a proper function. Although he chooses a name she cannot pronounce—that of the Hebrew trickster Rebecca—she is satisfied with the variant she can pronounce, Beccah ("Bek-hap"), because it means a pure white lily, the child who "keeps [Soon Hyo] from crossing over and roots [her] to this earth."[65] Soon Hyo's concern with names no doubt comes from having lost her own. For the majority of the book, she is referred to as Akiko, the name given to her in the camp as a reference to which cell she was assigned—she was Akiko #41 and the woman before her was Akiko #40, etc. She had had the opportunity at the mission to tell Rick her true name, but decided that Soon Hyo was dead and would never return. In the book, the name Soon Hyo is not used until the last chapter she narrates (ch. 16), just after Beccah first learns of it.[66]

Soon Hyo's decision not to correct Rick about her name recalls her inability to speak when she arrives at the mission.[67] This silence is symbolic to her since her predecessor, Akiko #40, chose death over silence.[68] It becomes even more symbolic in that Rick falls ill (and dies shortly thereafter) the same night Soon Hyo breaks her silence to Rick about her past and her name—"I know what I speak, for that is my given name. Soon Hyo, the true voice, the pure tongue. I speak of laying down for

63. Ibid., 21, 22.
64. Ibid., 21.
65. Ibid., 116–17.
66. Ibid., 173.
67. Ibid., 16.
68. Ibid., 20–21.

a hundred men . . . over and over, until I died. I speak of bodies being bought and sold, of bodies—."⁶⁹ Soon Hyo truly becomes Akiko, the one who breaks silence; but whereas Akiko #40 broke silence to bring about her own death, Soon Hyo brings Rick's. As she tells Beccah at the opening of the novel, "I killed your father."⁷⁰ For Soon Hyo, the power of words extends to the power to kill.

Silence has an interesting power as well, for it allows people to remain alive without truly living, since the silent ones, like Soon Hyo, lose control over their lives. Soon Hyo chooses silence in the camp, chooses it again at the mission, and after Rick's death, chooses it once more. For after learning her past, Rick begs her to keep her story to herself for Beccah's sake: "I ask you to protect our daughter, with your silence, from that shame."⁷¹ Although Rick's death seemingly allows her to be open about her past, she grants his request and retreats once more into silence, so that Beccah does not learn her mother's story until after her death.

Related to her lifetime of silence is the temporary deafness Soon Hyo experiences when she arrives at the mission.⁷² This deafness is stifling; although she remains able to perform her daily chores, she realizes that "without the sounds of these actions, [she] had no way to connect them to [her]self. No way to judge time, distance, action, reaction."⁷³ Her deafness renews old terrors, as her "ears were filled with memories of the comfort camps," and these sounds could only be blocked by the constant motion of work.⁷⁴ The trauma of the camps continues to lock her into her cell, shutting out the safety she now enjoys.

What brings Soon Hyo out of her deafness is language at its most intense, i.e., music. Soon Hyo regains her hearing via the missionaries' congregational singing.⁷⁵ Their style of singing is new to her—not solo or unison singing, but parts, "with notes so rich and varied that it sounded like many songs blended into one."⁷⁶ This Western style of choral singing opens her ears by bringing up "every sound from every day [she] spent

69. Ibid., 195.
70. Ibid., 1.
71. Ibid., 196.
72. Ibid., 63.
73. Ibid., 64.
74. Ibid.
75. Ibid., 70.
76. Ibid., 71.

in the camp all at once, . . . until, in a rush, [her] ears shattered,"[77] and she recovers positive sounds from the camp—sounds of nature and songs of resistance, defiance, rest, and freedom.[78]

Interestingly, Keller once again uses Western influence in a positive way in Soon Hyo's life, as it is not her native musical traditions that rescue her, but Western choral singing. The fact that this Western singing brings back positive memories of Korean monophonic singing from the camp may suggest that the harmonic basis of Western music symbolizes a diversity that Soon Hyo needs to experience in order to be healed; it may also suggest that Soon Hyo has been traumatized by inter-Asian conflict and must view the world from a non-Asian perspective in order to be healed.

Music also becomes important to Soon Hyo in the States as, for a time, only Rick's singing could calm the infant Beccah. As a result, Soon Hyo comes to hate his Bible songs and even his voice, "sounding so honest and joyful that you want to believe, even when you know the truth. The same voice that fools everyone but me."[79] In truth, however, she is simply jealous that he alone is able to calm *her* daughter.[80] This problem is resolved when, remembering a long-forgotten song, she uses it to quiet Beccah's crying.[81] Thus, music is most powerful when one can produce it: although the church's music restores her hearing and helps her remember the songs of strength from her past, she cannot claim her role as a mother until she can sing those songs herself. More importantly, however, with her recovery of her singing ability she also reclaims her powers as a *mudang* and thereby becomes a mother figure to the local Korean community.

Soon Hyo's recovery of her *mudang* ability is, from a Christian perspective, curious, because even though the church thinks it has delivered her from her non-Christian spiritual powers, Induk seems to use the church to preserve them. From Soon Hyo's perspective (which the novel's depictions of Beccah seem to corroborate), it is not Christ but Induk who rescues her from the Japanese, brings her to America, and gives her a daughter. Yet, Induk does not work in spite of Christianity.

77. Ibid., 70.
78. Ibid., 71.
79. Ibid., 69.
80. Ibid., 116.
81. Ibid., 71.

Instead, she seems to be using it to aid her own plans for Soon Hyo, as seen in Soon Hyo's encounter with Manshin Ahjima, who takes her to the mission, and in the way Western hymnody restores Soon Hyo's hearing.[82] Although Rick never understands Soon Hyo's culture or history, and Soon Hyo never accepts Rick's Christianity, the conflicts between them do not interfere with Induk's plans for Soon Hyo, as is seen in the way Induk uses Rick's intolerance for masturbation to achieve Beccah's conception, who is especially important as it is through her that Induk ensures not only that Soon Hyo has someone to perform the burial rites for her, but also that there will be someone to carry on the *mudang* tradition and minister to the Korean community in Hawaii. By the end of the novel, it seems as though everything Soon Hyo has gone through has been part of a larger plan by Induk to support Korean Americans in their native traditions. Whereas some scholars suggest that Korean shamanism is an aid rather than an obstacle to Christian evangelism, Keller's novel suggests the converse: Christianity is an aid rather than an obstacle to Induk.[83] Inverting the Apostle Paul's promise in Romans 8:28, Keller implies that in spite of the conflicts between Korean religion and Christianity, Induk is able to work all things for good, not just for Soon Hyo, but for Koreans everywhere.

---

82. Ibid., 61.
83. Chung, *Syncretism*, 178.

TWELVE

Christianity's Cross-cultural (Mis)Translation in Amy Tan's Fiction

Dí Gan Blackburn

Introduction

THEOLOGIANS AND HISTORIANS SUCH as Lamin Sanneh and Leslie Newbigin characterize Christianity as a cross-culturally translatable religion, by which they mean that it can and should be translated out of its Western cultural embodiment to the recipient cultures.[1] As Sanneh points out, Christianity has depended on cross-cultural translation from the beginning, first out of Aramaic and Hebrew and then out of Greek and Latin. In his view, the cross-cultural religious interaction between missionaries and the natives eventually leads to a realization that "no one cultural expression of the religion [is] the exclusive representation of the gospel."[2] When introduced cross-culturally, Christianity needs to discriminately break away from its Western cultural embodiments and embrace the recipient culture without losing its original gospel message. Christianity's cross-cultural translation is therefore not only a linguistic exchange but also a cultural transaction. Without such a proper cross-cultural translation, Christianity can seldom avoid being mistakenly labeled as a Western religion.

Amy Tan's fiction demonstrates the challenges and failures in Christianity's cross-cultural translation. In *The Joy Luck Club* (1989),

---

1. Leslie Newbigin, *Foolishness to the Greeks: The Gospel and Western Culture* (Grand Rapids: Eerdmans, 1986); Lamin Sanneh, *Translating the Message: The Missionary Impact on Culture* (Maryknoll, NY: Orbis, 1990).

2. Sanneh, *Translating the Message*, 65.

The Kitchen God's Wife (1991), *The Hundred Secret Senses* (1995), and *The Bonesetter's Daughter* (2001), Christianity is presented either as a Western religion with few Chinese cultural embodiments or as a syncretistic religion that embraces the recipient Chinese culture indiscriminately. On one hand, because the American missionaries present it as part of a Western cultural enterprise, church lives and mission works are often viewed by the Chinese recipients as foreign, alien, absurd, and consequently portrayed in the fashion of a laughable parody or farce. On the other hand, as the Chinese and Chinese American characters hold on to their deep-rooted Chinese religious mindset, Christianity is so syncretized that it mostly resembles folk Chinese religions. What is neglected by such mistranslations of Christianity is the basic message of the gospel, which is hardly internalized by either the missionaries or the Chinese recipients.

The Joy Luck Club

In *The Joy Luck Club*, the First Chinese Baptist Church is run by American missionary ladies who use English as its official language. Understanding little English and unfamiliar with American culture, the Chinese immigrants respond to the church's activities with "numbness in [their] faces."[3] For them, the major function of the First Chinese Baptist Church is to offer free training on how to become an American. Although the Joy Luck mothers adapt to the church's external cultural training willingly, they do not feel obliged to give up their Chinese religious beliefs for Christianity. For instance, Lindo "wanted [her] children to have the best combination: American circumstances and Chinese character."[4] The church is pragmatically accepted as part of the "American circumstances" as far as it does not challenge its members' "Chinese character."

The Joy Luck Club's philosophy of "joy" and "luck," which is fundamentally pragmatic, evidently influences its members' approach to Christianity. The Joy Luck Christians' focus on pursuing "joy" and "luck" is largely derived from the traditional Chinese "low-brow" Buddhist concept of *ch'iu-fu* (seeking blessings).[5] In popular practice, a Buddhist deity

---

3. Amy Tan, *The Joy Luck Club* (New York: Ivy, 1989) 6.

4. Ibid., 254.

5. In China, Buddhism and Daoism have been traditionally interpreted and practiced in "high-brow" and "low-brow" fashions. The "high-brow" approach is taken

is often regarded as someone to bargain with, and his worshippers are expected to exchange religious practices and offerings for his blessings in a "businesslike" manner.[6] Likewise, the Christian church to these Joy Luck Christians is merely a practical institution where one can bargain for more joy and luck, while the Christian God of their understanding only functions as another (often unsatisfying) provider of *fu* (blessings). As popular Buddhism is to layman practitioners, Christianity to these Chinese women "appears only as a matter of convenience, a means to more materialistic or social ends."[7] The relationship between the Joy Luck Christians and the church "is characterized by bribery: adopt our faith or you won't get these benefits."[8]

Since more gods means more benefactors of joy, luck, and *fu*, the Joy Luck Christians' pragmatic approach to beliefs is inevitably syncretistic and pluralistic, which is not atypical of their Chinese religious background. As Milton M. Chiu points out, "one of the distinctive characteristics of Chinese religion" is its syncretistic nature.[9] Holmes Welch also notes that the three major religions in China, Confucianism, Taoism, and Buddhism, have always borrowed from one another.[10] In addition, W. E. Soothill observes that most Chinese people "have no prejudices and make no embarrassing distinctions; they belong to none of the three religions, or, more correctly, they belong to all three." With this eclectic attitude toward religion, a Chinese religious laity would "use whichever form best responds to the requirement of the occasion."[11]

---

by scholars and the elite class, who produced theological, literary, artistic, historical, and cultural interpretations. The "low-brow" approach is taken by the less-educated, lower-class people, whose understandings of the two religions are often marked by their "fortune-seeing" motives, superstitious practices, and confusion of the two religions. For further readings on traditional religions in China, see books by Holmes Welch, Milton M. Chiu, and W. E. Soothill.

6. Holmes Welch, *The Practice of Chinese Buddhism*, 1900–1950 (Cambridge: Harvard University Press, 1967) 377.

7. Patricia Marby Harrison, "Genocide or Redemption? Asian American Autobiography and the Portrayal of Christianity in Amy Tan's *The Joy Luck Club* and Joy Kogawa's *Obasan*," *Christianity and Literature* 46:2 (Winter 1997) 155.

8. Ibid., 154.

9. Milton M. Chiu, *The Tao of Chinese Religion* (Lanham, MD: University Press of America, 1984) 378.

10. Welch, *The Practice of Chinese Buddhism*, 400.

11. W. E. Soothill, *The Three Religions of China* (London: Oxford University Press, 1923) 13.

Since faith is a matter of pragmatic and pluralistic choice rather than an ideological commitment, the church-going Joy Luck Christians freely incorporate other beliefs into their Christianity: Chinese astrology, the Five Elements, and *feng shui*, just to name a few.[12] An-mei's Christian God takes an equal position with the "house gods" and "ancestors" and co-labors with them in making sure that the family's "lucky streak would never break, that all the elements were in balance."[13] Although a churchgoer, An-mei takes *The Twenty-Six Malignant Gates* more seriously than the Bible. While often consulting this Chinese superstitious booklet to avoid the predicted days of danger, she merely carries the Bible to church on Sundays "[a]s proof of her faith."[14] Later, as An-mei's pragmatic Christian faith collapses under the weight of suffering, the Bible is further neglected. It ends up "wedged under a too-short table leg, a way for her to correct the imbalances of life."[15] Such a relocation of the Bible signifies the final subjection of An-mei's pragmatic Christianity to her Chinese beliefs such as the Five Elements and *feng shui*.

Because suffering opposes *fu*, Tan's Joy Luck Christians are reluctant to translate the basic Christian concept of the cross into their belief system. In fact, as they are easily disillusioned with the Christian God who does not answer all their *ch'iu-fu* prayers, they find the experience of the cross a stumbling block to their faith. Such a discriminatory interpretation of Christianity is best illustrated by An-mei's reaction to the loss of her son Bing. After Bing drowns by the beach, An-mei seeks help from all directions: the Christian God, the Chinese water god, her mother's spirit, and finally her own *nengkan* (capability). Christianity is performed by An-mei as a foreign religious form filled with Chinese content: "She held in her hand the white Bible [and] called to God ... It began with 'Dear God' and ended with 'Amen,' and in between she spoke in Chinese."[16] The Chinese prayer An-mei addresses to the Christian God is mostly a "low-brow" Buddhist prayer in disguise. Like a Buddhist

---

12. Patricia Hamilton, "*Feng Shui*, Astrology, and the Five Elements: Traditional Chinese Belief in Amy Tan's *The Joy Luck Club*," *Studies in Twentieth Century Literature* 24:1 (2000) 125–45.
13. Tan, *Joy Luck Club*, 129.
14. Ibid., 122.
15. Ibid.
16. Ibid., 136.

layman, she goes to the temple (church), asks for good fortune, and offers money and meritorious acts as the payment for her bargain:

> "I have always believed in your blessing," she praised God in that same tone she used for exaggerated Chinese compliments. "We knew they would come . . . You rewarded us for our faith.
>
> "In return we have always tried to show our deepest respect. We went to your house. We brought you money. We sang your songs. You gave us more blessings . . . And now I have come to take Bing back."[17]

Bing is not returned. Disappointed by the Christian God, who fails to answer her prayers, An-mei puts her Bible aside and takes out a thermos and a teacup. She pours tea into the ocean to "sweeten the temper of the Coiling Dragon who lives in the sea."[18] She then throws her mother's sapphire ring to the sea, believing that by sacrificing her most precious treasure she would soften the dragon's heart. Still, Bing is not returned. At this point, An-mei's "faith" is stripped to its core: it is her own *nengkan* that she has believed in. To her daughter's amazement, An-mei swiftly takes off the inner tube from the car and ties it to the fishing line. She throws the "life-saver" into the sea, but it drifts away instead of bringing back Bing.

As observed by her daughter Rose, An-mei's self-reliant faith is no more than "just an illusion that somehow you're in control":

> My mother believed in God's will for many years. It was as if she had turned on a celestial faucet and goodness kept pouring out. She said it was faith that kept all these good things coming our way, only I thought she said "fate," because she couldn't pronounce that "th" sound in "faith."[19]

An-mei could not pronounce "th" in "faith," and instead she says "fate," a semi-religious concept familiar to most Chinese. As a representative of the Joy Luck Christians, An-mei's cross-cultural translation of Christianity is more pragmatic and syncretistic than faithful. The real meaning of the Christian faith remains as foreign as a language that An-mei cannot pronounce.

17. Ibid.
18. Ibid., 137.
19. Ibid., 128.

The Kitchen God's Wife

In *The Kitchen God's Wife*, Winnie's Christian faith closely resembles that of the Joy Luck Christians. After suffering tremendously from an abusive previous marriage in China during WWII, Winnie finds love in a Chinese American GI, Jimmy Louie. Winnie becomes a Christian mainly because of Jimmy, who serves as a Christian minister after returning to America. After she arrives in America, Jimmy's Christianity, as well as his fluency in the English language, becomes the reminder of his Americanness that alienates Winnie and makes her uncomfortable: "In America, I saw your father and I had both changed, and yet we had not. Our love was the same, but he now had his love for God. He could always speak English, I still could not."[20]

When Jimmy is dying with cancer, neither Winnie nor their daughter Pearl finds much comfort in the Christian faith. At Jimmy's funeral, Pearl finds her father "colorless and thin. And he was not resting peacefully with God."[21] Pearl confesses that she has never truly taken in the Christian faith introduced by her father:

> It's the same guilt I've felt before—when my father baptized me and I did not believe I was saved forever, when I took Communion and did not believe the grape juice was the blood of Christ, when I prayed along with others that a miracle would cure my father, when I already felt he had died long before.[22]

According to Tan's interviews and biographies, Jimmy is modeled after her own father, who worked as a Baptist minister and suffered a painful death when he was still in his middle age.[23] Perhaps Pearl's confession here reveals much of Tan's personal feelings about Christian faith.

Just like in *The Joy Luck Club*, it is the strong mother, not the weak father, who determines the spiritual consciousness of the Chinese American daughter. Winnie in many ways carries biographical traits of Tan's own mother, who was married to an abusive man and left her three

---

20. Amy Tan, *The Kitchen God's Wife* (New York: Ivy, 1991) 504.
21. Ibid., 49.
22. Ibid., 47.
23. The biographical information about Tan's brother and father can be found in different biographies and interviews. For example, see David Stanton, "Breakfast with Amy Tan," *Paintbrush* 22 (1995) 5–19. Tan admits many times that as a writer she is deeply affected by the tragic deaths of her father and her brother.

children in China before immigrating to the United States. Like Winnie, Tan's mother was also a believer in the spirits.[24] In contrast to the father's Christian belief that "the only ghost was the Holy Ghost," Winnie's syncretistic spirituality incorporates mystic and superstitious beliefs: "[S]he was always trying to suppress certain beliefs that did not coincide with my father's Christian ones, but sometimes they popped out anyway."[25]

At the end of the story, Winnie looks for a goddess statue for Pearl to put inside the empty altar she inherited from an old family friend. Disillusioned with all the male gods, Winnie buys a female statue that the factory has forgotten to put a name on, "a mistake" that nobody wants.[26] This mistake is perfect for Winnie, who happily names her "Lady Sorrowfree," a goddess who "will use her stick to chase away everything bad" so that there will be "no regrets in this world."[27] Submitted to her worshipper's wish, this statue represents neither an orthodox male deity like the Chinese Kitchen God, nor a Western deity like the Christian God. She is a goddess who shuns suffering and promises joy, luck, and "sorrowfree." Winnie's worship of Lady Sorrowfree in *The Kitchen God's Wife* and An-mei's worship of her own *nengkan* in *The Joy Luck Club* are fundamentally in the same fashion.

The Hundred Secret Senses

If *The Joy Luck Club* and *The Kitchen God's Wife* demonstrate how Christianity is disfigured by pragmatic and syncretistic cross-cultural mistranslation, *The Hundred Secret Senses* shows how the lack of a proper translation can make Christianity appear totally foreign and absurd. In the novel, as neither the Western missionaries nor the Chinese recipients have enough knowledge of each other's culture and language, Christianity's cross-cultural translation falls into the hands of two mischievous translators, whose intentional distortions are often playful and satirical.

---

24. The best biography on this aspect of Tan's life is by Sarah Lyall, "At Home with Amy Tan: In the Country of the Spirits," *New York Times*, December 28, 1995, online: http://www.nytimes.com/books/01/02/18/specials/tan-home.html.
25. Tan, *Kitchen God's Wife*, 43, 44.
26. Ibid., 531.
27. Ibid., 532.

In the novel, Olivia's half sister Kwan arrives from China full of Chinese superstitious dreams and stories, most of which are about Kwan's previous life as a peasant Hakka woman named Nunumu, or Moo. Moo/Kwan worked for American missionaries in Southeastern China in the 1860s, a time when China was trapped in the interwoven power struggles among the corrupted Manchurian rulers, the Tai Ping (Heavenly Kingdom) rebels, and various kinds of foreign intruders.

As in *The Joy Luck Club*, Christianity in *The Hundred Secret Senses* is identified as Western and portrayed through Moo/Kwan's Chinese lens as culturally alien and absurd. Just like the Joy Luck mothers who appear superstitious and mysterious in their American daughters' eyes, Kwan looks and talks so bizarrely to her American half-sister and stepmother that she is put in a mental hospital soon after her arrival. Kwan is therefore "endowed with the peculiar traits resonant of the *personage* which, particularly in the Elizabethan drama, was termed as the *fool*."[28] As a "fool," Kwan is allowed to make truthful statements that would normally be considered offensive. With Moo/Kwan being the only Chinese convert of the American mission, the novel presents a "foolish" interpretation that highlights the absurdity of the mistranslated Christianity.

Kwan's superstitious story about her previous life goes back to the year 1858 when she first meets the American missionaries. She takes her name, Nunumu—which is simplified to Moo by the Americans—from a legendary "God Worshipper" martyr. Moo/Kwan is given the name because she had lost one eye the day the real Nunumu died, and "people said this was a sign that Nunumu had chosen [her] to be her messenger, just as the Christian God had chosen a Hakka man to be the Heavenly King."[29] In this sense, Moo/Kwan becomes a prophet figure who speaks of spiritual truth. In the following years, her life revolves around the Heavenly Kingdom members, whom she calls "God Worshippers," and the American Christian missionaries, whom she refers to as "Jesus Worshippers."

The God Worshippers are followers of Hong Xiuquan, who was a real historical figure that claimed to be chosen by God as the younger Chinese brother of Jesus. Hong, or the Heavenly King, declared that he

---

28. Lina Unali, "Americanization and Hybridization in *The Hundred Secret Senses* by Amy Tan," *Hitting Critical Mass: A Journal of Asian American Cultural Criticism* 4:1 (Fall 1996) 140; emphasis original.

29. Amy Tan, *The Hundred Secret Senses* (New York: Ivy, 1995) 35.

was called to lead the oppressed Chinese people to fight the Manchu rulers. Hong's religion is accurately defined by historians as a syncretistic Christian cult, supplemented with many Chinese religious practices. Since Christian monotheism conflicts with the syncretistic Chinese religious tradition, Hong had a hard time incorporating Christian concepts such as monotheism and the Holy Trinity. Instead, he located the Christian God in a Chinese family diagram and regarded himself a member of it. Hence he had God the Father, Jesus the Elder Brother, and himself the younger brother of Christ.[30]

The God Worshippers' syncretistic adoption of Christianity, which is not unlike the Joy Luck Christians' approach, confuses Moo/Kwan, who "no longer [knows] what [she] should believe, whom [she] could trust."[31] For example, "to prove they abided by a Western calendar of fifty-two Sundays and not the sacred days of the Chinese almanac," the God Worshippers renounce the traditional Chinese Chong Yan festival, a day for people to climb up highlands in honor of their ancestors. When the day arrives, Moo/Kwan finds herself "walk[ing] down the mountain" instead of climbing up.[32]

If the God Worshippers' syncretistic Christian cult religion seems confusing, the Jesus Worshippers' Christianity is almost completely absurd to Moo/Kwan. The God Worshippers at least are Chinese (it is the "Christian," or "foreign," part of their religion that confuses Moo/Kwan), but the Jesus Worshippers are complete foreigners. As a Chinese peasant girl, Moo/Kwan knows neither the English language nor the cultural background of the American missionaries. To achieve a sense of familiarity with these Westerners, she has to first translate their names into Chinese expressions. For example, Moo/Kwan calls the missionary lady "Miss Mouse" because her name Lasher sounds like *laoshu* (mouse) in Chinese and she often appears "nervous" like a little scared mouse. In the same fashion, doctor Swan is called "Dr. Too Late" because Swan sounds like *suan-le* (too late) in Chinese. Moo/Kwan even adds a mocking comment about "Dr. Too Late": "no wonder sick people were scared to see him."[33] Moo/Kwan's playful translation of the missionaries'

30. Jordan Paper, *The Spirits Are Drunk: Comparative Approaches to Chinese Religion* (Albany, NY: SUNY Press, 1995) 248–58.

31. Tan, *Hundred Secret Senses*, 40.

32. Ibid., 40.

33. Ibid., 68.

names reflects the lighthearted attitude she takes toward their mission in general.

According to Sanneh, "vernacular translation begins with the effort to equip the gospel with terms of familiarity."[34] In *The Hundred Secret Senses*, however, such familiarity is never achieved as both the Western missionaries and Chinese recipients fail to overcome their cultural differences. As Moo/Kwan comments, the missionaries' "Chinese was so bad it sounded just like their English." Without knowing Chinese at all, Pastor Amen preaches sermons that are merely "a lot of sounds that only the other missionaries could understand."[35] The novel's depiction of the broken communication between the missionaries and the Chinese audience reflects the exact absence of Christianity's cross-cultural translation as proposed by Sanneh and Newbigin. In *Foolishness to the Greeks: The Gospel and Western Culture*, Newbigin warns that a Christian missionary "may simply fail to communicate: he uses the words of the language, but in such a way that he sounds like a foreigner; his message is heard as the babblings of a man who really has nothing to say."[36] The case of Pastor Amen is certainly worse, since he cannot even use "the words of the [Chinese] language."

To communicate with the Chinese, the missionaries have to depend on their interpreter Miss Banner, who "wasn't a religious kind of person" at all.[37] Resembling the Joy Luck Christians, Miss Banner adopts a pragmatic and superficial interpretation of the Christian faith. She joins the mission for food and housing and becomes the interpreter involuntarily. Like An-mei, Miss Banner abandons her faith after personal tragedies: "I prayed to God to save my brothers . . . . Religion teaches you that faith takes care of hope. All my hopes are gone, so why do I need faith anymore?"[38] Such a pragmatic approach to Christianity is frequently revealed in Miss Banner's translation of every Sunday service.

For example, Pastor Amen's "Welcome, welcome!" is translated into "Hurry-come into God's House! Eat rice after the meeting!"[39] At the end of the service, the three missionaries would sing along with Miss

34. Sanneh, *Translating the Message*, 208.
35. Tan, *Hundred Secret Senses*, 67.
36. Newbigin, *Foolishness to the Greeks*, 7.
37. Tan, *Hundred Secret Senses*, 65.
38. Ibid., 65.
39. Ibid., 66.

Banner's music box a song about Christian martyrdom and commitment. While "Mrs. Amen had tears pouring from her eyes," none of the Chinese understand her emotional reaction. Instead, "[s]ome of the old country people asked out loud if the box contained tiny foreigners."[40] We are told by Moo/Kwan that the music is originally "a German song about drinking beer, dancing, and kissing pretty girls." Although Mrs. Amen has turned it into a song with new spiritual words about following Jesus and having eternal life after death, to her Chinese audience, "that was the song . . . telling everyone to go outside to eat a bowl of rice, a gift from Jesus."[41]

To make the poorly understood service more entertaining, Miss Banner decides to ignore the pastor completely. Whenever Pastor Amen pauses for her to translate, she tells the Chinese congregation children's stories about an ancient giant and a princess. After about five minutes, she "would stop at a very exciting part and say something like: '"Now I must let Pastor speak for five minutes. But while you wait, ask yourself, Did the tiny princess die, or did she save the giant?"' At the end of the service, she would "[tell] people to shout 'Amen' if they were ready to eat their free bowl of rice. Ah, big shouts!"[42]

Miss Banner's intentional mistranslation intensifies the emptiness and absurdity of the message brought by the missionaries to their Chinese recipients. As a result, the mission bears no fruit. Although asked by the Jesus Worshippers every Sunday, Moo/Kwan has to confess her unbelief, until one day, she dreams of seeing Jesus as "a foreign man with long hair, long beard, many followers."[43] Moo/Kwan's dream of the foreign Jesus is immediately taken by the missionaries as an evidence of her conversion. This foreign image of Jesus suggests that, to both the Western missionaries and their Chinese "convert" Moo/Kwan, Christian faith is a superficial identification with Western culture. According to such an interpretation, Christianity cannot be translated cross-culturally but always remains trapped in its Western captivity.[44]

40. Ibid., 68.
41. Ibid.
42. Ibid., 69.
43. Ibid., 70.

44. In his book *The Christian Tradition: Beyond Its European Captivity* (Philadelphia: Trinity Press International, 1992), Joseph Mitsuo Kitagawa argues that Christianity has always been caught "captive" in Western culture. His opinions are challenged by Sanneh and Newbigin.

The Bonesetter's Daughter

The same pattern of mistranslation, which is pragmatic, syncretistic, and playful by nature, is exemplified in *The Bonesetter's Daughter*. A large portion of the novel is about LuLing's life in China during WWII, when she lives and works in an American mission orphanage. Associated with foreigners of "strange" ways, Christianity is assumed to be an American religion. Echoing Kwan, the Chinese convert LuLing declares that "the Christian heaven [is] like America, a land that [is] far away, filled with foreigners, and ruled by their laws."[45] Like those of the Joy Luck Christians, LuLing's belief is deeply rooted in Chinese folk religions, which are fundamentally pragmatic and syncretistic. Mirroring Moo/Kwan's comical interpretation of Christian beliefs and rituals in *The Hundred Secret Senses*, LuLing's playful involvement with the American Christian missionaries in *The Bonesetter's Daughter* also reveals the same external focus on Christianity's Western cultural embodiments.

For instance, to prevent either the Communist or the Japanese from burning down the Chinese temple, which they need for housing, the American missionaries decide to "convert the Chinese gods into Christians" by "baptiz[ing] them with paint."[46] By gluing sheep hair, noodles, and feathers to the temple statues, they manage to transform the Chinese gods into long-bearded, long-haired biblical figures and winged angles. LuLing describes the hilarious scene with a mocking tone typical of Tan's Chinese and Chinese American Christian characters:

> Buddha became fat Jesus, the Goddess of Mercy was Mary of the Manger, The Three Pure Ones, boss gods of the Taoists, turned into the Three Wise Men, and the Eighteen Lohan of Buddha were converted to the Twelve Apostles with six sons. Any small figures in hell were promoted to angels.[47]

Although some Chinese students are scared to affront the Chinese deities, LuLing pragmatically reasons that "[t]he Chinese gods understood that we were living in a Western household run by Americans. If the gods could speak, they, too, would insist that the Christian deities have the better position."[48] Echoing An-mei in *The Joy Luck Club*, LuLing fur-

---

45. Amy Tan, *The Bonesetter's Daughter* (New York: Putnam's, 2001) 267.
46. Ibid., 240.
47. Ibid., 241.
48. Ibid., 240.

ther declares, "I believed that if I was respectful to both the Chinese gods and the Christian one, neither would harm me."[49]

In *The Theory and Practice of Translation*, Eugene A. Nida and C. Taber assert that for accurate translation "the meaning must have priority over stylistic forms" whenever there is a conflict.[50] A proper cross-cultural translation of Christianity should, therefore, distinguish the basic meaning of the gospel from its Western cultural embodiment or style. In Tan's novels, however, most of the Chinese and Chinese American Christian characters seem to see little meaning of Christianity apart from its Western cultural forms. In *The Bonesetter's Daughter*, Christianity is reduced to its Western cultural shell, which, instead of carrying its original gospel, is filled with disguised Chinese gods. Under the cover of paint, sheep hair, noodles, and feathers are the same old Chinese religious idols, whose "baptism" is merely an external transformation into Western forms.

Tan's (Mis)Translation in Historical and Theological Perspective

Tan's characters' Chinese mistranslation of Christianity is by no means atypical. Historically speaking, Christianity's Chinese translation has encountered great obstacles in determining the right level of cultural compromise.[51] Instead of using the Scripture as the criteria for cultural evaluation and compromise, Chinese recipients of Christianity often indiscriminately cling to the Chinese religious framework. For instance, although the Jesuit missionaries in the seventeenth century introduced all the basic Christian doctrines to the Chinese, their Chinese recipients often (mis)translated the message selectively and eventually came up with their own version of Christian theology: "hexagrams proclaiming the glory of the Trinity; a *Tianzhu*-ism without Jesus; the primordial Chinese revelation that suffices to redeem our souls."[52] Under such an

49. Ibid.

50. Eugene A. Nida and C. Taber, *The Theory and Practice of Translation* (Leiden: Brill, 1969) 19.

51. For more information on this topic, see D. E. Mungello, editor, *The Chinese Rites Controversy: Its History and Meaning* (Nettetal, Germany: Steyler, 1994).

52. Erik Zürcher, "Jesuit Accommodation and the Chinese Cultural Imperative," in ibid., 31–64.

interpretation, heaven (*Tian*) preserves its Confucian and Buddhist connotations, and the Christian Lord of heaven (*Tianzhu*) only supplements instead of challenging the old beliefs. Consequently, other basic Christian notions such as "Original Sin, Incarnation and Redemption tend to become marginalized."[53]

In *People of the Book*, David Lyle Jeffrey asserts that Christianity is to embrace "riches from an alien source . . . if they can be properly baptized."[54] The Christian approach toward cultural appropriation "is not a syncretism but a discriminating borrowing according to fixed and ordinate principles laid down in Scripture itself."[55] Echoing Jeffrey, Sanneh cautions that "[t]he degree to which Christianity became integrated into a particular culture . . . was also a means of determining the level of compromise."[56] The apostle Paul, for example, is brought to a "radical tension with his own cultural roots" at his conversion.[57] To achieve a proper level of cultural compromise, the recipient translator's conversion is the crucial prerequisite. In Newbigin's words, after the gospel is translated into the recipient culture's language, what follows should be a "radical *metanoia*, a U-turn of the mind" on the recipient's part.[58] Perhaps these three scholars have best pointed out what is fundamentally lacking in Tan's characters' mistranslation of Christianity: a proper and discriminative cultural compromise achieved through the translator's sufficient knowledge of Scripture and internalized conversion.

Christianity's cross-cultural mistranslation in Tan's fiction reveals many compromises made at the cost of basic Christian doctrines, such as Christ's incarnation, sin, repentance, and the way of the cross. For instance, "the name of Jesus Christ," which "sums up everything" for Christianity," is almost never mentioned by Tan's Christian characters in *The Joy Luck Club*.[59] In *The Hundred Secret Senses*, Christ's image is presented in caricatures, either as a long-bearded foreign man in Kwan/Moo's dream or as a portrait hung next to that of Chairman Mao in Du Lili's room. In conflict with the monotheism of Christianity, Jesus is only

---

53. Ibid., 52.
54. David Lyle Jeffrey, *People of the Book* (Grand Rapids: Eerdmans, 1996) 107.
55. Ibid., 87.
56. Sanneh, *Translating the Message*, 37.
57. Ibid., 24.
58. Newbigin, *Foolishness to the Greeks*, 6; emphasis original.
59. Quoted in Sanneh, *Translating the Message*, 44.

one of the many gods in Kwan's interpretation: "You love Jesus, go Jesus House. You love Allah, go Allah Land. You love sleep, go sleep."[60]

The concept of sin has a twist of meaning in Tan's Chinese mistranslation. In the West, not all sins are crimes, and a sinner is not necessarily a criminal. To a Chinese mind, however, sin and crime are not strictly differentiated. The Chinese word for "sin/crime," *zui*, means "guilt" and "crime," and has social as well as religious connotations.[61] Therefore, it is understandable that Tan's characters consistently avoid being identified as sinners/criminals, and their confessions and repentances have little to do with sin. For example, in An-mei's most earnest confession delivered after Bing's death, she "repents" of being "careless."[62] With such distorted interpretations of sin and repentance, redemption becomes a self-help project that depends on the circumstance of "luck" and the human effort of *nengkan*.

Although suffering is an experience constantly shared by all of Tan's Chinese and Chinese American Christian characters, it is not understood in connection with the cross. Unable to recognize its redemptive power, Tan's characters regard suffering as the failure of *ch'iu-fu* and consider a Christian faith that cannot prevent suffering of little value. An-mei in *The Joy Luck Club* and Miss Banner in *The Hundred Secret Senses* both admit that they lost their faith after personal tragedies. Pastor Amen in *The Hundred Secret Senses* "lost not just his faith, but also his mind" after being cheated by General Cape, stoned by the God Worshippers, and deprived of food and other living supplies. As a parodic echo of Jesus's last words, "My God, my God, why have you forsaken me?" Pastor Amen cries out "'God, why did you betray me? Why?'" when he "lost his faith."[63] In contrast to Jesus who pleads to God to forgive his persecutors—"Father, forgive them; for they do not know what they are doing"—Pastor Amen shouts that he hates China and the Chinese people, who "have no souls to save."[64]

In *Foolishness to the Greeks*, Newbigin points out two mistakes that commonly appear in Christianity's cross-cultural translation. First, the

---

60. Tan, *Hundred Secret Senses*, 110.

61. Wolfran Eberhard, *Guilt and Sin in Traditional China* (Berkeley: University of California Press, 1967) 12–13.

62. Tan, *Joy Luck Club*, 136.

63. Mark 15:34; Tan, *Hundred Secret Senses*, 204.

64. Luke 23:34; Tan, *Hundred Secret Senses*, 204.

translator "may simply fail to communicate" if he translates the message superficially into the vernacular language without sufficiently understanding the recipient culture. Second, the translator may know the recipient's language and culture so well that "he is accepted all too easily as a familiar character" and his message is "simply absorbed into the existing world-view." The first kind of translation fails as "irrelevant" and the second "fall[s] into syncretism."[65] Both cases are evident in Tan's fiction. On one hand, the American missionaries/translators "simply fail to communicate"; on the other hand, the Chinese recipients/translators constantly and selectively program Christianity into their "existing world-view."

In *Real Presences*, George Steiner calls for a "responsible response" to the "real presences" of the authorial intention of a text.[66] Likewise, in *People of the Book*, Jeffrey notes that a responsible interpretation is a moral act hinged on "the *will* of the reader."[67] A responsible reader/translator should respect the authorial intention of the original text/message/Scripture; otherwise, "the interpreter can falsify the text by egocentrism in [her] own intentions."[68] In the case of Tan's characters, Christianity is often falsified into a religion that expresses the believers' "own intentions." As they manipulate Christianity into a religion of pragmatic benefits, they "see in the text just what [they want] to see, rather than the vision of its author."[69] Perhaps this explains the fundamental cause of their mistranslation: focusing on their own "will" to seek joy, luck, and *fu*, while neglecting the authorial intention of the gospel, Tan's characters often fail to make a "responsible response" to the "real presences" of Christianity.

Conclusion

As a cross-culturally translatable religion, Christianity should not be presented as a mere Western cultural enterprise, in spite of its many Western

---

65. Newbigin, *Foolishness to the Greeks*, 7.

66. George Steiner, *Real Presences* (Chicago: University of Chicago Press, 1989). Steiner attributes the playful or irresponsible reading of the text to the poststructuralist and deconstructionist notion of the "death of the author."

67. Jeffrey, *People of the Book*, 175; emphasis original.

68. Ibid., 183.

69. Ibid.

cultural embodiments. Instead, with the joint effort of both missionaries and the recipients, Christianity should always be cross-culturally translated into the recipient culture. An accurate cross-cultural translation of Christianity requires both the missionaries and the recipients to be responsible readers who are willing to submit their will to the authorial intention of the gospel. In Tan's fiction, however, essential Christian doctrines such as sin, incarnation, redemption, and the cross are never properly translated due to the lack of responsible and faithful translators. Christianity is either captive to its Western cultural embodiment or dissolved into a Chinese religious framework. Demonstrating the many obstacles and mistakes in Christianity's cross-cultural translation, Tan's fiction depicts Christianity's Chinese mistranslation.

THIRTEEN

Images of Religion in South Pacific Fiction

An Interpretation of Albert Wendt's *Pouliuli*

Jack A. Hill

Introduction

THE EMERGENCE OF AN indigenous South Pacific literary tradition in English is a relatively recent phenomenon. Most North Americans still associate literary works about the South Pacific with the novels of Western authors, such as James Michener (*Hawaii, Return to Paradise* and *Tales of the South Pacific*), Somerset Maugham (*The Trembling of a Leaf*), Herman Melville (*Typee: A Peep at Polynesian Life*), and Jack London (*The Cruise of the Snark: A Pacific Voyage*). While providing interesting and occasionally insightful sketches of island life, such classics have also perpetuated negative stereotypes of Pacific Islanders. For example, London depicts Melanesian hunters as ferocious cannibals, and Melville views Polynesian women as sexual playmates. But while island scholars have debunked the ethnocentric biases and distortions of Western authors, few North Americans have become familiar with literary developments in the region itself.[1]

---

1. See Raymond Pillai, "Directions in Fiji and Pacific Literature," in *Class and Culture in the South Pacific*, edited by Antony Hooper et al. (Auckland, New Zealand: Centre for Pacific Studies, University of Auckland, 1987) 104–14. See also Albert Wendt, "Novelists and Historians and the Art of Remembering," in Hooper, *Class and Culture*, 78–91.

Since World War II, Islanders throughout the South Pacific have begun to publish a variety of literary works in English.[2] This new wave of writing has arisen in tandem with the founding of both the University of Papua New Guinea in 1966 and the University of the South Pacific in Fiji in 1968, along with the concomitant rise of nation-states in the post-colonial era. In many respects, it represents a post-colonial literary development. It emerges in the midst of a modification of oral traditions and literatures, the dissipation of traditional worldviews, and the introduction to the islands of literacy and Western education. Although it entails discontinuities in terms of the use of oral forms of expression, it also preserves continuities by utilizing myths and legends. And, as one of the leading authorities on this genre of literature has argued, "These new directions are found at their best in the innovative adaptation of Western style fictional forms by the Samoan author, Albert Wendt."[3]

Albert Wendt's Fiction as Evocative of Religious Imagery

Perhaps the region's most prolific writer, and clearly the most important figure in this nascent tradition, Wendt has published numerous poems, essays, short stories, and novels, in addition to editing several anthologies of creative writing.[4] Although born into a Samoan family on October 27, 1939, in Apia, Samoa (formerly Western Samoa), he inherited his surname from a German ancestor. He received an MA in history at Victoria University in Wellington, New Zealand, was principal of Samoa College, taught at the University of the South Pacific (USP) in

---

2. For overviews of this nascent literature, see *Readings in Pacific Literature*, edited by Paul Sharrad (Wollongong, Australia: New Literatures Research Centre, University of Wollongong, 1993); and Ken Arvidson, "The Emergence of a Polynesian Literature," *World Literature Written in English* 14 (April 1975) 91–115. Albert Wendt provides a succinct overview of social and cultural antecedents of this literature in his "Introduction," in *Lali: A Pacific Anthology*, edited by Albert Wendt (Auckland: Longman Paul, 1980) xiii–xix.

3 Subramani, *South Pacific Literature: From Myth to Fabulation*, (rev. ed.; Suva, Fiji: Institute of Pacific Studies of the University of the South Pacific, 1992) ix–x. In the above paragraph, I draw heavily on Subramani's account of this nascent literary tradition in his "Preface" in *South Pacific Literature*, ix–xx.

4 For details on Wendt's publications, see Paul Sharrad and Karen Peacock, "Albert Wendt: Bibliography," *The Contemporary Pacific* 15:2 (2003) 378–420.

Suva, Fiji, and in 1988 became a professor of New Zealand literature at Auckland University.[5]

Wendt's career as a writer took a quantum leap with the publication of his third novel, *Pouliuli* (1977). Because the novel's protagonist has affinities with the tragic hero of *King Lear*,[6] reviewers tended to interpret it as a tragedy, focusing on the existential themes of madness, terror, and emptiness.[7] And indeed, at one level it can be read as a story of bitter despair in which an old village chief gradually loses his sanity while his family quarrels over who should succeed him. At another level, it is also a post-colonial, sociological critique of missionary Christianity, the old Samoan chiefly system, and the anomie associated with invasive Western social mores. But, as far as I am aware, none of the reviewers have explored the degree to which *Pouliuli* can also be read as a rich text that is evocative of images of religion. Although Wendt has gone on to write several other novels, including *Leaves of the Banyan Tree* (1979), *Ola* (1991), and *Black Rainbow* (1992), *Pouliuli* represents a particularly fresh and penetrating exploration of notions of religious transcendence.

Here, I argue that Wendt's multifaceted account of mythic traditions and the limits of human existence in *Pouliuli* is a potential resource for deepening our understanding of Pacific Islander's views of religion. However, although Wendt's fiction can be read as evoking religious imagery, I am not arguing that Wendt views himself as a religious person or that he would describe what he writes as expressive of a religious perspective. On the contrary, Wendt has frequently been maligned by fellow Pacific Islanders for his trenchant critiques of religious ideas and rituals. My argument is that while he is not viewed as a "religious voice" in any conventional sense of the term, he nevertheless provides positive images of religion (understood in a phenomenological way), which represent creative post-colonial responses to invasive missionary Christian forms.

---

5 For details on Wendt, see Robert Ross, editor, *International Literature in English* (New York: Garland, 1991); and Eugene Benson et al., editors, *The Routledge Encyclopedia of Post-Colonial Literature* (London: Routledge, 1994).

6 See K. O. Arvidson's review of Wendt's *Flying Fox in a Freedom Tree*, in *Land Fall* 29:1 (March 1975) 72–76.

7 Representative reviews include: Chris Tiffin, *Mana* 3:1 (Oct 1978) 140-42; *World Literature Today* 52 (Autumn 1978) 696; *World Literature Today* 52 (Spring 1978) 247; Sally Lodge, *Publishers Weekly* 218 (October 31, 1980) 83; and *Library Journal* 106 (February 15, 1981) 473.

Indeed, his critical approach to Christian motifs presupposes a complex moral and spiritual sensibility that is rarely articulated in the region today. Since the earliest "discoveries" of the islands by Europeans in the sixteenth century, indigenous religious traditions have been characterized as "pagan," relatively insignificant, and secondary to missionary Christian beliefs and practices, which were progressively introduced in the past three centuries. Consequently, the bulk of literature about religion in the Pacific islands has tended to focus on either the interaction between Christianity and indigenous traditions[8] or on the development of Christianity itself.[9] In fact, Christianity has become so widespread and entrenched in the region that the South Pacific has arguably become the most Christianized region in the world.[10]

And yet, as one travels throughout the region today, one senses disaffection with the life of the church. Youth, academics, and urban professionals are expressing frustrations with what they perceive as rigid structures and overly conservative theologies. There is a particular concern that churches perpetuate a neo-colonialist heritage where European hymns, liturgical forms, and architectural styles continue to characterize religious experience. This criticism has coincided with a revival of interest in indigenous "primal" or "local" religious traditions. However, the recovery and articulation of these pre-Christian roots has proved extremely difficult, although elements of these roots are still manifest in Pacific Islander experience today. Indeed, one of the reasons it is illuminating to focus on Wendt's work is that he makes numerous references to vestiges of pre-Christian religious ideas and attitudes in his fiction.

By looking at Wendt's work carefully then, my aim is to explore the cutting edge of post-colonial perspectives on religious life today in the South Pacific. I am thus not concerned with recapitulating conventional understandings of Christian faith or with rediscovering pre-Christian roots. Rather, I seek to shed light upon how at least one of the region's most creative scholars and artists is conceiving what is most important

---

8 See in this regard the classic study by Ernst Beaglehole, *Social Change in the South Pacific: Rarotonga and Aitutaki* (New York: Macmillan, 1957).

9 See the authoritative studies of the history of the church in the South Pacific by John Garrett: *To Live among the Stars: Christian Origins in Oceania* (Suva, Fiji: Institute of Pacific Studies, University of the South Pacific, 1982), and *Footprints in the Sea* (Suva, Fiji: Institute of Pacific Studies, University of the South Pacific, 1991).

10 See Manfred Ernst, *Winds of Change: Rapidly Growing Religious Groups in the Pacific Islands* (Suva, Fiji: Pacific Conference of Churches, 1994).

or ultimate in Pacific Islander experience. Drawing on both literary and social-scientific interpretive perspectives, I believe that popular narrative texts represent some of the best sources for understanding contemporary religious experience.[11] As the phenomenologist Alfred Schutz argues, the lyrical world of art constitutes a province of meaning in which there are virtually infinite spatial and temporal horizons.[12] However, before examining how Wendt portrays religion in a novel, it is important to clarify what is meant by the term "religion."

Toward a Definition of Religion

In order to investigate images of religion in literary texts, it is helpful to view religion as a distinct mode of consciousness. In the course of our daily routines, each of us attends to the world in different ways. On awaking in the morning, we may be aware of having just dreamed about a pleasant image or scenario. As we dress for the day, we may fantasize about actualizing that dream by, say, flying to a far away vacation destination. Working through a crossword puzzle over breakfast, we may focus our attention in a highly analytic way. But as we set aside the puzzle, we may also momentarily ponder the very nature of crossword puzzles as forms of recreation. We might ask, "What skills do they utilize?" or "What makes them enjoyable?" When we ruminate in this vein we are adopting a philosophical mode of consciousness.

As we drive to work, we ordinarily stop and go with a very mundane, matter-of-fact consciousness of driving. But the sight of a sunrise may evoke in us a sublime sense of beauty and wonder. That is, we may suddenly adopt an aesthetic mode of awareness. But, the starkness of the landscape beneath the colors on the horizon may also evoke a shudder deep within us. We may sense a profound loneliness or estrangement in creation. We may be overcome with a sense of dread. Or, conversely, we may be moved to an ecstatic experience of joy and grace—to a sense of being accepted and welcomed into creation. In either case, at this moment, we come up against the very limits of our mortality. In such

---

[11] See my discussion of Martha Nussbaum's approach in "Doing Ethics in the Pacific Islands: Interpreting Moral Dimensions of Prose Narrative," *The Annual of the Society of Christian Ethics* 12 (2001) 1–20.

[12] Alfred Schutz, *Collected Papers*, vol. 1: *The Problem of Social Reality* (Hague: Nijhoff, 1967) 347.

moments, we have a genuinely religious consciousness. But how is such a consciousness to be described?

Although this is not the place for a full-fledged account of religious consciousness, it is possible to delineate a preliminary point of departure by focusing on the concepts of symbol, lifeworld, and transcendence.[13] In the most basic sense, religion is a way of "seeing" the world that is mediated by symbols. A "symbol" can be defined as any object, person, act, event, or context that evokes a shift in modes of awareness within the lifeworld. The "lifeworld" can be understood as the broadest context of human experience. It includes all of our different modes of awareness or the entire range of our human experience. To exist is to exist totally within our lifeworld. But that existence is marked by numerous and continuous shifts between different modes of awareness. For the sake of argument, each of these shifts can be viewed as representing a "transcendence" from one way of being conscious to another. Consequently, in the course of a typical day, we experience many "transcendences," often between an ordinary commonsense, workaday attitude and other ways of attending to experience, such as fantasizing, philosophizing, and playing.

"Religion" can now be understood as a mode of awareness that evokes a transcendence of other transcendences. That is, it prompts a way of attending to human experience *as if* from a perspective beyond our lifeworld. Referring to the above illustration, what is happening when one shudders in dread at the starkness of a landscape is that an aesthetic mode of awareness has suddenly (and perhaps mysteriously) evoked a reflection on the self and the quality and meaning of one's existence, as if one were looking at it in its totality. In other words, in this moment of dread (or, conversely, in other moments of grace) the self comes up against the limits of its existence. It is acutely conscious of the potential of "not being" or, conversely, of "being" in a way not vulnerable to the precarity or the constraints of mortality. Accordingly, the transcendent character of religious consciousness is distinct in that it constitutes a transcendence of the other transcendences we experience in the lifeworld. However, it does not necessitate a belief in some other world, although it may entail, and traditionally has entailed, such beliefs.

---

13. See my appropriation of Alfred Schutz's description of the lifeworld for conceptualizing a religious mode of awareness in Jack A. Hill, *I-Sight: The World of Rastafari* (Evanston, IL: American Theological Library Association; Lanham, MD; Metuchen, NJ: Scarecrow, 1995) 121–37.

To sum up what has been said thus far, religion is mediated by symbols. Symbols evoke shifts in awareness within the broadest context of human experience, or the lifeworld. Religious symbols evoke ways of attending to experience as if from a perspective beyond the lifeworld. Let us now turn to an analysis of religious symbols in Albert Wendt's seminal novel, *Pouliuli*.

Discerning Images of Religion

Escape to Freedom

Pouliuli depicts the triumphs and tribulations of the *Fa'a Samoa* (Samoan way of life) in the latter part of the twentieth century.[14] The novel centers on Faleasa Osovae, the aging patriarch of the *Aiga Faleasa* (an extended kin group). When we first meet him, Faleasa, now 76, has been a model *alii* (high ranking traditional leader) throughout his lifetime. He has been a faithful husband, generous and stern father, deacon, lay preacher, powerful force on the *matai* council (a regional ruling authority), successful farmer and a nationally respected orator. While we are told that he is renowned for his "unimpeachable integrity" and "perfect health,"[15] the plot unfolds immediately when Faleasa abruptly and unexpectedly appears to go berserk.[16] He throws an extraordinary tantrum. Ranting, raving, and vomiting at will, he kicks everyone out of his *fale* (traditional Samoan home), tosses all the family's belongings into the yard, and demands to be left alone. We are told that he suddenly feels a deep revulsion about everything he has ever done or achieved. He is afflicted with an acute awareness of the hypocrisy and deceit of virtually all those around him. He regrets that he has given his whole life in *tautua* (service) to an *aiga* that essentially takes him for granted. The reader is struck by the regularity and intensity of this service when Faleasa, reflecting on his wild outburst, observes that this is the first day in his adult life that he

> . . . hadn't said any prayers, hadn't sung any hymns, hadn't read the Bible, hadn't pretended to like his thirty or so snotty-nosed

---

14. Albert Wendt, *Pouliuli* (Auckland: Longman Paul, 1977). *Pouliuli* is pronounced, "Pooh-lee-oo-lee."

15. Ibid., 1.

16 Samoans sometimes refer to persons "going under a cloud" as a way of describing seemingly irresponsible behavior which defies rational explanation.

grandchildren ... hadn't sacrificed a little bit more of himself for the sake of his *aiga*, village, and church.[17]

Faleasa's shocking behavior poses a primary question for the reader: "How do we understand what is going on with Faleasa?" After failing to placate him with his favorite foods, his wife and other family members quickly conclude that he has become temporarily insane. The cause of his sickness is attributed to possession by a vindictive *aitu* (spirit). Faleasa of course knows full well how his tantrums will be interpreted, and he decides to play along with the idea that he is possessed. In fact, the entire opening chapter can be read as a hilarious commentary on subtle twists in oratory and human naivety. When the pastor is sent to exorcise the *aitu*, Faleasa pretends to give voice to the soul of his dead mother, through which he castigates the wrongdoings of his *aiga*. This is a delightfully amusing sequence. After a trio of high-ranking leaders fails to gain ground with him, a *fofo* (traditional healer) is finally contacted. After conversing with the *fofo*, Faleasa sends him away with an arm full of family treasures, much to the chagrin of his immediate family.

Before commenting further on the plot development, let us note several ways in which Faleasa's tantrums represent the foreground of a background of religious experience.[18] Because the author writes from the perspective of the subjectivity of the protagonist, the reader is offered numerous insights into Faleasa's own self-conscious frame of reference. In contrast to the public perceptions of his behavior, Faleasa describes what is happening as a rebirth:

> Nothing about his past, he reflected, seemed real, important, vital, necessary—he had shed it all like a useless skin. Yes, he had been *reborn*; but he realized they would not accept his *new self* ...[19]

Faleasa's rebirth entails liberation from a self-definition that is thoroughly constrained by the way his kin and culture define him. Near the end of the first chapter he confides to his lifelong friend that he has been

---

17. Wendt, *Pouliuli*, 11.

18. Faleasa's tantrums can be interpreted in several ways. See Joseph Chadwick, "Allegories of the Novel in *Pouliuli*," in *Comparative Literature: East and West: Traditions and Trends: Selected Conference Papers*, edited by Cornelia N. Moore and Raymond A. Moody (Honolulu: University of Hawaii and the East-West Center, 1989) 151–61.

19. Wendt, *Pouliuli*, 6; emphasis added.

transformed from "'cannibal meat' into a 'free angel.'"[20] This new self is antithetical to the conventional Samoan Christian understanding of self. Whereas in the past Faleasa epitomized the "generous, always-willing-to-sacrifice-himself-for-them . . . provider, arbitrator, floor mat," now he embarked upon an "exhilarating battle for survival as a free man."[21] This new freedom overlaps with a rejection of familiar Christian practices. Faleasa plays with the local pastor and stops leading the evening *lotu* (worship) in his *fale*. He even attempts to drown out the *lotu* being conducted next door by playing loud secular music on his radio. In fact, his rebirth coincides with revulsion for what he now describes as a nonsensical Christianity.

Liberation in Darkness

At the same time that he rejects Christianity, Faleasa appears to embrace ancient Samoan cosmology. He discovers that it is "extremely healing to contemplate the Void."[22] The Void is dark, and the title of the novel, *Pouliuli*, is Samoan for "the Darkness." Later, Faleasa reflects upon the salvific role of Pouliuli in a story of a mythic hero, Pili.[23] Faleasa believes that this saga discloses the essence of pre-contact Samoan beliefs about the cosmos and humanity's place in it. In the story, Pili appears as an ugly lizard who is the offspring of the Supreme Creator, Tagaloaalagi, and a human woman, Sina, whom Tagaloaalagi had abducted. When Pili realizes that his father is Tagaloaalagi, he resolves to beg him to restore him to human form. However, approaching the Supreme Creator is taboo and so Pili enlists the support of three spirits, one of which is Pouliuli.

In a fascinating and complex narrative, Pili eventually does get restored to human form, but only by drawing upon Pouliuli's powers. Pili leaps into Pouliuli's huge mouth in order to vanish into thin air. From this invisible vantage point, Pili is empowered to negotiate his return to earth as a handsome youth. But although his reign is just and peaceful, discord ensues when he divides his kingdom among his offspring. When his pleas for peace are ignored and his only daughter calls him a useless old man, Pili vanishes from the village. It is said that he has jumped into

20. Ibid., 16.
21. Ibid., 6, 10.
22. Ibid., 7.
23. Ibid., 94–98.

the mouth of his friend, Pouliuli, and would refuse to become visible again. Identifying with Pili, Faleasa feels that he too had "voluntarily jumped up . . . into a living death, into the living darkness of Pouliuli."[24] Rather than being frightened, Faleasa is consoled by this image. It was "like being suspended in the core of a timeless sea, without a beginning or an end; [where] . . . all is well."[25]

Viewed in relation to Wendt's earlier work, this voluntary leap into Pouliuli might well represent a significant personal resolution and/or discovery. In his previous novel, *Sons of the Return Home*, the legend of the death of Maui is a recurring motif. Here Maui is a proud, Promethean figure who fails in his final self-imposed task of conquering death by re-entering the body of the Polynesian goddess, *Hine-nui-te-po* (the Great Woman of Darkness). She crosses her legs, barring him from immortality. But in *Pouliuli*, the leap into Darkness is portrayed as a free, genuine option that is metaphysically satisfying.[26]

Politics and Sensuality

Beyond his identification with Pili's leap into Darkness, Faleasa's contemplation of the Void is also linked to practical political activity. We are told that, after going up into the dark healing Void, he hatched a plot to oust an inept pastor. But, while anticipating the destructive thrust of the ouster, Faleasa also plans to save some of his closest friends. As if to stress the salvific character of Faleasa's plotting, the novelist employs a rare use of italics when he introduces the term "save" in this context. Faleasa is particularly concerned with "saving" his closest friend, Laaumatua, who is virtually the only member of the community who has not been deceitful or disloyal.[27] Faleasa's saving actions have added significance because Laaumatua, who hobbles around on a clubfoot, has heretofore been somewhat of an outcast in the community.

24. Wendt, *Pouliuli*, 97.

25. Ibid., 98. In his short story "Prospecting," Wendt explores the salvific and protective character of *Pouliuli*. The story appears in a special issue on Albert Wendt in *Echos du Commonweal*, edited by Jean-Pierre Durix, online: http://www.u-bourgogne.fr/ITL/echo_w1.htm.

26. This of course represents only one possible interpretation of the legend and its function in the novel. See K. O. Arvidson's discussion of Wendt's use of the legend of the death of Maui in his review of *Sons for the Return Home*, in *Land Fall* 28:3 (September 1974) 256–60.

27. Wendt, *Pouliuli*, 19–28.

In a reversal of motifs, Faleasa refers to Laaumatua and kindred spirits as "missionaries" to the rest of the conventional Christians, who are now viewed as "cannibals."[28] Later, after ousting the hypocritical pastor, Faleasa undermines a greedy *matai*'s quest for supremacy in the *aiga*. Near the end of the novel, he masterminds the election defeat of a crooked parliamentarian. In each of these episodes, under the guise of insanity, Faleasa acts as if on a mission, via his appointed "missionaries," Laaumatua and Moaula (Faleasa's favorite son), to try—albeit unsuccessfully—to bring about an iota of justice in an unjust situation.[29]

In addition to his political machinations, Faleasa also experiences a new consciousness of himself as an embodied being:

> —he realized that here was another marvelous quality of his new self. His wrinkled, scarred, thick hide had achieved a new and *miraculous sensitivity*: he could see with it, feel with it, think with it.[30]

This fresh consciousness represents a religious transcendence in the sense that it involves a whole new full life through sensuous awareness.[31] Faleasa even senses a new vitality in the scent of the stench of his own vomit. The novelist does not overtly develop this aspect of the protagonist's rebirth, but it underscores the degree to which Faleasa's transformation is *not* an otherworldly flight.

Moral Courage

These "free angel," "Pouliuli," politically activist, and embodied images of religion are all associated with the main plot in the novel, but the bulk of the development of the narrative consists of a series of minor subplots

28. Ibid., 17.

29 The bulk of Faleasa's gamesmanship has a recreational as well as a vindictive intent. He clearly revels in sticking it to adversaries. His actions may be interpreted on a number of levels, but our point is that his "rebirth," "spiritual transformation," and "freedom quest" are not divorced from renewed and intensified political activity.

30. Wendt, *Pouliuli*, 7; emphasis mine.

31 See the discussion of the full life through sensuality as a non-traditional way of being religious in Frederick J. Streng, Charles L. Lloyd, and Jay T. Allen, editors, *Ways of Being Religious: Readings for a New Approach to Religion* (Englewood Cliffs, NJ: Prentice-Hall, 1973). In Wendt's writings, the "sensual" is correlated with the self's willingness to embrace the night and engage in self-examination. See Evelyn Ellerman, "Intertextuality in the Fiction of Camus and Wendt," in Moore and Moody, *Comparative Literature*, 43–50.

woven into the fabric of the larger story. These subplots are depicted as flashbacks to Faleasa's childhood memories and represent micro-tales that suggest insights regarding the novelist's implicit understandings of religion. For example, in the second chapter we are introduced to Faleasa and Laaumatua as young boys. While Faleasa was born the only legitimate son of the most powerful *matai* in the village, Laaumatua was born the illegitimate son of a wayward daughter of the poorest *aiga* in the village. Whereas Faleasa enters the world at night as a healthy, screaming baby during a violent thunderstorm (viewed as a favorable omen), Laaumatua arrives during the glaring light of midday as a whimpering clubfooted infant. As a youngster, Laaumatua refers to his physical disability as "my burden," and he is stigmatized in the village as abnormal because of it.[32] But he compensates for his burden by being the fastest, toughest, strongest youth in the village.

In spite of these differences, the two quickly became friends. The main action in the chapter revolves around their surreptitious killing of someone else's pig and their subsequent efforts at a cover-up. As with all of Wendt's vignettes, this story can be interpreted on a number of levels. For our purposes, it is especially interesting to focus on the nature of Faleasa's confession to his father. At the moment of truth, Faleasa refuses to shift the blame for the wrongdoing onto his friend, even though Laaumatua had encouraged him to kill the pig. Moreover, when Faleasa's father derisively refers to Laaumatua as a "cripple," Faleasa holds his ground and vehemently denies that that is the case.[33] Faleasa's father is so stunned by his son's courageous audacity (to talk back to a father of such status would have been a severe breech of mores) that he does not even punish him.

Two redemptive elements surface in the story. One, Faleasa assumes his share of responsibility for the misdeed. Two, he steadfastly defends his friend, who is perceived as abnormal in the eyes of the community. These types of moral responses could be contrasted with those of Adam in the Genesis 3 creation story. Whereas, in the biblical narrative, Adam tries to shift the blame for his own disobedience onto Eve, in Wendt's vignette, Faleasa not only owns up to his complicity in wrongdoing, but also refuses to participate in the demeaning labeling of his co-conspirator—

---

32 Wendt, *Pouliuli*, 21.
33. Ibid., 28.

even given the likelihood of severe punishment. Here Wendt suggests that humans do have a capacity to transcend moral duplicity.

Spiritual Brokenness

Finally, underneath the surface of Wendt's apparent satirical realism lies a profound spiritual sensibility. This is illustrated in one of the most poignant vignettes in the novel: Faleasa's childhood memory of the sudden appearance of the mysterious "German." One day a scrawny, "strange-looking old man," covered with dark scars and sores and wearing only a "tattered *lavalava*" (wrap-around skirt traditionally worn by Samoan men), was seen sitting in front of the church. After some time he stood up, stretched his arms skyward, gazed fiercely into the light and opened his mouth "as if he was screaming in terrifying soundless pain."[34]

After collapsing, the old man is nursed back to health by the women and "the most skillful healer" in Faleasa's *aiga*.[35] Faleasa's father refers to him as an "important guest" and treats him as if he were a "blessing from God."[36] As the old man gradually regains his health, Faleasa becomes enchanted with him. He dreams that the old man is his father, but that rather than raising him in the traditional way, he encourages him to freely express his emotions and to talk about his thoughts:

> The dream ended with the old man picking him up gently and—laughing until the whole earth and sky and sea were alive with his joy—releasing him up into air as soft as feathers, where he floated, wheeled, swam, and turned cartwheels in limitless, endless freedom.[37]

The striking recovery of the old man reminds the youngster of a dazzling monarch butterfly before it frees itself from its cocoon. Referring to the German, Faleasa's father says, "fragile beauty had been born out of the crucible of madness and suffering."[38]

As the old man converses with villagers and leads morning prayers, he sparks a "contagious feeling of generous goodwill."[39] Faleasa's father

---

34. Ibid., 98; see also 99–114.
35. Ibid., 100.
36. Ibid.
37. Ibid.
38. Ibid., 101.
39. Ibid.

instructs Faleasa to be his companion, telling his son that he could learn much from the old man. The German breaks eating taboos by asking Faleasa to come and eat with him. Though illiterate, he repeats lengthy biblical passages from memory, noting that he was "merely an ignorant creature with an insatiable memory that wouldn't leave him alone."[40] Then the old man waxes philosophical about the gulf between the ancient oral traditions and the new literacy. He laments to the young Faleasa that he is imprisoned in his memory—that he cannot escape the "rapacious, fearless appetite of memory."[41] He praises the *papalagi* missionaries for bringing the magic of the written word to Samoa. And yet, at the same time that he extols the freedom associated with the printed word, he fears the word will not be capable of exorcising "the horror being born out of the world's collective memory."[42] Although Faleasa does not understand what the old man is talking about, he senses that he "had suffered as no man had suffered before, and that he was full of *alofa* [compassion], understanding and wisdom."[43]

Soon after he arrives, the old man begins to roam the village at night, taking objects from the church, the store, and various *fales*. Everywhere he pilfers things he leaves three circles of pebbles. When Faleasa discovers the petty thefts, the villagers decide to graciously tolerate them as small payments for the blessings he brings to the village. In an act of disobedience and betrayal, Faleasa then follows the old man in his nightly ritual and drives him from the village by disrupting his ritual behavior. In a dramatic scene, Faleasa rips the pebble from the old man's hand and hurls it into the darkness. The old man utters his soundless scream "unable to bear the world's pain any longer."[44]

In the course of this vignette, we learn that the old man was a Samoan raised by English missionaries, educated in Europe and became fluent in German. But after his missionary stepparents died of a mysterious illness, he accused them of having stolen his soul and replaced it with a crippled *papalagi* one. The London Missionary Society missionaries told their congregations that he was crazy. However, word spread that he could heal all kinds of diseases, that God was working through his

40. Ibid., 104.
41. Ibid.
42. Ibid., 105.
43. Ibid., 108.
44. Ibid., 113.

madness to cure illnesses and reward those who were kind to the unfortunate. He would not mention his parents and denied his education in Europe. He now spoke only Samoan and said that he was trying to find his true soul. The belief spread that he was in his own unique way a messenger of God—living proof of God's ability to suffer the world's pain.

Early in his encounter with the German, Faleasa senses that he has "suffered as no man suffered before."[45] Wendt depicts his outcry as a terrifying "soundless scream."[46] The source of his personal suffering is rooted in the discovery that his missionary parents (his real mother died while giving birth to him) and his mentors at the local theological college had stolen his soul and replaced it with a crippled *papalagi* soul. When he refuses to speak any other language than German and organizes military parades with his students at the college, he is kicked off the faculty and branded crazy by the missionaries. Rumors circulate that he fell in love with a generous widow who then died a horrible death, and that he once vowed to stay in a particular village for the rest of his life, but a famine had struck and to save the people he had moved out. From this time on he never again speaks English or German, but becomes fluent in Samoan, and tells all whom he visits that he is trying to find his true soul.

The redemptive quality of his suffering becomes evident when Faleasa's father remarks that "fragile beauty" has been born out of "the crucible of (his) madness and suffering."[47] The German's compassion is reflected in his reputation as a healer. Wherever he goes he is a catalyst for generating contagious feelings of well-being and rewards those who are kind to the unfortunate. Perhaps most significantly, he evokes a spirit of freedom in those he encounters. He encourages Faleasa, contrary to the way he has been raised according to the *Fa'a Samoa*, to freely express his emotions and thoughts—to say that he is, and to be in his saying. He has dreams of "limitless, endless freedom."[48] By extending an invitation to the young Faleasa to eat with him, the old man crosses one of the most sacred boundaries in the *Fa'a Samoa*. In response to his audacious hospitality, Faleasa falls in love with him. But this love proves too great, too radical, and too explosive, and Faleasa—socialized to control, repress,

45. Ibid., 108.
46. Ibid., 113.
47. Ibid., 101.
48. Ibid., 108.

and dominate—drives him away by violating the old man's fragile performance of sacred ritual in his liminal space.

Conclusion

I have sought to show that *Pouliuli* represents a rich resource for reflecting on fresh images of religion in today's rapidly changing South Pacific islands. Let us conclude by summarizing those images and elaborating upon the senses in which they are continuous with traditional cultural and religious experience.

First, in coming to be a "free angel," Faleasa begins the process of deconstructing his identity as a Samoan LMS Christian. He experiences a new mode of awareness as if from beyond the perspective of his lifeworld by being "reborn" in a way that appears to negate the taken-for-granted norms and meanings of the *Fa'a Samoa*. As his friend Laaumatua states, "The individual freedom you have discovered . . . is contrary to the very basis of our way of life."[49] Indeed, Faleasa's quest to live as a "free angel" appears to entail a self-preoccupation that flies in the face of the altruistic principle of service to others which is basic to the *Fa'a Samoa*. Only by radically disentangling himself from the chain of societal expectations associated with that ethos, as well as from European education, can he begin a genuine search for rebirth, for his true soul. It is by deconstructing himself as a Samoan LMS Christian that he prepares the ground for reuniting with his indigenous religious roots as they are evoked in the symbol of Pouliuli.

Second, by vicariously leaping into Pouliuli he experiences a mystical detachment from his ordinary everyday lifeworld. This identification with the Darkness represents a non-theistic and non-Trinitarian image of transcendence that is rooted in ancient Samoan cosmology. Just as Faleasa's rebirth as a free angel represents an anti-thesis in relation to the *Fa'a Samoa*, so his identification with Darkness represents an antithesis in relation to the imagery of light in Christianity. Again, the autonomy and agency of the self are highlighted. The act of leaping into Pouliuli is intrinsically an active, voluntary religious response. Here religious experience is not so much something done to the self as something done by the self.

---

49. Ibid., 17.

Moreover, being in relation to Pouliuli is to experience a living death: to be at least figuratively invisible to others in this world. It is to pass beyond the realm of ordinary perception into the unseen and to move into an ambiguous realm where one both lives in and is dead to this life at the same time. Here there may be some affinities with the Christian (Pauline) notion of being in the world yet not of the world. There is a peace, a sense that, in spite of the world's tension and violence, all is well. But to exist in Pouliuli is also to live in a mystical detachment. It is to be "suspended in a timeless sea, without beginning and without end."[50] This literary use of the image of Pouliuli suggests that research on religious experience in the Pacific islands might fruitfully explore how religious symbols in ancient myths and legends are appropriated in the contemporary lifeworlds of Pacific Islanders.

Third, Faleasa's efforts to save the "missionaries" in the midst of the "cannibals" highlight the down-to-earth, practical political dimension of his religious quest. By enlisting his newly ascribed missionaries to subvert and dissemble a hypocritical pastor, a greedy *matai*, and a crooked parliamentarian, Faleasa embarks upon a course of saving activity. To the extent that his political maneuvers are connected to his new consciousness, Faleasa's actions express a this-worldly image of religion that is not divorced from political behavior. Faleasa neither leaves the *aiga* nor retreats into a self-imposed isolation within it (even though he pretends to take himself out as a player by mimicking insanity). And once again, paradoxically, his missionary endeavors are in defense of some implicit sense of preserving what is good and just in the *Fa'a Samoa* itself.

Moreover, Faleasa experiences a transformed awareness of himself as a sensuous embodied being. He can know the other by sensing him through the pores of his skin. Even the sharp, penetrating stench of his vomit is evocative of a new feeling of vitality and freedom. Wendt's description of this sensitivity as miraculous suggests that there is a religious aspect to this heightened awareness of embodiment. Unlike the somewhat disembodied missionaries, Faleasa is now more firmly alive and aware of his self as a created being.

Fourth, the nature of Faleasa's bald confession regarding the killing of the pig evokes deep-seated moral sensibilities in the Samoan ethos. When Faleasa courageously stands up for his physically challenged friend, his father does not mete out the proscribed punishment for

---

50. Wendt, *Pouliuli*, 98.

disrespectful comeuppance. One implication for images of religion is that though humanity is certainly vulnerable to a full range of moral imperfections, it is not necessarily fallen. There is a latent capacity for authenticity, truth telling, and loyalty to the other who is outside the normative community. Though we act in ugly and duplicitous ways, we are not condemned to wallow in an unending cycle of self-delusion and defensiveness. We can and do transcend the limitations of the patterns of moral imperfections institutionalized in our lifeworlds. We possess, at heart, the potential to act, as we know we ought to act—without recourse to the intervention of external powers.

And finally, the centrality of the narrative of the old man in the novel suggests that the motifs of suffering, freedom, and compassion are paradigmatic for a contemporary Samoan religiosity. Faleasa's decision to escape into the "madness or silence" of the old man illuminates a significant religious subtext that has been overlooked in critical discussions of *Pouliuli*. While Faleasa's quest for meaning unfolds within a nihilistic horizon dominated by power struggles, self-abnegation, vanity, violence and the terror of two World Wars, the subtext is the enduring reality of the religio-moral vision of *Pouliuli*. In such a decaying social and moral order, in such a liminal period between the dissolution of the traditional *Fa'a Samoa* and the concomitant moral and spiritual vacuum of what Max Weber once described as the "Iron Cage" of the emerging technological order, Faleasa's escape becomes a form of liberating praxis. It is madness when viewed from the perspective of either the *Fa'a Samoa* or the technological order, but it represents a creative counter-space when viewed from a perspective beyond these lifeworlds. It is silence because the prevailing religious vocabulary is powerless to bring it to consciousness. As Faleasa laments, the language of Christianity no longer gives "meaning to the Void," and the missionaries did a thorough job of condemning ancient religious phenomena.[51] Silence thus represents a way of preserving the viability of a religious domain—evoked in Wendt's image of the soundless scream.

In the final analysis, this vignette is particularly significant because it becomes the paradigm for answering our question, "What is happening with Faleasa?" At the conclusion of the vignette we see Faleasa recollecting the story of the old man and his youthful betrayal of him. In retrospect, he views it as a vain betrayal of the love offered to him by

51. Ibid., 136.

the German. He then recognizes that his bid for freedom from the *Fa'a Samoa* is vanity. As the novel concludes, we see Faleasa on the church steps, a virtual mirror image of the German, with "arms outstretched, his mouth fixed in a soundless scream."[52] His friend Laaumatua comes to comfort him and takes him back to his *fale*. Faleasa's eyes reveal a profound vulnerability. He touches Laaumatua with a warm hand and smiles at him. While Faleasa sleeps, Laaumatua concludes that all life is vanity, that persons like Faleasa and himself—persons with heart and deep moral sensibilities—have lost out to the deceitful and hypocritical creatures of the new world. He passes a final benediction on Faleasa:

> Sleep on, my most precious friend, safe in the embrace of *Pouliuli*, the Great Darkness out of which we came and to which we must all return. Sleep on.... You have escaped.... Sleep on, my friend, while the world dreams of terror...[53]

In the end, Faleasa (like the German before him) is seen to be sitting in front of the church in the village "as if he had emerged out of the fabric of the church itself."[54] The church is dead or dying. The old man, and by implication, Faleasa, are now taking up the quest of searching for a true soul. The way or path of the old man, with which Faleasa now aligns himself, is fraught with an almost unbearable suffering. But this suffering is the potential crucible for an extraordinary freedom and vulnerable compassion. It does not yet have a vocabulary, but it is continuous with ancient mythopoeic experiences. It aims toward a transformation or discovery that entails a reintegration or reunion with the Great Darkness.

52. Ibid., 144.
53. Ibid., 145.
54. Ibid., 144.

PART FIVE

Christianity in Native America

FOURTEEN

Native-Christian Syncretism in Two Louise Erdrich Novels

Sinéad Moynihan

> The woman shall not wear that which pertaineth unto a man,
> neither shall a man put on a woman's garment:
> for all that do so *are* abomination unto the Lord thy God.
>
> Deuteronomy 22:5

Introduction

THIS CHAPTER EXAMINES THE ways in which the possibilities and limitations of Native-Christian (specifically, Roman Catholic) syncretism emerge in two novels by Louise Erdrich, a contemporary writer of Ojibway and German American ancestry. If, as Dennis Walsh asserts, the clear opposition Erdrich draws between Catholicism and shamanic religion in *Love Medicine* (1984) yields to a perceptible blurring of the two in *Tracks* (1988), I take Walsh's hypothesis further to argue that the figure of Father Damien Modeste in *The Last Report on the Miracles at Little No Horse* (2001) represents the ultimate crisis in the categories of Native versus Christian.[1] While Alison A. Chapman attributes the "complex web of borrowings, reappropriations, and transformations" of Ojibway and Catholic beliefs in *The Last Report* to Erdrich's rewriting of a series of saints' narratives, I argue that the potential and/or inadequacies of Native-Christian interactions are mapped upon the bodies

---

1. Dennis Walsh, "Catholicism in Louise Erdrich's *Love Medicine* and *Tracks*," *American Indian Culture and Research Journal* 25:2 (2001) 107–27.

of two women who "pass" in order to take up their Catholic vocations.[2] Pauline Puyat, a mixedblood who passes as white in becoming the nun Sister Leopolda, is one of two narrators in *Tracks*. Agnes DeWitt, the protagonist of *The Last Report*, cross-dresses as Father Damien Modeste from 1914 until her death in 1996. Racial/gender passing thus becomes an appropriate metaphor for the subjects' (in)ability to negotiate what are, apparently, opposing categories: Native versus Christian beliefs. By offering the reader two alternative—one "positive," one "negative"— embodiments of Native-Christian alliances, I argue that Erdrich's view of religious syncretism emerges as ultimately ambivalent.

Passing from Nun to Priest

The persistence of the notion that certain raced and gendered identities —socially constructed or otherwise—deviate from a norm that is white and male, is widely acknowledged. Passing as a strategy, though undoubtedly problematic, with the potential to expose the artificiality of the edifices of race and gender as tools of oppression is also a given. What happens, then, when raced and gendered identities collide with religious affiliation as a third category of identification? What if the religion in question is Christianity, which has historically responded in an ambiguous fashion to, and has been deeply implicated in, racial and gender oppression? If, in Western culture, the ascendancy is granted to those who are white, male, and Christian, what happens when one belongs to the dominant caste in some respects, but the subjugated group in (an)other(s), like Agnes/Father Damien in Erdrich's *The Last Report*?

In *Tracks* and *The Last Report*, Erdrich makes the Catholic clergy the starting point for her interrogation of Catholicism. The texts pose the question of whether Catholicism's colonialist function necessarily distances it irreconcilably from Native beliefs, or if the two might, in some contexts, actually prove compatible. In *Tracks*, which covers the years 1912 to 1924, two narrators, Nanapush and Pauline/Sister Leopolda, chart the decline of the Ojibway way of life on a North Dakota reservation through the combined forces of Old World diseases, harsh winters, and the General Allotment (Dawes) Act of 1887.[3] Spanning the

---

2. Alison A. Chapman, "Rewriting the Saints' Lives: Louise Erdrich's *The Last Report on the Miracles at Little No Horse*," *Critique* 48:2 (2007) 151.

3. The Dawes Act "divided reservation lands into allotments of 160 acres and 80 acres which were assigned, respectively, to the heads of families and other individuals

years from 1910 to 1996, *The Last Report*, published thirteen years after *Tracks*, traces through flashbacks the life of Agnes DeWitt. After a brief and unsuccessful spell as Sister Cecilia, a postulant in a Minnesota convent (1910–12), Agnes embarks on a romantic relationship with farmer Berndt Vogel. Following Berndt's death, Agnes takes the place and the name of Father Damien Modeste, a Catholic priest who dies in a flood while en route to the Indian mission at the same North Dakota reservation featured in *Tracks*. Agnes lives as Father Damien, dispatching regular epistles to the pope on various matters of importance to reservation life, until her suicide by drowning in 1996.

It is no coincidence that both Pauline and Agnes begin their religious lives as nuns, for the nun has, since the nineteenth century, functioned as a vexed figure in American literature. Escaped nuns' tales, such as Maria Monk's *Awful Disclosures of the Hôtel Dieu Nunnery* (1836)—the bestselling novel in the U.S. prior to the appearance of Harriet Beecher Stowe's *Uncle Tom's Cabin* (1852)—purported to be true accounts of their Protestant heroines' horrific experiences at the hands of nuns and priests. The salacious, titillating tales of convent life which began to appear in the 1830s—in which convents are depicted as "essentially priests' brothels"[4]—are deeply embedded in a more general "othering" of Catholicism throughout United States history.[5] In particular, the appearance of escaped nuns' tales coincided with a sharp increase in the number

---

over the age of eighteen." The act was designed "to hasten the integration of Indians into American society by promoting the growth of commercial agriculture on reservations. Allotted lands were held in trust for a period of twenty-five years, during which it was hoped that Indians would learn to become efficient farmers and acculturate to white ways through converting to Christianity and pursuing formal education at off-reservation schools" (Helena Grice et al., *Beginning Ethnic American Literatures* (Manchester: Manchester University Press, 2001) 41.

4. Susan M. Griffin, "Awful Disclosures: Women's Evidence in the Escaped Nun's Tale," *PMLA* 111:1 (1996) 95.

5. Interestingly, this "othering" of Catholicism has, in some cultural contexts outside the United States, taken the form of a preoccupation with cross-dressing nuns, priests, and monks. As Marjorie Garber observes, in eighteenth- and nineteenth-century British gothic novels, and novels inspired by the gothic form, the "notorious deployment of gender travesty in a religious context provided not only titillating shock value but also a 'reading' of Catholicism as hypocritical and erotic, something to be unmasked." The significance of the religious transvestite figures in Matthew Lewis's *The Monk* (1796) and Charlotte Bronte's *Villette* (1853), respectively, is, according to Garber, "as much England/France and Protestant/Catholic as it is male/female: the phantom appearance of the transvestite, once again, marks a category crisis *elsewhere*" (Marjorie Garber, *Vested Interests: Cross-Dressing and Cultural Anxiety* [London: Penguin, 1993], 218).

of predominantly Catholic German and Irish immigrants to the United States. This fascination with nuns in nineteenth-century convert tales is thus reflective of the ambiguous position occupied by Catholicism, as opposed to other Christian denominations, in the United States. For while Catholicism has undoubtedly performed a colonising function in its mission to Christianize Native Americans, it has itself always been considered "other" in the United States through its association with various immigrant groups.

It is not surprising, given this historical context, that Erdrich draws upon—sometimes seriously, sometimes playfully—the escaped nuns' tales in her novels, toying with the legacy of the literary nun as a vexed figure. This is most apparent in the postulant Marie Lazarre's encounter with the sadistic Sister Leopolda in Erdrich's first novel, *Love Medicine*. Like the Protestant girls in the nineteenth-century stories, Marie is seduced by the iconography and symbolism of Catholicism, imagining herself becoming a saint "carved in pure gold. With ruby lips. And [her] toenails would be little pink ocean shells, which they would have to stoop down off their high horse to kiss."[6] That a Native girl might be so devout echoes *Awful Disclosures*, in which Monk claims that "[m]any of the Indians were remarkably devoted to the priests, believing everything they were taught."[7] At the convent, however, Leopolda (who, unbeknownst to Marie, is her mother), subjects Marie to relentless abuse in the name of holiness—pouring boiling water on her back and stabbing her with a fork. Having failed to "run back down the hill" after the first violent incident, Marie finally decides to "[r]ise up and walk!", escaping the nun and the convent.[8] In *The Last Report*, meanwhile, Erdrich recalls the conflation of convent and brothel in the nineteenth-century nuns' tales. When Sister Cecilia (Agnes DeWitt) leaves the convent and arrives at Berndt Vogel's farm, Berndt thinks at first that the stranger "must be a loose woman, fleeing a brothel."[9]

---

6. Louise Erdrich, *Love Medicine* (New York: Bantam, 1987) 40.

7. Maria Monk, *Awful Disclosures of the Hotel Dieu Nunnery*, in Maria Monk and Rebecca Reed, *Veil of Fear: Nineteenth-Century Convent Tales*, edited by Nancy Lusignan Schultz (West Lafayette, IN: Purdue University Press, 1999) 47.

8. Erdrich, *Love Medicine*, 49, 56.

9. Louise Erdrich, *The Last Report on the Miracles at Little No Horse* (London: Flamingo, 2001) 13.

Central to Erdrich's interrogation of Christianity is her construction of Agnes DeWitt/Father Damien Modeste and Pauline Puyat/Sister Leopolda as narrative doubles. Like Pauline Puyat, who becomes Sister Leopolda, Agnes also begins her religious life in a convent as the novice nun Sister Cecilia. Both Pauline and Agnes undergo symbolic deaths in undertaking their Catholic vocations, their rebirths demanding changes of nominal and physical identity. Pauline becomes Sister Leopolda and has her hair "chopped from [her] head with a pair of shears."[10] Agnes assumes the name Father Damien Modeste, and a masculine identity along with it. Agnes keeps Leopolda's "secret" (that she murdered Napoleon Morrissey) in order that her own secret identity will not be revealed. A section of the novel entitled "Leopolda's Passion" is followed directly by a chapter called "Father Damien's Passion."[11] The identities of Father Damien and Sister Leopolda are thus intimately bound up with one another. However, the relationship between Damien and Leopolda is deeply antagonistic because Damien knows that the supposed miracles for which Leopolda is responsible are, in fact, merely a means of covering up her violent acts.

Theology of the Body

In the conflict between Leopolda and Damien, the body becomes the principal battleground. In Catholic teaching, of course, the body emerges as a site of profound ambivalence. On the one hand, it appears to be preoccupied with circumscribing and delimiting the body; on the other, it seems to affirm the possibility of transcending one's body. The Catholic hierarchy, intervening through canon law and papal encyclicals, seeks to regulate the body, sex, and reproduction, issues that in some other Christian religions are considered matters of individual conscience. The Church's opposition to and prohibition of pre-marital sex, artificial methods of contraception, abortion and homosexuality, are well known. In fact, the basic symbol of Christianity, the cross, is "the shape of an object whose significance is the body that was nailed to it."[12] This image is remarkable for evoking the body as a fixed, immobile entity—contained by and within the cross shape—and is thus an effective metaphor for the

---

10. Louise Erdrich, *Tracks* (London: Hamish Hamilton, 1988) 205.
11. Erdrich, *Last Report*, 336–41, 342–51.
12. Richard Dyer, *White* (London: Routledge, 1999) 15.

Catholic Church's attempts to impose bodily boundaries. Father Jude Miller, who comes to the reservation to establish whether the now-deceased Leopolda is eligible for sainthood, is the mouthpiece for some of these views when he claims that "[i]ntercourse outside the boundaries of marriage hurts the order or things. Creates disorder. Breaks traditions, vows, families. Creates such . . . problems."[13] Agnes's cross-dressing as Father Damien thus appears to contravene several key tenets of Catholic dogma. Most obviously, she assumes the role of priest, a vocation still denied to Catholic women. Formerly a novitiate nun, Agnes's decision to cross-dress as a priest in 1912 coincides roughly with the circumscription of the autonomy of the women's orders in 1917.[14] Indeed, Agnes, in her priest's garb, immediately notices that Kashpaw, who meets her off the train to take her to the reservation, "treated her with much more respect as a priest than she'd ever known as a nun."[15] The Catholic Church's persistent refusal to ordain women, even as other Christian churches do, is one of the reasons for which many feminists find the Church inherently misogynistic.

In ostensible contradistinction to this obsession with containing the body as symbolized by the crucifix, in English language usage, *cross* and *crossing* often evoke the very opposite connotations of bodily mobility and transgression. Furthermore, Catholicism embraces a non-essentialist conception of the self that is not contained *in* or *by* the body. The self in traditional Christianity is intangible, indefinable, and is usually called the soul. It is the soul that accedes to eternal life after the earthly body has expired. In *The Last Report*, it is this more liberating politics of the cross that (in Agnes's case) Erdrich seeks to explore, privileging the receptiveness of Christianity—specifically Catholicism—to notions of bodily transformation and finding therein the potential for reconciling Agnes's lifelong gender disguise with her Catholicism. Of course, disguise is far from anathema to the Catholic faith. In reminding adherents that God is omnipresent and to encourage them to see God in all his creatures, Catholicism teaches that God may appear in many guises.

The coexistence of these apparently incongruent conceptions of the body enables Erdrich to interrogate Christianity, and the potential

---

13. Erdrich, *Last Report*, 135.

14. Sara Maitland, *A Map of the New Country: Women and Christianity* (London: Routledge and Kegan Paul, 1983) 58.

15. Erdrich, *Last Report*, 62.

for a melding of Christian and Native beliefs, through the bodies of Sister Leopolda and Father Damien. A war is waged over the extent to which each can exert corporeal control, master their own bodies, become subjects rather than objects. Leopolda's marriage of the two belief systems leads to paralysis, Damien's to mobility. Leopolda's conversion to Catholicism is accompanied by attempts at bodily mortification; Damien's Catholicism enables bodily transformation. Leopolda ultimately strives for bodily containment, Damien for bodily transcendence. As a cross-dressing priest, Agnes/Damien corroborates Marjorie Garber's observation that

> the apparently spontaneous or unexpected or supplementary presence of a transvestite figure in a text (whether fiction or history, verbal or visual, imagistic or "real") that does not seem, thematically, to be primarily concerned with gender difference or blurred gender indicates a *category crisis elsewhere*, an irresolvable conflict or epistemological crux that destabilizes comfortable binarity, and displaces the resulting discomfort onto a figure that already inhabits, indeed incarnates, the margin.[16]

In *The Last Report*, the categories in crisis are Ojibway religious beliefs versus Catholicism.

As in many passing narratives, the passer's ambiguously gendered or raced body is often presented in terms of his or her mobility between places, races, genders, and cultures. If Damien is "welcome where no other white man was allowed," Pauline is aware that if she never sees Nanapush, Fleur, or the Kashpaws again, they will not miss her.[17] Damien's association with mobility is evident from his very first appearance in *Tracks*. During the harsh winter of 1912, Fleur and Nanapush almost become frozen statues, "the slivers of ice" collecting and covering them so that they "become so heavy, weighted down with the lead gray frost, that [they] could not move."[18] Significantly, the pair are liberated from their immobility by the arrival of Father Damien, who bursts through their cabin door, "causing that great crack of light to interfere with death."[19] By contrast, Pauline Puyat is associated throughout with immobility, which is similarly wrought in terms of congealing, particularly after she enters

---

16. Garber, *Vested Interests*, 17.
17. Erdrich, *Last Report*, 276; Erdrich, *Tracks*, 196.
18. Erdrich, *Tracks*, 6.
19. Erdrich, *Last Report*, 80.

the convent. During a cold winter spent there, her blood "never thawed." When Nanapush tempts her with hot, sweet tea in an effort to force her to urinate and thus violate her self-imposed twice-a-day rule, she tries to resist by making herself "into a block of ice."[20]

Elsewhere in *Tracks*, her immobility takes the form of paralysis. When she witnesses Fleur's rape at the hands of the men with whom they both work, she realizes, in retrospect, that she "should have gone to Fleur, saved her, thrown [herself] on Dutch the way Russell did once he unlocked [her] arms."[21] Instead, she experiences a kind of paralysis and is powerless to rescue her. After they return to the reservation and Fleur, pregnant with her second child, enters premature labor, Pauline again undergoes a type of paralysis that renders her useless. She claims that "the Lord overtook [her] limbs and made them clumsy," ensuring that she cannot "work [her] arms, [her] hands properly, [her] fingers."[22] In contrast, when she is inflicting violence on others, she is finally able to overcome her paralysis. In strangling her former lover, Napoleon Morrissey, "the only things left of intelligence" are her hands: "What I told them to, then, they accomplished."[23]

While Pauline is all "angles and sharp edges, a girl of bent tin," she longs for the fluidity that marks the bodies of the lovers Fleur Pillager and Eli Kashpaw, who "swelled and shrank" in relation to each other.[24] Pauline greatly envies Fleur's mobility and the power that accompanies it. In mediating between Misshepeshu, the water monster, and the people, Fleur is "the one who closed the door or swung it open."[25] Pauline hopes that through converting the Ojibway people to Christianity, she will fulfill a similar intermediary function: "There would have to come a turning, a gathering, another door. And it would be Pauline who opened it, same as she closed the Argus lockers."[26] But if Fleur is the "hinge," then Pauline is merely "a piece of wall," attempting to shore up boundaries rather than sidestep them.[27] By contrast, Agnes's mobility between genders and

20. Erdrich, *Tracks*, 136, 150.
21. Ibid., 26.
22. Ibid., 157.
23. Ibid., 202.
24. Ibid., 71, 72.
25. Ibid., 139.
26. Ibid., 139.
27. Ibid., 139, 76.

cultures is most explicitly depicted through Damien's friendship with Nanapush, named for the Ojibway trickster.[28] Her cross-dressing, which becomes a metaphor for her ability to transcend linguistic and cultural barriers, recalls the trickster's "transformational powers to escape from difficult situations" and his/her "control over . . . physical boundaries."[29]

Passing between Native and Christian Beliefs

Damien's at-one-ness with his ambiguously gendered body and Pauline's alienation from her racially mixed body are reflected in the ways in which they fuse Catholic and Ojibway traditions. While Damien begins to practise a mixture of faiths, discovering that *"[t]he ordinary as well as esoteric forms of worship engaged in by the Ojibwe are sound, even compatible with the teachings of Christ,"* Pauline can only substitute one for the other. For Damien, Ojibway and Christian figures can coexist with no apparent difficulty: *"Saint Augustine, Nanabozho, whoever can hear me, give me a little help now,* he prayed."[30] For Pauline, by contrast, this is an uneasy alliance, signalled by her attempt to dispel her nightmares by hanging a Native American dreamcatcher alongside the crucifix above her bed. But this "only spun the dreams through, thicker, faster, until [she] ceased to sleep at all."[31] Pauline sees Native and Christian beliefs in completely oppositional terms. Her rejection of Ojibway practices in favor of Christianity is symbolically evoked when she shoots a bear who invades Fleur Pillager's cabin while Fleur is giving birth to her daughter, Lulu.[32] Among the Ojibway, "[b]ear hunting was conducted according to complex religious procedures." Treatment of the bear "approached the level of veneration."[33] Although she does so to protect the inhabitants of Fleur's cabin, in shooting the bear, Pauline fails to respect the procedures by which Ojibway bear-hunting rites ought to be conducted. Significantly,

---

28. Several critics have discussed Nanapush's affinities with the mythical trickster. See, for example, Sheila Hassell Hughes, "Tongue-Tied: Rhetoric and Relation in Louise Erdrich's *Tracks*," MELUS 25:3/4 (2000) 91.

29. Jeanne Rosier Smith, *Writing Tricksters: Mythic Gambols in American Ethnic Literature* (Berkeley: University of California Press, 1997) 73–74.

30. Erdrich, *Last Report*, 49, 266; emphasis original.

31. Erdrich, *Tracks*, 66.

32. Ibid., 60.

33. Sam D. Gill, *Native American Religions: An Introduction* (Belmont, CA: Wadsworth, 1982) 117.

Father Damien, en route to Fleur's cabin to baptize Lulu, encounters the banished bear and by instinct, splashes it with holy water.[34] Performing the ritual of baptism, an important Christian ceremony for initiating infants into God's community, Damien (somewhat comically) registers his respect for the bear, and by extension, Ojibway customs.

Of course, the most obvious and effective way in which Erdrich reveals the compatibility of Christian and Native traditions is through Damien's embodiment of the cross-dresser-as-spiritual-leader. When Kashpaw first encounters Damien, he mistakes the priest for a (male) berdache:

> The priest was clearly not right, too womanly. Perhaps, he thought, here was a man like the famous Wishkob, the Sweet, who had seduced many other men and finally joined the family of a great war chief as a wife, where he had lived until old, well loved, as one of the women.[35]

Rather than the more well-known male-to-female role in certain Native traditions, Father Damien, a cross-dressing female, recalls, more accurately, the existence of a female cross-gender role in at least thirty-three Native American tribes.[36] What is interesting about this role is the extent to which it mirrors the priest's duties and responsibilities in Catholicism, including priestly celibacy and its concomitant childlessness. Female *berdaches* eschewed marriage,[37] and, like a priest, cross-gender females did not bear children once they assumed their masculine occupations:

---

34. Erdrich, *Last Report*, 183.

35. Ibid., 64. I use the term "berdache" because it is the most commonly used and accepted anthropological term. However, some critics, such as Paula Gunn Allen, understandably take exception to the application of this term because its Arabic etymology connotes "sex-slave boy" (see Allen, *The Sacred Hoop: Recovering the Feminine in American Indian Traditions* [Boston: Beacon, 1992], 199).

36. Evelyn Blackwood, "Sexuality and Gender in Certain Native American Tribes: The Case of Cross-Gender Females," *Signs* 10 (1984) 29. Will Roscoe calls this figure a "female berdache," which he defines as "anatomical females occupying a named social status involving cross- or mixed-gender economic and social behavior, sometimes partial and/or occasional cross-dressing, and sometimes relationships with (non-berdache) women" (*Changing Ones: Third and Fourth Genders in Native North America* [New York: St. Martins, 1998], 73). Although I am only concerned with Father Damien's berdachism here, Julie Barak notes these kind of crossovers in many other Erdrich characters. See Barak, "Blurs, Blends, Berdaches: Gender Mixing in the Novels of Louise Erdrich," *Studies in American Indian Literatures* 8:3 (1996) 49–62.

37. Roscoe, *Changing Ones*, 73.

"Their kin considered them nonreproductive and accepted the loss of their childbearing potential, placing a woman's individual interests and abilities above her value as a producer."[38] Most significantly, the female *berdache* role often comprehended a spiritual element. Cross-gender females "were inspired by dreams or visions, had shamanic powers, or were sanctioned by tribal myths."[39] Like the shamanic female *berdache*, Agnes's call to the priesthood occurs in a dream. She claims to have been nursed back to health after the flood by a man whom she believes to be Christ: *"Be thou like as me, were His words, and I took them literally to mean that I should attend Him as a loving woman follows her soldier into the battle of life, dressed as He is dressed, suffering the same hardships."*[40]

Significantly, this passage is as evocative of the Catholic tradition of female-to-male transvestite saints as it is of the female *berdache* that figures in certain Native cultures, echoing the words of Saint Jerome that a woman who "wishes to serve Christ more than the world ... will cease to be a woman and will be called man."[41] The most celebrated of these saints is, of course, Saint Joan of Arc (1412–31).[42] Indeed, it was for transvestism, not for heresy, that Joan was put on trial by the Inquisition.[43] There was even, according to legend, a ninth-century female pope. Pope Joan, whose real name is believed to have been Agnes, was exposed as a woman when she gave birth during a papal procession.[44] Thus, although such transformations were acceptable only in the sense that it was believed that the status of manhood was closer to God than womanhood, these saints are nevertheless remarkable for their "destabilization of gender identity" in "a tradition usually seen to cast gender in fairly fixed and dualistic terms."[45]

38. Blackwood, "Sexuality and Gender," 31.

39. Roscoe, *Changing Ones*, 73.

40. Erdrich, *Last Report*, 43–44; emphasis original.

41. Quoted in Garber, *Vested Interests*, 214.

42. Other famous transvestite saints include Saint Eugenia of Alexandria, who lived as a monk until she was rejected the romantic attentions of Melanthia, a woman she had cured. Melanthia responded by accusing the monk of forcing himself sexually upon her. At the subsequent trial, over which her father presided, Eugenia was forced to disrobe to prove her innocence.

43. Garber, *Vested Interests*, 215.

44. Ibid., 215.

45. Elizabeth Castelli "'I Will Make Mary Male': Pieties of the Body and Gender Transformation of Christian Women in Late Antiquity," in *Body Guards: The Cultural*

Erdrich constructs Damien's mobility between his own Catholic faith and that of the Ojibway people by evoking imagery, incidents, and characters that are meaningful—indeed common—to both belief systems. For instance, Agnes becomes Father Damien after a flood, one of the great apocalyptic images in the Judeo-Christian tradition. Swept away atop her grand piano, Agnes encounters a dead priest, killed in the flood, whom she knows to have been en route to an Indian mission. Assuming his clothes and his name, Agnes is reborn as Father Damien Modeste and makes her way to Little No Horse to take his place. In the centrality of flood imagery, Erdrich echoes Ojibway folklore, in which the woodland trickster Nanabozho is credited with making the world new after a great flood.[46] Indeed, while Damien, through his female-to-male cross-dressing, is reminiscent of the shaman in Native traditions, "the most provocative cosmological symbol in Ojibway shamanism is the character of Nanabozho."[47] The friendship that develops between Father Damien and Nanapush—named after Nanabozho—thus highlights the complementary nature of their respective roles as spiritual leaders. The Ojibway woodland trickster, Nanabozho, "served as the intermediary between the power spirits and the people, and, as such, had the power to transform himself at will in order to perform his tasks."[48] A priest carries out a similar kind of intermediate function between God and the devout, and in Agnes's case she actually transforms herself into a man in order to do this.

Through Pauline's and Damien's diametrically-opposed interpretations of their shared religious affiliation, Erdrich configures Catholicism as a permeable membrane through which subjects of different gender or racial/ethnic and cultural identities may "pass." For Pauline, the incorporation of the trappings of Catholicism leads to violence. After all, she strangles Napoleon Morrissey with a rosary made of barbed wire[49]

Politics of Gender Ambiguity, edited by Julia Epstein and Kristina Straub (New York: Routledge, 1991) 47.

46. Christopher Vecsey, *Traditional Ojibwa Religion and Its Historical Changes* (Darby, PA: Diane, 1993) 84.

47. John A. Grim, *The Shaman: Patterns of Religious Healing among the Ojibway Indians* (Norman: University of Oklahoma Press, 1987) 85.

48. Connie A. Jacobs, *The Novels of Louise Erdrich: Stories of Her People* (New York: Peter Lang, 2001) 73.

49. Erdrich, *Tracks*, 201–2; Erdrich, *Last Report*, 163.

and stabs her daughter, Marie, with a fork, subsequently claiming that the stigmata have been miraculously bestowed upon her.[50] However, the sympathetically-drawn Father Damien suggests that Catholicism and Ojibway beliefs may be fused in a healthy, rewarding manner. Louise Erdrich's work thus provides an example of a writer who addresses "the conflicts between Catholicism and their individual cultures with an ambivalence, an internally divided attitude informed in part by the fact that Catholicism was imported into those cultures through colonialism."[51] Jeana DelRosso's analysis of the attitudes of certain women writers towards Catholicism, "positions from which they variously and often simultaneously view the church as vehicle of repression, of subversion, or of liberation," holds true for Pauline and Agnes.[52] The unforgiving portrait of Catholic/Ojibway syncretism that appears in *Tracks* yields, thirteen years later in *The Last Report*, to a sympathetic portrayal of Father Damien. Across Erdrich's oeuvre as a whole, therefore, her view of religious syncretism emerges as ultimately ambivalent.

---

50. Erdrich, *Last Report*, 136; idem, *Love Medicine*, 55–56.

51. Jeana DelRosso, "The Convent as Colonist: Catholicism in the Works of Contemporary Women Writers of the Americas," *MELUS* 26:3 (2001) 183.

52. Ibid., 185.

Contributors

Isabel Asensio-Sierra is Assistant Professor of Spanish at Weber State University, Utah. Originally from Spain, she graduated with a doctorate in comparative literature from Vanderbilt University, Tennessee. She has authored several publications and has presented numerous papers at various international, national, and regional conferences. Her research and teaching focus on contemporary Spanish American and Brazilian women's writing. She is currently working on the translation of Chilean writer Pía Barros's book *La Grandmother y otros* (2007).

Di Gan Blackburn graduated from Beijing International Studies University in 1995. She received a master's degree in American studies in 1998 and a doctorate in English in 2004, both from Baylor University, Texas. Her dissertation is entitled "Christianity in Contemporary Asian American Literature: (Mis)-Translations of the Word." Her publications include "Chinatown, Home, and the Trapped Daughters: Novels by Chinese American Women Writers of the 1990s" in *Captive and Free: Colonial Incarceration* (2001), as well as articles in *Asian American Poets: A Bio-bibliographical Critical Sourcebook* (2002). Her current research interest is Christian life in Communist China, especially from the 1950s to the 1970s.

Mini Chandran is Associate Professor of English in the Department of Humanities and Social Sciences at the Indian Institute of Technology, Kanpur, Uttar Pradesh, India. She is currently working on issues of literary censorship in India. She was a journalist for four years before coming to academics and has also translated numerous short stories and essays from English to Malayalam (a regional Indian language).

Evgenia V. Cherkasova is Associate Professor of Philosophy at Suffolk University, Boston. She holds a doctorate in philosophy from Pennsylvania State University and a bachelor's degree in mathematics from Moscow State University. Originally from Russia, Cherkasova is a generalist whose scholarly and pedagogical interests include ethics, moral psychology, philosophy of art, phenomenology, and existentialism. She is the author of many articles in peer-reviewed journals, essay collections, and encyclopedia. Her most recent publication is a book entitled *Dostoevsky and Kant: Dialogues on Ethics* (2009).

John Estes has published poetry and prose in over seventy journals. He is the author of *Kingdom Come* (2010) and two chapbooks: *Swerve*, which won a 2008 National Chapbook Fellowship from the Poetry Society of America, and *Breakfast with Blake at the Laocoön* (2007). He holds a doctorate in English and creative writing from the University of Missouri.

Jack A. Hill is Associate Professor of Religion (Social Ethics) at Texas Christian University, Fort Worth. He has authored books on Rastafarian ethics (*I-Sight: The World of Rastafari* [1995]), visions of a new South Africa (*Seeds of Transformation: Discerning the Ethics of a New Generation* [1998]), and most recently, *Ethics in the Global Village: Moral Insights for the Post 9-11 USA* (2008). He has also published three textbooks for extension education programs in theology and ethics in the South Pacific, as well as seminal articles on pedagogical theory and practice. He is the recipient of his college's Distinguished Lecture Series Award. Besides research and teaching, Hill is an ordained minister of the Christian Church (Disciples of Christ), and he facilitates workshops on ethics and teaching for diversity around the country.

J. A. Jackson is Assistant Professor of English at Hillsdale College, Michigan. His most recent publications include an article on the Revelation to John and apocalyptic hermeneutics, entitled "'And They Sang a New Song': Reading John's Revelation from the Position of the Lamb" (in *Contagion* 12 [2006]), and *Levinas and Medieval Literature: The "Difficult Reading" of English and Rabbinic Texts* (2009), coedited with Ann W. Astell. He has been invited to give lectures on Eastern Orthodoxy at various venues, has presented numerous times on Eastern Orthodoxy at international conferences, and has taught a seminar on Eastern Orthodox Christianity.

Ellin Sterne Jimmerson has a doctorate in U.S. history from the University of Houston, a Master of Theological Studies with a concentration in Latin American liberation theology from Vanderbilt Divinity School, Tennessee, and is an ordained Baptist minister. A writer, her interests include the liberationist poems of Nicaragua's Ernesto Cardenal and illegal migration. Her essay "In the Beginning—Big Bang: Violence in Ernesto Cardenal's Cosmic Canticle" will appear in *Subverting Scripture*, edited by Beth Benedix, in 2009. Her documentary on illegal migration, *DESCONOCIDA unidentified female*, narrated by Martin Sheen and shot in Alabama, Arizona, and Mexico, brings major migration issues into focus. It will be released in 2009.

Ymitri Mathison is Associate Professor of English at Prairie View A&M University, Texas. Her areas of specialization are nineteenth- and twentieth-century British literature, postcolonial literature, children's literature, and American multicultural literature. She has published articles on Hanif

Kureishi, Farrukh Dhondy, Robert Louis Stevenson, R. M. Ballantyne, and H. Rider Haggard, and has an article forthcoming on Kenneth Grahame. She has also published numerous encyclopedia entries on African American and Asian American fiction writers.

Catherine Winn Merritt is currently pursuing a master's degree in early modern studies at the University of Alabama. She plans to continue into a PhD program and focus predominantly on cultural studies and literature, including oral traditions of mythology and folklore. In 2007 she graduated summa cum laude from Auburn University Montgomery, Alabama, where she was recognized as an Outstanding Student of English. She continues to participate in Omicron Delta Kappa, Phi Kappa Phi, and Sigma Tau Delta.

Darren J. N. Middleton is Professor of Religion at Texas Christian University, Fort Worth. Born and raised in England, he has published six books, including *Theology after Reading: Christian Imagination and the Power of Fiction* (2008), and he recently received one of TCU's highest honors, the AddRan College of Humanities and Social Sciences Award for Distinguished Achievement as a Creative Teacher and Scholar. He is currently working on a book entitled *Globalizing Rasta: Film, Literature, Music, Religion*.

Mozella G. Mitchell is Professor and Chair of the Department of Religious Studies at the University of South Florida, Tampa. She received her doctorate in literature and theology from Emory University, Georgia. In addition to numerous articles in professional journals and edited collections, she is the author of *Crucial Issues in Caribbean Religions* (2006), *New Africa in America: The Blending of African and American Religious and Social Traditions among Black People in Meridian, Mississippi, and Surrounding Counties* (1995), and *Spiritual Dynamics of Howard Thurman's Theology* (1986).

Sinéad Moynihan is a Leverhulme Early Career Fellow in the School of American and Canadian Studies at the University of Nottingham, England, where she completed her doctorate on narratives of passing in 2006. A monograph based on her doctoral dissertation, entitled *Passing into the Present: Contemporary American Fiction of Racial and Gender Passing*, is forthcoming. She is currently working on a book project entitled *"Other People's Diasporas": Negotiating Race in Contemporary Irish and Irish-American Culture*.

J. Stephen Pearson recently received his doctorate in comparative literature from the University of Georgia and now teaches English at the University of Tennessee, Knoxville. His research examines analogies and intersections between ethnic minority and religious literatures. His publications include discussions of the Americanization of the Chinese Monkey King character in novels by Gerald Vizenor and Patricia Chao, the application of borderlands theory to the Vita of St. Catherine of Genoa, and the depiction of Benedictine community as a form of diaspora in Kathleen Norris. He is currently expanding the topic of his chapter in this volume by exploring the role of Christianity in Asian American literature.

Eric J. Sterling is Distinguished Research Professor of English at Auburn University Montgomery, Alabama. Originally from Queens, New York, he has published three books: *The Movement Towards Subversion: The English History Play from Skelton to Shakespeare* (1996), *Life in the Ghettos During the Holocaust* (2005), and *Arthur Miller's Death of a Salesman: Dialogue* (2008). His book *Continuum Handbook to Seventeenth-Century Literature* will be published in 2010. Sterling teaches composition, business writing, dramatic literature of various eras, Shakespeare, and Jewish literature of the Holocaust.

For Further Reading

IN ADDITION TO THE sources included elsewhere in this volume, the following represents a selected list of sources for the study of Christianity in the non-Western world. We have divided this section into two main areas, fiction and non-fiction:

Fiction

Achebe, Chinua. *Arrow of God*. London: Heinemann, 1977.
Adichie, Chiamanda Ngozi. *Purple Hibiscus: A Novel*. Chapel Hill, NC: Algonquin Books of Chapel Hill, 2003.
Alfeyeva, Valeria. *Pilgrimage to Dzhvari: A Woman's Journey of Spiritual Awakening*. New York: Bell Tower, 1993.
Anaya, Rudolfo A. *Bless Me, Ultima*. New York: Grand Central, 1994.
Bacho, Peter. *Cebu*. Seattle: University of Washington Press, 1991.
Beti, Mongo. *The Poor Christ of Bomba*. Translated by Gerald Moore. London: Heinemann, 1971.
Bulgakov, Mikhail Afanas'evich. *The Master and Margarita*. Translated by Mirra Ginsburg. New York: Grove, 1987.
Cha, Teresa Hak Kyung. *Dictée*. Berkeley, CA: Third Woman, 1995.
Clitandre, Pierre. *Cathedral of the August Heat*. Translated by Bridget Jones. New York: Readers International, 1987.
Craven, Margaret. *I Heard the Owl Call My Name*. Garden City, NY: Doubleday, 1973.
Davis, Thomas R. A. H. *Vaka: Saga of a Polynesian Canoe*. Suva, Fiji: Institute of Pacific Studies, University of the South Pacific, 1992.
Endō, Shūsaku. *Deep River*. Translated by Van C. Gessel. New York: New Directions, 1994.
―――. *Silence*. Translated by William Johnston. New York: Taplinger, 1980.
Grace, Patricia. *Cousins*. London: The Women's Press, 1993.
Greene, Graham. *The Honorary Consul*. New York: Penguin, 2008.
Kamakau, Samuel M. *Ka Po'e Kahiko: The People of Old*. Honolulu, HI: Bishop Museum Press, 1991.
Kazantzakis, Nikos. *The Greek Passion*. Translated by Jonathan Griffin. New York: Simon and Schuster, 1953.
Kingsolver, Barbara. *The Poisonwood Bible: A Novel*. New York: HarperFlamingo, 1998.
Kogawa, Joy. *Obasan*. New York: Anchor, 1981.
Lawton, Harry, and George Knox. *Buddha, Confucius, Christ: Three Prophetic Plays*. New York: Herder and Herder, 1971.
Lee, Li-Young. *The Winged Seed: A Remembrance*. New York: Simon and Schuster, 1995.

Mandelstam, Osip. *Modernist Archaist: Selected Poems*. Edited by Kevin M. F. Platt, with translations by Charles Bernstein et al. Santa Monica, CA: Whale and Star, 2008.

Montero, Mayra. *The Messenger: A Novel*. Translated by Edith Grossman. New York: HarperFlamingo, 1999.

Ngũgĩ wa Thiong'o. *The River Between*. London: Heinemann, 1965.

Papadiamantēs, Alexandros. *The Boundless Gardens: Selected Short Stories*. Edited by Lambros Kamperidis and Denise Harvey. Limni, Greece: D. Harvey, 2007.

Wiebe, Rudy Henry. *The Blue Mountains of China*. Grand Rapids: Eerdmans, 1970.

Ziedan, Youssef. *Beelzebub*. Cairo, Egypt: Dar al Shoruk, 2008.

Non-Fiction

Adeyemo, Tokunboh, editor. *Africa Bible Commentary: A One-Volume Commentary Written by 70 African Scholars*. Grand Rapids: Zondervan, 2006.

Adogame, Afe, et al., editors. *Christianity in Africa and the African Diaspora: The Appropriation of a Scattered Heritage*. New York: Continuum, 2009.

Alba, Richard, et al., editors. *Immigration and Religion in America: Comparative and Historical Perspectives*. New York: New York University Press, 2008.

Alvarez, Alma Rosa. *Liberation Theology in Chicana/o Literature: Manifestations of Feminist and Gay Identities*. New York: Routledge, 2007.

Amireh, Amal, and Lisa Suhair Majaj, editors. *Going Global: The Transnational Reception of Third World Women Writers*. New York: Routledge, 2000.

Anderson, Allan. *An Introduction to Pentecostalism: Global Charismatic Christianity*. New York: Cambridge University Press, 2004.

Aponte, Edwin David, and Miguel A. De La Torre, editors. *Handbook of Latina/o Theologies*. St. Louis: Chalice, 2006.

Balling, Jakob. *The Story of Christianity: From Birth to Global Presence*. Grand Rapids: Eerdmans, 2003.

Banchoff, Thomas, editor. *Religious Pluralism, Globalization, and World Politics*. New York; Oxford: Oxford University Press, 2008.

Barrett, David J., et al., *World Christian Encyclopedia: A Comparative Survey of Churches and Religions in the Modern World*. 2 vols. New York: Oxford University Press, 2001.

Bastide, Roger. *The African Religions of Brazil: Toward a Sociology of the Interpenetration of Civilizations*. Translated by Helen Sebba. Baltimore: Johns Hopkins University Press, 2007.

Bauman, Chad M. *Christian Identity and Dalit Religion in Hindu India, 1868–1947*. Grand Rapids: Eerdmans, 2009.

Bautista, Julius, and Francis Lim Khek Gee, editors. *Christianity and the State in Asia*. New York: Routledge, 2009.

Bays, Daniel H., and Ellen Widmer, editors. *China's Christian Colleges: Cross-Cultural Connections, 1900–1950*. Stanford: Stanford University Press, 2009.

Bediako, Kwame. *Christianity in Africa: The Renewal of a Non-Western Religion*. Maryknoll, NY: Orbis, 2002.

Bednarowski, Mary Farrell, editor. *Twentieth-Century Global Christianity*. A People's History of Christianity 7. Minneapolis: Fortress, 2008.

Benson, Bruce Ellis, and Peter Godwin Heltzel, editors. *Evangelicals and Empire: Christian Alternatives to the Political Status Quo*. Grand Rapids: Brazos, 2008.

Biddle, Arthur W., et al. *Global Voices: Contemporary Literature from the Non-Western World*. Upper Saddle River, NJ: Prentice Hall, 1994.

Blewett, Timothy, et al., editors. *British Foreign Policy and the Anglican Church: Christian Engagement with the Contemporary World*. Burlington, VT: Ashgate, 2008.

Bonk, Jonathan J., editor. *Encyclopedia of Missions and Missionaries*. New York: Routledge, 2007.

Brinkman, M. E. *The Non-Western Jesus: Jesus as Bodhisattva, Avatara, Guru, Prophet, Ancestor, or Healer?* London: Equinox, 2008.

Brock, Rita Nakashima, et al., editors. *Off the Menu: Asian and Asian North American Women's Religion and Theology*. Louisville, KY: Westminster John Knox, 2007.

Chesnut, R. Andrew. *Competitive Spirits: Latin America's New Religious Economy*. New York: Oxford University Press, 2007.

Chidester, David. *Christianity: A Global History*. San Francisco: HarperOne, 2001.

Chung, David. *Syncretism: The Religious Context of Christian Beginnings in Korea*. Edited by Kang-nam Oh. Albany, NY: SUNY Press, 2001.

Clark, Donald N. *Christianity in Modern Korea*. Lanham, MD: University Press of America; New York: Asia Society, 1986.

Collins, Paul M. *Christian Inculturation in India*. Burlington, VT: Ashgate, 2007.

Compier, Don H., Kwok Pui-lan, and Joerg Rieger, editors. *Empire and the Christian Tradition: New Readings of Classical Theologians*. Minneapolis: Fortress, 2007.

Cox, Harvey Gallagher. *The Silencing of Leonardo Boff: The Vatican and the Future of World Christianity*. Oak Park, IL: Meyer-Stone, 1988.

Cushner, Nicholas P. *Why Have You Come Here?: The Jesuits and the First Evangelization of Native America*. New York: Oxford University Press, 2006.

Damrosch, David. *What Is World Literature?* Princeton: Princeton University Press, 2003.

Dawson, Andrew. *New Era, New Religions: Religious Transformation in Contemporary Brazil*. Burlington, VT: Ashgate, 2007.

Deena, Seodial Frank H., and Karoline Szatek. *From Around the Globe: Secular Authors and Biblical Perspectives*. Lanham, MD: University Press of America, 2007.

De La Torre, Miguel A., editor. *Handbook of U.S. Theologies of Liberation*. St. Louis: Chalice, 2004.

Dube, Musa W. *Postcolonial Feminist Interpretation of the Bible*. St. Louis: Chalice, 2000.

Ecklund, Elaine Howard. *Korean American Evangelicals: New Models for Civic Life*. New York: Oxford University Press, 2006.

Ehshete, Tibebe. *The Evangelical Movement in Ethiopia: Resistance and Resilience*. Waco, TX: Baylor University Press, 2009.

Ellis, Stephen, and Gerrie Ter Haar. *Worlds of Power: Religious Thought and Political Practice in Africa*. London: Hurst and Co., 2004.

Elmore, Mark, and Caleb Heart Lyer Elfenbein, editors. *Missions, Management and Effects: A Reader in Religion and Colonialism*. London: Equinox, 2009.

Freston, Paul. *Evangelical Christianity and Democracy in Latin America*. New York: Oxford University Press, 2008.

Frykenberg, Robert Eric. *Christianity in India: From Beginnings to the Present*. New York; Oxford: Oxford University Press, 2008.

Gabriel, Theodore P. C. *Christian Citizens in an Islamic State: The Pakistan Experience*. Burlington, VT: Ashgate, 2007.

Gallagher, Susan VanZanten, editor. *Postcolonial Literature and the Biblical Call for Justice.* Jackson, MS: University of Mississippi Press, 2007.

———. "Reading and Faith in a Global Community." *Christianity and Literature* 54:3 (2005) 323–40.

Garrard, John, and Carol Garrard. *Russian Orthodoxy Resurgent: Faith and Power in the New Russia.* Princeton: Princeton University Press, 2009.

Gillquist, Peter E. *Becoming Orthodox: A Journey to the Ancient Christian Faith.* Ben Lomand, CA: Conciliar, 1992.

Goodwin, Stephen R., editor. *World Christianity in Local Context.* Essays in Memory of David A. Kerr 1. New York: Continuum, 2009.

———. *World Christianity in Muslim Encounter.* Essays in Memory of David A. Kerr 2. New York: Continuum, 2009.

Guadeloupe, Francio. *Chanting Down the New Jerusalem: Calypso, Christianity, and Capitalism in the Caribbean.* Berkeley: University of California Press, 2008.

Gunn, Giles. "Introduction: Globalizing Literary Studies." *PMLA* 116 (2001) 16–31.

Gupta, Suman. *Globalization and Literature.* Cambridge, UK: Polity, 2009.

Hanciles, Jehu J. *Beyond Christendom: Globalization, African Migration, and the Transformation of the West.* Maryknoll, NY: Orbis, 2008.

———. *Euthanasia of a Mission: African Church Autonomy in a Colonial Context.* Westport, CT: Heinemann, 2002.

Hansen, Holger Brent, and Michael Twaddle, editors. *Christian Missionaries and the State in the Third World.* Athens: Ohio University Press, 2001.

Hassett, Miranda K. *Anglican Communion in Crisis: How Episcopalian Dissidents and Their African Allies Are Reshaping Anglicanism.* Princeton: Princeton University Press, 2007.

Hastings, Adrian, editor. *A World History of Christianity.* Grand Rapids: Eerdmans, 1999.

Hawley, John C. *Christian Encounters with the Other.* New York: New York University Press, 1998.

Held, David, et al. *Global Transformations: Politics, Economics and Culture.* Stanford: Stanford University Press, 1999.

Hopkins, Dwight N., and Marjorie Lewis, editors. *Another World Is Possible: Spiritualities and Religions of Global Darker Peoples.* London: Equinox, 2009.

Jacobsen, Knut A., and Selva J. Raj, editors. *South Asian Christian Diaspora: Invisible Diaspora in Europe and North America.* Burlington, VT: Ashgate, 2008.

Jenkins, Philip. *The New Faces of Christianity: Believing the Bible in the Global South.* New York: Oxford University Press, 2006.

———. *The Next Christendom: The Coming of Global Christianity.* Rev. and expanded editor. New York: Oxford University Press, 2007.

Jewett, Robert. *Mission and Menace: Four Centuries of American Religious Zeal.* Minneapolis: Fortress, 2008.

Johnson, Todd M., and Kenneth R. Ross, editors. *The Atlas of Global Christianity.* Edinburgh: Edinburgh University Press, 2009.

Jongeneel, Jan A. B., et al., editors. *Christian Mission and Education in Modern China, Japan, and Korea: Historical Studies.* Frankfurt: Peter Lang, 2009.

Kalu, Ogbu U., editor. *Interpreting Contemporary Christianity: Global Processes and Local Identities.* Grand Rapids: Eerdmans, 2008.

Kang, Wi Jo. *Christ and Caesar in Modern Korea: A History of Christianity and Politics.* Albany, NY: SUNY Press, 1997.

Keller, Catherine, et al., editors. *Postcolonial Theologies: Divinity and Empire*. St. Louis: Chalice, 2004.
Kieh, George Klay, Jr., editor. *Africa and the New Globalization*. Burlington, VT: Ashgate, 2008.
Kim, Sebastian, and Kirsteen Kim. *Christianity as a World Religion*. New York: Continuum, 2008.
Koschorke, Klaus, et al., editors. *A History of Christianity in Asia, Africa, and Latin America, 1450-1990: A Documentary Sourcebook*. Grand Rapids: Eerdmans, 2007.
Kunhiyop, Samuel Waje. *African Christian Ethics*. Grand Rapids: Zondervan, 2008.
Leopold, Anita Maria, and Jeppe Sinding Jensen, editors. *Syncretism in Religion: A Reader*. London: Equinox, 2004.
Leustean, Lucian, editor. *Eastern Christianity and the Cold War, 1945-91*. New York: Routledge, 2009.
Lewis, Donald M., editor. *Christianity Reborn: The Global Expansion of Evangelicalism in the Twentieth Century*. Grand Rapids: Eerdmans, 2004.
Lumsdaine, David Halloran, editor. *Evangelical Christianity and Democracy in Asia*. New York: Oxford University Press, 2009.
Marks, Darren C., editor. *Shaping a Global Theological Mind*. Burlington, VT: Ashgate, 2008.
Marty, Martin E. *The Christian World: A Global History*. New York: Modern Library Classics, 2008.
Matsuoka, Fumitaka, and Eleazer S. Fernandez, editors. *Realizing the America of Our Hearts: Theological Voices of Asian Americans*. St. Louis: Chalice, 2003.
Mathewes-Green, Frederica. *Facing East: A Pilgrim's Journey into the Mysteries of Orthodoxy*. San Francisco: HarperOne, 2006.
McGuckin, John Anthony. *The Orthodox Church: An Introduction to Its History, Doctrine, and Spiritual Culture*. Malden, MA: Wiley-Blackwell, 2008.
Miller, Donald E., and Tetsunao Yamamori. *Global Pentecostalism: The New Face of Christian Social Engagement*. Los Angeles: University of California Press, 2007.
Moore, Rebecca. *Voices of Christianity: A Global Introduction*. Boston: McGraw-Hill, 2006.
Muck, Terry C., and Frances S. Adeney. *Christianity Encountering World Religions: The Practice of Mission in the Twenty-First Century*. Grand Rapids: Baker Academic, 2009.
Mullin, Robert Bruce. *A Short World History of Christianity*. Louisville, KY: Westminster John Knox, 2008.
Niles, D. Preman. *From East and West: Rethinking Christian Mission*. St. Louis: Chalice, 2004.
Norris, Frederick W. *Christianity: A Short Global History*. Oxford: Oneworld, 2002.
Oden, Thomas C. *How Africa Shaped the Christian Mind: Rediscovering the African Seedbed of Western Christianity*. Downers Grove, IL: InterVarsity, 2008.
Ott, Craig, and Harold A. Netland, editors. *Globalizing Theology: Belief and Practice in an Era of World Christianity*. Grand Rapids: Baker Academic, 2006.
Owen, Suzanne. *The Appropriation of Native American Spirituality*. New York: Continuum, 2009.
Pabst, Adrian, and Christoph Schneider, editors. *Encounter between Eastern Orthodox and Radical Orthodoxy: Transfiguring the World through the Word*. Burlington, VT: Ashgate, 2009.

Paige, Hugh R, Jr., et al., editors. *The Africana Bible: Reading Israel's Scriptures from Africa and the African Diaspora*. Minneapolis: Fortress, 2009.

Paramore, Kiri. *Ideology and Christianity in Japan*. New York: Routledge, 2008.

Park, Chung-shin. *Protestantism and Politics in Korea*. Seattle: University of Washington Press, 2003.

Parry, Ken, editor. *The Blackwell Companion to Eastern Christianity*. Malden, MA: Wiley-Blackwell, 2007.

Pears, Angie. *Doing Contextual Theology*. New York: Routledge, 2009.

Prior, Michael. *The Bible and Colonialism: A Moral Critique*. Sheffield: Sheffield Academic, 1997.

Pui-lan, Kwok. *Postcolonial Imagination and Feminist Theology*. Louisville, KY: Westminster John Knox, 2005.

Ranger, Terence O., editor. *Evangelical Christianity and Democracy in Africa*. New York: Oxford University Press, 2008.

Raschke, Carl. *GloboChrist: The Great Commission Takes a Postmodern Turn*. Grand Rapids: Baker Academic, 2008.

Reader, John. *Reconstructing Practical Theology: The Impact of Globalization*. Burlington, VT: Ashgate, 2008.

Reid-Salmon, Delroy A. *Home Away from Home: The Caribbean Diasporan Church in the Black Atlantic Tradition*. London: Equinox, 2008.

Rieger, Joerg. *Christ & Empire: From Paul to Postcolonial Times*. Minneapolis: Fortress, 2007.

Riordan, Patrick. *A Grammar of the Common Good: Speaking of Globalization*. New York: Continuum, 2008.

Robert, Dana L. *Mission: A Brief History*. Malden, MA: Wiley-Blackwell, 2008.

Rowland, Christopher, editor. *The Cambridge Companion to Liberation Theology*. New York: Cambridge University Press, 1999.

Sanneh, Lamin. *Disciples of All Nations: Pillars of World Christianity*. New York: Oxford University Press, 2008.

———. *Translating the Message: The Missionary Impact on Culture*. Rev. and expanded ed. Maryknoll, NY: Orbis, 2008.

———. *Whose Religion Is Christianity?: The Gospel beyond the West*. Grand Rapids: Eerdmans, 2003.

Sanneh, Lamin, and Joel A. Carpenter, editors. *The Changing Face of Christianity: Africa, the West, and the World*. New York: Oxford University Press, 2005.

Schouten, Jan Peter. *Jesus as Guru: The Image of Christ among Hindus and Christians in India*. Translated by Henry and Lucy Jansen. New York: Rodopi, 2008.

Seat, Leroy. "The Future of Christianity in Asia." *Review and Expositor* 103.3 (2006) 541–78.

Sharkey, Heather J. *American Evangelicals in Egypt: Missionary Encounters in an Age of Empire*. Princeton: Princeton University Press, 2009.

Shih, Shu-Mei. "Global Literature and the Technologies of Recognition." *PMLA* 119 (2004) 16–30.

Smilde, David. *Reason to Believe: Cultural Agency in Latin American Evangelicalism*. Berkeley: University of California Press, 2007.

Smith, Allyne. *Eastern Christianity: A Brief History*. Malden, MA: Wiley-Blackwell, 2008.

Smith, David I. *Learning from the Stranger: Christian Faith and Cultural Diversity*. Grand Rapids: Eerdmans, 2009.

Soothill, Jane E. *Gender, Social Change and Spiritual Power: Charismatic Christianity in Ghana*. Boston: Brill, 2007.
Stanley, Brian, editor. *The World Missionary Conference, Edinburgh 1910*. Grand Rapids: Eerdmans, 2009.
Stinton, Diane B. *Jesus of Africa: Voices of Contemporary African Christology*. Maryknoll, NY: Orbis, 2004.
Sugirtharajah, R. S. *The Bible and the Third World: Precolonial, Colonial and Postcolonial Encounters*. New York: Cambridge University Press, 2001.
———. *Postcolonial Reconfigurations: An Alternative Way of Reading the Bible and Doing Theology*. St. Louis: Chalice, 2003.
Tan-Chow, May Ling. *Pentecostal Theology for the Twenty-First Century: Engaging with Multi-Faith Singapore*. Burlington, VT: Ashgate, 2007.
Tate, Andrew. *Contemporary Fiction and Christianity*. New York: Continuum, 2008.
Tennent, Timothy C. *Theology in the Context of World Christianity: How the Global Church Is Influencing the Way We Think About and Discuss Theology*. Grand Rapids: Zondervan, 2007.
Tinker, George E. "Tink." *American Indian Liberation: A Theology of Sovereignty*. Maryknoll, NY: Orbis, 2008.
———. *Missionary Conquest: The Gospel and Native American Cultural Genocide*. Minneapolis: Fortress, 1993.
Tomlinson, Matt. *In God's Image: The Metaculture of Fijian Christianity*. Berkeley: University of California Press, 2009.
Vilaça, Aparecida, and Robin M. Wright, editors. *Native Christians: Modes and Effects of Christianity among Indigenous Peoples of the Americas*. Burlington, VT: Ashgate, 2009.
Varghese, Baby. *West Syrian Liturgical Theology*. Burlington, VT: Ashgate, 2004.
Walls, Andrew F. *The Cross-Cultural Process in Christian History: Studies in the Transmission and Appropriation of Faith*. Maryknoll, NY: Orbis, 2002.
Webster, John C. B. *A Social History of Christianity: Northwest India Since 1800*. New York: Oxford University Press, 2007.
Wijsen, Frans, and Robert Schreiter, editors. *Global Christianity: Contested Claims*. New York: Rodopi, 2007.
Wuthnow, Robert. *Boundless Faith: The Global Outreach of American Churches*. Berkeley: University of California Press, 2009.
Yong, Amos. *The Spirit Poured Out on All Flesh: Pentecostalism and the Possibility of Global Theology*. Grand Rapids: Baker Academic, 2005.

www.ingramcontent.com/pod-product-compliance
Lightning Source LLC
Chambersburg PA
CBHW051053230426
43667CB00013B/2278